Forgotten Patriot

ROBERT MORRIS

THE MACMILLAN COMPANY
NEW YORK · BOSTON · CHICAGO
DALLAS · ATLANTA · SAN FRANCISCO

MACMILLAN AND CO., LIMITED
LONDON · BOMBAY · CALCUTTA
MADRAS · MELBOURNE

THE MACMILLAN COMPANY
OF CANADA, LIMITED
TORONTO

ROBERT MORRIS
Portrait by Gilbert Stuart

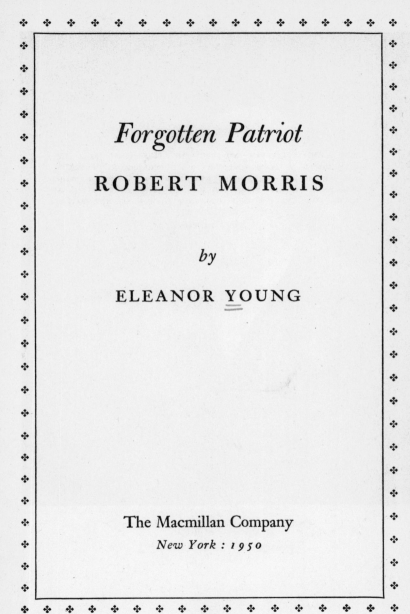

Forgotten Patriot

ROBERT MORRIS

by

ELEANOR YOUNG

The Macmillan Company

New York : 1950

Printed in the United States of America

TO THE MEMORY OF MY FATHER

William Henry Young

WHO BEGAN THIS STUDY OF

Robert Morris

AND IN LOVING REMEMBRANCE OF WHOM

I HAVE COMPLETED IT

PREFACE

TODAY, when America especially needs to renew her faith and to restore her courage, it is profitable to study the lives of those Americans who have exemplified these traits. Chief among our Revolutionary forefathers is one whose unswerving faith sustained the doubters, and whose courageous optimism revived the flagging spirits of his countrymen. Yet for a century and a half his memory has been ignored. Today the name of Robert Morris is virtually unknown by the majority of educated persons in the country that he served so zealously and so ably in its most critical period. In our United States histories a single line is sometimes vouchsafed his distinguished services. In our national capital there is not one memorial to honor him. No stamp issue has made his name and face familiar.

This is the man of whom his earliest biographer, David Gould, wrote: "If our country, in the war of the Revolution, was as much indebted to any other man as she was to her Washington, that man was Robert Morris of Philadelphia. . . . Of the Signers of the Declaration not one contributed so much of property or labour as Robert Morris."

Other early writers also praised him, often extravagantly. In *Eminent Philadelphians* the author, Henry Simpson, states that Robert Morris deserves to be placed "on the highest pinnacle of Revolutionary fame, next to Washington"; for, as he points out, "without Morris, Washingon could not have carried out his plans." John Kennedy in his two works, *Robert Morris and the Holland Purchase* and *The Genesee Country*, has called him "the second great genius of the Revolution," "the opportune Titan," and in most extravagant eulogy, "the most remarkable man that has appeared at any time in any country." "Without the sums raised by Robert Morris," Mr. Kennedy asserts, "even Washington could not have saved the country. . . .

vii

Without him the Revolution would have been the history of glorious despair, the history of gibbets, the history of the wreck of human hopes."

Even the more impartial historian John Fiske has this to say concerning the achievements and rightful place in history of the Superintendent of Finance: "That the government had in any way been able to finish the war after the downfall of its paper money was due to the gigantic efforts of one great man—Robert Morris of Pennsylvania. It was he who supplied the money which enabled Washington to complete the great campaign of Trenton and Princeton. By dint of every imaginable device of hard-pressed ingenuity he contrived to support the brilliant work which began at Cowpens and ended at Yorktown. . . . In his devotion to the common weal he drew upon his private resources—and in later years—for shame be it said—an ungrateful nation allowed one of its noblest and most disinterested champions to languish in a debtors' prison."

Despite Morris's patriotic services, however, there have appeared in the last century only two biographies of the Financier of the Revolution: the life by Professor Sumner and that by Dr. Oberholtzer, the latter published almost forty years ago. Since then no voice has been raised to sound the name of Robert Morris. During that time from old trunks and desks have come to light hundreds of personal letters reflecting the rich humanity as well as the patriotic fervor of this great man. It was my privilege to read more than three hundred of these letters in the Huntington Library—letters which completely change the picture of his later years. From Liverpool, moreover, has come word that his correct date of birth has never heretofore been given.* Thus it is my purpose to raise the curtain again upon this able, zealous public servant, who helped to establish our independence and to lay a solid foundation for our national life.

Although I feel keenly the injustice done Morris by our neglect of him through all these years, I have tried to maintain an open mind concerning his life and achievements. If he seemed praiseworthy, I

---

* On the other hand, concerning certain aspects of his life, such as his part in the Constitutional Convention, material is lacking. This is one of the inevitable hazards with which a biographer contends.

have so depicted him—despite the debunking tendencies in biographies today. If he erred, I have made no deliberate effort to shield him, although I may have attempted to interpret his actions. Above all, I have found him intensely human, consequently far from perfect. It is my earnest desire to present the many facets of his personality: as husband, father, merchant, land speculator, and debtor, as well as unselfish patriot, generous host, and resourceful financier. Through his *Diary* and the thousands of letters to him and from him, I have been impressed by the simple humanity and inherent nobility of the man. I hope that I may pass that picture on to the readers of this biography.

As this work is intended for the ordinary reader, I have not broken the narrative by reference notations, which usually prove distracting. For the sake of those who seek authorities, however, I have placed notes at the end of the book, corresponding to each chapter. Most of the source material, unfortunately, can be found only in the manuscript departments of a few libraries and historical societies.

The chronological order of events has been maintained unless it seemed necessary to follow one thread of narrative and later return for another. The objective viewpoint has been adhered to throughout except in a few instances, since the words and actions of Robert Morris best depict his character. Therein also lies the evidence that, in support of the Declaration of Independence (of which at first he did not approve), he pledged his life, his fortune, and his sacred honor to his adopted country—and kept the pledge.

ELEANOR YOUNG

Mount Vernon, New York

CONTENTS

xi

ILLUSTRATIONS

PART ONE

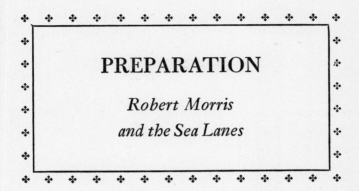

PREPARATION

Robert Morris
and the Sea Lanes

CHAPTER I

SEA SQUALLS

❖　❖　❖

EARLY on a mid-July morning in 1750, there strode along Front Street in Philadelphia a sturdy youth of fifteen. There was a west-of-England look about the boy with his round, florid face, his sandy-red hair, his tall, robust figure, and his general air of vitality. With a spring in his step he was on his way to the offices of Charles Willing, Merchant, where he had recently become a clerk in the accounting section. Robert Morris—clerk! His bright blue eyes sparkled with pleasure at the thought and his cheeks flushed more deeply. It was not so long ago that he had been apprenticed to Charles Willing, serving at first as janitor and office boy, sweeping the floors, tidying the offices, and labeling boxes and barrels. Nor was it so very long, only three years, since he had sailed from Liverpool, England, to Oxford, Maryland, to meet a father he had scarcely known. In the last three years this father had become very dear to him, in their life together in Oxford and more recently through their correspondence.

For the past few days Robert Morris had been worried about his father. Some danger faced him, his son felt, or some illness. It was a queer sensation, this vague feeling of threatened disaster. Perhaps it was because of his not having received a letter for many days. Perhaps it was just "a feeling in his bones." Someone had told him, grandmother probably, that his father's family had "second sight," the ability to foresee coming events. Whatever the cause, the sensation was uncomfortable.

In order to forget his uneasiness, he looked across the street at the wharves and beyond them at the river with its ships like seagulls sailing toward the sea, or like homing pigeons gliding to the docks. He turned towards Carpenter's Wharf, at the foot of Walnut Street, where lay the *Mayflower*, one of Willing's three boats. Leaping over boxes of tea, of cheese, of hammers, of window glass, and threading his way among barrels of beer, cider, and rum, he mingled with the sailors, listening to the jargon of old tars from many lands. This scene reminded him of the Old Dock or the newer Salthouse Dock at Liverpool, where he had played as a boy. Here was the same rough, disorderly crowd: sailors with their prize money heading for the taverns, sailors already reeling from their visits to the "pubs," sailors singing or swearing at their work. Their tales of privateering had widened his eyes in earlier years. Occasionally he caught a whisper here in America of French or Spanish ships caught and plundered, but there were no such insinuations on Willing's dock. As an employer Charles Willing was kind but firm. The sailors knew as well as their captains that he would not tolerate any piracy or unfair practices in connection with his mercantile ventures. Here all was business.

When Robert turned away from the wharf toward the accounting house across the cobble-stoned street, his worries were forgotten. Ships had always fascinated him. The love of the sea was in his blood. His grandfather, Andrew Morris, had been a sailor; his father, Robert Morris, was a factor or agent for a Liverpool firm dealing in tobacco, and thus necessarily had ships consigned to him. As interesting as shipping to young Morris was the mercantile business itself, especially the accounting end of it. In Charles Willing's office the great variety of activities held his enthusiasm at the peak. This was a wholesale house dealing in hardware, liquor, grains, coffee, clothing, and furniture. In order to facilitate its business, the firm dealt in notes of exchange, thus serving as international bankers. Few details of this business escaped Morris's eager mind and penetrating eye.

After a long day in the accounting office, Robert returned to the home of his guardian, Robert Greenway, a close friend of the elder Morris, who for more than a year had supervised his ward's education and apprenticeship. There he found a letter in a strange handwriting, which a messenger had just delivered. Robert's large hands trembled as he tore it open.

His eyes, skipping over forms, pierced to essentials. Over the signature "Henry Callister," Robert Morris read the tragic news of his father's death as a result of an accident, a cannon-shot in the arm. The writer, so the letter continued, was the last person with whom the elder Morris had spoken. Mr. Callister had been reading to him from Plato's *Phaedo* at Morris's request just before his death, while Tray, the faithful spaniel, lay beside the sick man's bed. Here, too, was news of the burial of Robert Morris in the cemetery of White Marsh Church, Talbot County, Maryland, five miles from Oxford. His father, only thirty-nine years old, dead in his prime! What was the accident? How could it have happened?

Later Robert heard all the details of the tragedy. In those days it was customary, after the arrival of a ship from a foreign port, for the captain to give a dinner and entertainment to the consignee and his friends and, as a compliment, to fire a salute at their departure from the vessel. As American agent of his firm, Foster Cunliffe & Sons, Morris had had consigned to him at Oxford a new ship, the *Liverpool*. Consequently he had invited a party of friends to accompany him to the ship to enjoy the captain's hospitality. The night before the gala event, however, Morris dreamt that, after a pleasant day on shipboard, he had received a fatal wound from the salute fired in his honor. Try as he would, he could not shake off the memory of this dream. The vivid details seemed branded upon his imagination. All morning he brooded upon them and before noon had decided not to join the party.

Calling Captain Mathews into his office, he very apologetically related his dream to the captain, telling him of the powerful effect produced upon his mind and spirits, and offered this as an excuse for not attending the celebration that afternoon.

The captain, indignant at this last minute change in plans, rebuked Morris and taunted him at this display of superstition. "Will not your decision seem inhospitable to the friends you have invited? Surely you will not let a foolish dream interfere with your obligation."

Morris compressed his lips at the captain's rebuke, then smiled as he ran his hand over his tightly curled wig.

"Better inhospitable than inanimate," he replied. "Call it superstition if you like, but our family is reputed to have the gift, or curse, of receiving premonitions of impending disaster."

Captain Mathews, unable by taunts or entreaties to persuade Morris to come aboard the vessel, at last promised that no salute would be fired. Thereupon Morris reluctantly consented to attend the celebration. In a pinnace, a small tender propelled by oars and sails, he set out with his friends for the *Liverpool*, moored farther down the bay. The day was bright, the water sparkling, his companions, ladies and gentlemen of Oxford, lively and amusing. Soon Morris had forgotten his strange foreboding. The fish and Burgundy were especially fine; the sailors' dances entertaining. All declared the celebration a great success.

After the festivities, as the guests were preparing to leave, Captain Mathews called Morris aside. "The crew don't take kindly to the arrangements, sir. They insist on firing the usual salute. You know a glass of grog is served every sailor immediately afterward."

"Why not serve the grog without the salvo?" Morris suggested.

"Too irregular, sir—destructive of ship discipline. The ceremony is part of the occasion. Certainly you would not let a mere dream interfere with the pleasure of so many," the captain concluded earnestly. He knew how to appeal to Morris's customary geniality and consideration of others.

"Very well," Robert Morris agreed, "but do not fire the salute until I or someone else gives the signal."

"I will accompany you to shore, sir, and give the signal myself when we are far enough away." Captain Mathews thereupon made the necessary arrangements, instructing the gunner not to fire until he (the captain) raised his hand.

The members of the jolly party were lowered over the side of the *Liverpool* and started rowing back to shore. What happened after that none of the spectators could tell accurately. According to one account, a lady's handkerchief fluttered from her hand, and this was considered the prearranged signal. According to another story, told by Jeremiah Banning, a young "ear witness" of the event, a fly lodged on the captain's nose before the boat had rowed clear of the gun range. Thoughtlessly Mathews, forgetting for the moment his responsibility, raised his hand to brush the fly away. Seeing the motion and considering this the signal, the gunner fired the salute. The next moment Morris felt a sharp pain in his upper arm. His companions solicitously examined the wound to discover that the wadding from one of the guns had passed through the backboard of the pinnace, striking his arm above the elbow, breaking the bone, and lodging in the flesh. Now that the much-feared event had actually occurred, Morris showed remarkable fortitude. Always genial, unwilling to mar the gaiety of the occasion, he minimized the injury.

"Pray do not let this accident disturb you," he replied to his friends' inquiries.

No physician was available that evening. Indeed there was little expert medical advice to be had outside the largest cities. An immediate operation would have saved Morris's life and even the arm itself, but none was performed. A few days afterward mortification set in. Still he lingered while his friends read to him, and Tray lay beneath his bed or rose to lick his hand.

Later his son visited his grave in the White Marsh churchyard, where Tray had followed the body and had remained for many days. With tears in his eyes Robert Morris read the epitaph written by his father's friends:

In Memory of
Robert Morris, a Native of Liverpool, in Great Britain
Late Merchant of Oxford
in this Province.
Punctual Integrity influenced his dealings.
Principles of Honour governed his actions.
With an uncommon degree of Sincerity,
He despised Artifice and Dissimulation.
His friendship was firm, candid and valuable.
His Charity frequent, secret and well adapted.

His Zeal for the Publicke good, active and useful.
His Hospitality was enhanced by his Conversation,
Seasoned with cheerful wit and a sound judgment.
A Salute from the cannon of a ship,
The wad fracturing his arm,
Was the signal by which he departed
Greatly lamented as he was esteemed
In the fortieth year of his age,
On the 12th day of July
MDCCL

His son learned, too, that his father's neighbors, as evidence of their respect and affection for him, enjoined in their wills that his grave should be preserved untouched.

Robert's thoughts turned naturally to his early days in America when he had first become acquainted with his father. As the ship from Liverpool approached the dock in Oxford, he recalled the sight of that robust figure on the wharf and the smile of welcome on his father's round face. With a pang he remembered their days together in his father's home, especially the hours in the library with its fine classical books, where he had browsed, educating himself. Most of all, however, it was of the man himself he thought. What a remarkable character his father was—so genial, so kind, so industrious and intelligent! No wonder he was popular. His many friends had proved their affection for him. His hospitality was noted. There were always the choicest wines and food on his table, and conversation that sparkled like the Burgundy. He was more than a good host; he was a fine character—honest, sincere, public-spirited. And what a business man! His industry and intelligence had made him a most successful agent. Robert would try to grow like him.

Another boy of this period, Jeremiah Banning, later Captain Banning, corroborated the son's estimate of the elder Morris in his *Recollections*, written many years afterward:

"As a mercantile genius, 'twas thought he had not his equal in the land. In carrying political points he defeated all opposition. He gave birth to the inspection law in tobacco—and carried it—though opposed by a powerful party." He introduced methods of keeping books in money instead of in tobacco and other commodities. The same writer spoke of him as steady, sincere, and a warm friend, always generous and ready to relieve real distress. "At repartee he bore down all before him." The greatest foibles mentioned by the captain were those of a haughty bearing, a vindictive spirit, and extreme severity to his servants.

Hospitable, generous, industrious, public-spirited, courageous—these characteristics of his father imprinted themselves indelibly upon the impressionable mind of his son. In him, too, there was evident the intelligence and initiative of the elder Robert Morris—traits and abilities soon to be called into play.

Those were days that required grave decisions, which could not be made by guardian or friends, but only by Morris himself, a fifteen-year-old boy left alone in the world. His thoughts turned back inevitably to the home he had known in early years when he had lived with Grandmother Murphet, his mother's mother, in Chorley Court, Liverpool. There he was born January 20, 1735 (January 31, 1734, Old Calendar), and a few days later was christened at St. George's Church on Castle Street, a new church consecrated the preceding August.* Of course he had merely heard of these events through his grandmother. His mother, Elizabeth Murphet Morris, he could not remember. But he could recall, with a pang of homesickness, his rambles about Liverpool, up to old St. Peter's where his father had been baptized on April 23, 1711, and where, under the lime trees of the churchyard, his grandfather, Andrew Morris, "saylor," was buried in 1728 and his grandmother, Maudlan (or Magdalen) Simpson Morris, the following year. He remembered the jasmine growing in Paradise Street and the apples and pears (irresistible temptations to small boys) on Church Street. There were visits, too, in those days to his aunt Ellin (or Ellener) Eccleston, his father's sister, who had married a butcher in Liverpool. Another aunt, Margaret, had married a Mr. Trout and moved to London, where her husband served as a clerk or merchant's assistant.

The revival of old memories did not lure Robert Morris away from

* See Notes on Chapter I.

his new life, far though he was from his remaining family. He was launched on an adventure and apparently never thought of turning from it. Loneliness served merely to strengthen his independence and initiative. Moreover, he was vitally interested in the mercantile business.

As a result of his father's death, he inherited a small legacy, about $7,000, which might enable him to gain an education or a start in business. Robert Greenway, executor of this estate, was requested to keep it in trust and to deliver it upon Robert's demand. His father's gold watch, another small bequest, he treasured through days of prosperity and misfortune, and bequeathed to his son at his own death.

There was another legacy of which he learned much later—to his sorrow—a half brother, an illegitimate son of Robert Morris, Senior and his "dear friend," Sarah Wise. To the latter Morris had left £250; to her daughter Sarah, £100; and to her unborn child (the aforementioned illegitimate son, Thomas), £100. Sarah also inherited a mourning ring, several silver tankards, six silver spoons, and all his wearing apparel. She evidently had the status of a common law wife. Apparently this relationship was well known to his friends and neighbors, who respected him nonetheless, praising his "integrity and principles of honour." To Robert the acknowledgment of his father's relationship to the Wise family must have come as a shock. He did not suspect then, however, what a liability this half brother would prove in later years.

CHAPTER II

THE MARKET CORNERED

❖　　❖　　❖

WITH the loss of his father Robert Morris threw himself even more whole-heartedly into his clerical duties. There was little temptation to attend school although the College of Philadelphia had just been established. In Oxford he had been tutored by the Reverend William Gordon, an indentured servant, who had quickly dispensed all his intellectual wares. Robert probably smiled to think of the day his father had scolded him for inattention to his studies. "I have learned, sir," he had replied somewhat cockily, "all that the master could teach me." Thereupon his father had sent him to Philadelphia, where there were more opportunities for cocksure young men. During his first year there he had received instruction from "Annan," the leading schoolmaster in the city. Whether he exhausted this pedagogue's store of knowledge or merely "quit," at all events within a year or two he had become an apprentice to Charles Willing. This highly successful, respected merchant took an exceptional interest in his youthful apprentice and clerk, treating him with consideration and affection. This mercantile office was Robert Morris's university, where he rapidly matured into young manhood.

At this time Charles Willing's son, Thomas, a little more than three years Robert Morris's senior, returned from London, where he had been reading law at the Inner Temple. He was a tall, slender, handsome man with a healthy, fresh complexion, blue eyes, and firm, thin lips. In later years his face resembled Washington's—a face of granite. Because of the square-toed shoes he wore and perhaps also because of his own "squareness," his integrity, and sense of justice, young Willing was dubbed "Square Toes." He and Robert Morris, so similar in character and in general abilities, were sufficiently dissimilar in their talents and temperament to supplement each other. They soon became firm friends and, before many years had passed, business associates. They both were courteous, kind, affectionate, and upright. In temperament, however, they differed widely. Thomas Willing was calm, deliberate, cautious; Robert Morris, enthusiastic, optimistic, audaciously enterprising, and resourceful. The former was the brake; the latter, the ignition in their car of progress.

Their cooperative efforts, although not their partnership, began almost immediately. As soon as his son returned from abroad, Charles Willing decided to visit his father, also Thomas Willing, in Bristol, England, and to attend to the business of the firm in the British Isles. Upon his departure he left his son in charge of the business, but placed Robert Morris in a responsible position, with orders that no one should interfere with his decisions—an unusual tribute to a fifteen-year-old clerk.

Willing's confidence was not misplaced. One day, soon after his employer's departure, young Morris heard that the price of flour had advanced in foreign markets. Here was an opportunity, he felt, to show his appreciation of his employer's trust. At once he called in the firm's agents in the city and environs and gave the order: "Buy up all the flour you can lay hold of to ship abroad." Contract after contract received his signature.

There was an increasing buzz of activity that day on Carpenter's Wharf. Wagon-loads of flour arrived. Ships were loaded and prepared to sail with their precious cargoes. An ominous thunder of protest from the other Philadelphia merchants rumbled through the city.

"Price of flour is up fifty per cent."

"No flour to be purchased for love or money."

"Willing has bought it up."

"Willing's abroad. Young Morris, you say—the—"

"This young upstart has cornered the market!"

"We and our children will starve."

"Just wait until Willing returns!"

Thomas Willing withdrew into an inner office. Robert Morris answered all callers politely but refused to release the flour. Despite his friendliness he could be as unyielding as a rock. He may have felt a few qualms of conscience when he considered the plight of the other merchants and the townsfolk. But wasn't he justified in acting in his employer's interest? Wouldn't Mr. Willing approve? Thus Charles Willing's return from England was awaited by everyone with breathless eagerness.

No sooner had his boat docked than the indignation of the merchants was unleashed. They greeted him with stormy protests against Morris's business maneuvers.

"Business transacted by a mere boy!"

"Who is this Robert Morris, that you should trust his judgment?"

"Very unethical practice to buy up all available flour."

Willing listened courteously, smiling to himself. Practices interfering with anyone else's interest are always dubbed "unethical." After the angry merchants had departed, Charles Willing called Robert Morris to his office.

"What is this I hear, my boy, about your having purchased and shipped abroad all available flour in the Philadelphia market?"

Morris's boyish face flushed. "I had to decide quickly, sir. When I heard that the price had advanced abroad, it seemed wise to contract for as much flour as we could lay our hands on. Didn't the other merchants have the same opportunity?"

"But you were there first, Robert; is that it?" His employer smiled. "Whatever they say, my boy, I commend your initiative and business judgment. You have proved yourself bold and resourceful."

Robert's eyes sparkled as he thanked his employer.

Not long after this, a new firm was established, that of Charles Willing & Son. Thomas, having inherited part of an aunt's estate, bought a partnership with his father. As Charles Willing had been elected Mayor of Philadelphia, he needed younger men to relieve him of detailed attention to business.

During the following years Robert Morris laid the foundations of his successful career as a merchant. One of the cornerstones of that career was system, organization, based on attention to minute details. His double entry ledger was kept meticulously. As young as he was at this time he had an eye to detail—to invoices and bills of lading, that they should be accurate. It was not long before Morris, with his alert mind and love of figures, assumed control of the firm's finances, Thomas Willing with his legal training and conservative attitude attending to contracts and other legal matters. For four years they collaborated in this manner.

In 1754 during one of Philadelphia's ever-recurring epidemics of yellow fever, Charles Willing fell a victim. As he lay on his death bed, he sent a message to Morris: "Robert, always continue to act as you have done." Thus he placed his seal of approval upon his young clerk's character and actions.

Now that "old Square Toes" was head of the firm, even more responsibility devolved upon his friend, Robert Morris, in whom he placed utter confidence. Philadelphia, a city of about nineteen thousand inhabitants, was the new world's largest emporium of that time. There the merchant aristocracy ruled the city with a rod of iron. Country peddling was discouraged. The working class, consisting of shopkeepers, ropemakers, sailmakers, sailors, coopers, smiths, and a host of others, remained unorganized, held rigidly under the capable thumb of the merchant princes of the city. The merchants themselves, on the other hand, were organized, undertaking jointly certain actions toward the merchants of Great Britain and the West Indies. The Committee of Merchants of Philadelphia wrote the Merchants of London: "We consider the Merchants here and in England as the Links of the Chain that binds both Countries together."

Cooperation such at this was another of the foundation stones in Morris's Temple of Success. "No man liveth unto himself," he believed most devoutly. It was through his cooperation with Thomas Willing and with the firm's employees that Charles Willing & Son had grown with the years. It was through cooperation that the merchants of the city had made themselves a force to be reckoned with—a force which Morris did not then suspect was destined to build a new nation, a "brave new world."

Since much of the firm's trade was with the West Indies, Robert Morris wished to visit the "Sugar Islands," as they were called. Aglow with boyish love of adventure and eager to learn at first hand of the ships and commerce of the firm, he requested Thomas Willing's permission to sail as supercargo on the *Severn* to Jamaica. With him he carried letters from Willing recommending him to all and sundry as "an honest, worthy young fellow." Taking advantage of Morris's vacation, the firm gave him the responsibility of selling ship and cargo in Jamaica—a task which he performed successfully.

Shortly after his return Charles Willing & Son purchased a new brigantine, also named the *Severn*, in which Morris bought one-fourth interest. In this way he was broadening his business ventures. In October, 1756, soon after the purchase of the ship, Morris sailed again as supercargo on what was destined to be a most eventful voyage.

The first adventure was wholly of a business nature. While Morris was in Jamaica, Mr. Sharp, a merchant of Kingston, invited him to become his partner and wrote Thomas Willing with reference to the arrangement. Willing replied that he wished to see Morris "advantageously engaged anywhere" as he held him "in great esteem." Here was a grave decision facing the twenty-one-year-old clerk. Should he leave Philadelphia where he had already achieved a measure of success and reputation? Or should he refuse a business opportunity that might bring fame and fortune? Thomas Willing had not yet broached the subject of a partnership. Perhaps he never would. Morris pondered the matter. At last having decided against the partnership with Sharp, he sailed for Philadelphia in February on the *Severn*.

The brig had been out only a day when a French privateer was sighted, then another. The French ships had already caught sight of the American vessel and were pursuing her. The *Severn* shifted her course and headed for the southern tip of Cuba. The privateers gave chase. They were gaining.

"What do you see?" shouted the captain to the lookout.

"Land—a bay."

"Port the helm!" he cried to the helmsman.

"We'll beach her and try to escape with the cargo," the captain told Morris.

But the French were closing in for the "kill." The nerves of all aboard the *Severn* were taut. As the brigantine nosed into the beach, the privateers entered the bay. There was no escape now. Before Captain Apowen and the crew could remove part of the cargo and escape, the French ships had grappled and boarded the *Severn* and bound Morris, the captain, and the crew. Like chattering magpies, the French crews fell lustily upon the cargo, ripping open boxes of sugar and spices, removing bungs from the rum barrels and drinking the contents. In drunken glee they stripped their captives of their possessions and most of their clothing as they danced around them mockingly.

For days Morris, Captain Apowen, and the American crew remained captive near the shore, half clothed, starving. One dark night after days of privation they stole away into the interior of the island. Through fields and forests they passed, the sun beating down mercilessly upon their exposed bodies by day, the rains pelting them by night. The country was hilly, the footing difficult. They had no food, no water. An occasional rabbit was trapped; once or twice a wild turkey was surprised on its nest. The wanderers had no firearms as their guns had been taken from them by the French; consequently they could not kill the birds that flew through the forests of ebony, mahogany, and rosewood. Painfully they at last emerged, a band of scarecrows, on the shore not far from the ruined city of Havana, destroyed by the French three years before.

Morris and the other Americans were in a sad plight. They were stranded in Cuba without money or any means of transportation. They even lacked food and clothing. In these dire straits, Morris's ingenuity suggested a method of obtaining supplies. One day he saw a Frenchman shaking his watch and holding it to his ear.

"It has stopped?" Morris inquired. The Frenchman shrugged and broke into voluble French which Morris could not understand.

"Perhaps I can repair it for you," the latter offered holding out his hand. The Frenchman with another shrug handed it to him. Morris possessed a natural mechanical skill, fostered by years of tinkering with clocks, watches, and household utensils. With a borrowed knife and improvised instruments he repaired the watch successfully and returned it to its owner in working order. The Frenchman in addition to paying him sent others to him for repair work. Thus Morris secured money for food and other necessities.

At last an American vessel arrived at the port and Morris and Captain Apowen sailed back home, reaching Philadelphia on April 6. Fortunately the *Severn*, captured by the privateers, was insured for £5,000. Morris presumably received his quarter of the insurance. He had received more than his share of adventure.

A few weeks later, Thomas Willing, delighted at Morris's safe return, invited him to become his business partner. The articles were drawn up, and the partnership, called sometimes Willing & Morris, sometimes Willing, Morris & Company, became effective May 1, 1757, just ten years after Morris's arrival in America. The young partner was now only twenty-two years old, yet in reality a man of mature judgment, familiar with merchandise, accounting, and the sea lanes. The ocean with its ships, bringing tragedy and fortune, had already left its imprint upon his character.

Philadelphia was a busy port in those days. Hundreds of ships docked there. Because of the so-called French and Indian War (1754-1763) England had begun to regulate trade by many acts offensive to the colonies. At first these trade laws were considered a war measure "for the duration," but they proved so lucrative that they were continued even after the war. The most troublesome act in the eyes of the Colonial merchants and shipmasters was that requiring ships to take return cargoes from Europe and Africa to America by way of England. This caused a loss of time and money. Consequently smuggling throve. Suppression of smuggling, originally a war measure, became a permanent peace policy. Customs officials, the F.B.I. of that day, investigated merchants and shopkeepers, developing a far-reaching spy service. Warships also were vigilant. Nevertheless, the temptation to smuggle in wine, coffee, and indigo, to escape the British import duties, became overwhelmingly strong.

Apparently the firm of Willing & Morris, with its vast amount of foreign freightage, remained above reproach. Robert Morris, as honest as his "square-toed" partner, believed that "Confidence is the source of credit, and credit is the soul of all pecuniary operations." Confidence, he felt, was inspired by honest, straight dealing, by precision and integrity. Willing placed in his partner an ever-increasing trust and fuller responsibility with the years. The senior partner was somewhat timorous and pessimistic whenever a financial crisis threatened or whenever bills of exchange were protested. Morris, on the contrary, rose to meet a challenge like a war-horse at the smell of gunpowder. Once when Willing heard that the firm's bills of exchange, amounting to £30,000 sterling, had been protested, he turned to Morris with an almost pathetic reliance upon his judgment and ability. "Ruin and gaol stare me in the face," he wrote his partner despairingly. "If the news is true, I fear I shall sink under it. You alone can calm my fears if it is false, or put me in a way to extricate myself if it is true. I therefore conjure you by the ties of friendship to write fully on this head directly." Morris sent him the details of the transaction, which evidently proved satisfactory to his partner as Willing thanked him heartily for his trouble in "stating so fully and particularly the situation."

When Thomas Willing, like his father, was elected Mayor of Philadelphia in 1763, at the end of the French war, Morris managed the business of the firm. In fact, for a period of almost twenty years, he was the acting and very active head. Under his management the house of Willing & Morris reached the summit of its commercial reputation as the largest, wealthiest firm in the country. Through these years he erected a solid structure based upon a foundation of honesty, economy, system, daring, perseverance, and attention to the most minute details. It was a house not "builded upon the sand" but destined to endure the stormy years ahead.

What of the stature of the builder? He also was growing with the years of struggle. A young man in his twenties, pitting his wits against those of the greatest merchants of his day, he more than held his own. In those earlier years, diligently engaged in building up a business, working day and night, he was too busy to question his own motives, to ask himself, "Where am I going?" A decision and a goal lay just ahead.

Business, never without its perplexities, faced even graver issues. On March 22, 1765, the Stamp Act received the royal assent. This act, levying duties on legal documents, commercial papers, news-papers, advertisements, and liquor licenses in the Colonies, placed an economic burden on the commercial provinces, of which Pennsylvania was the most important. If this went into effect, trade would stagnate. The load would fall most heavily upon merchants and lawyers, who faced imminent ruin.

Here was a new challenge to Morris. As a merchant directly af-fected by this act, he resisted its enforcement. The Committee of Philadelphia Merchants, of which he was a member, held indigna-tion meetings. At one such meeting, five members were chosen as a committee to visit John Hughes, the Philadelphia shopkeeper and a friend of Franklin, who had been appointed to receive the first stamps. Morris headed the committee. When they called upon Hughes, he was too ill to meet them. He sent down word, however, that he would not enforce the Stamp Act until it was put into execu-tion by the other colonies. At first this satisfied the committee, but, as they considered the matter, they felt more and more uneasy over the situation. "Until put into execution by the other colonies" —the other colonies might not object since they had fewer com-mercial interests. After talking the subject over among themselves and reporting to the Committee of Merchants, they determined to pay Hughes a second visit. This time they saw him person-ally and demanded an unequivocal promise not to distribute the stamps.

In order to secure peace, Hughes promised, "I will not distribute them until the citizens of Pennsylvania and Delaware desire me to do so."

Even this pledge did not entirely allay the fears of Morris and the other merchants. They soon held a meeting at Davenport's Tavern, Thomas Willing acting as chairman. There, amid vociferous arguments, more than four hundred merchants of Philadelphia drew up and signed the Non-Importation Resolutions. According to the terms of these resolutions, the subscribers agreed to receive no merchandise from England and sell none on commission to that country after January 1, 1766, unless the Stamp Act were repealed. Orders when placed with British firms must stipulate that goods should not be shipped until the objectionable act was repealed. All orders already placed were canceled unless the ships containing the merchandise had left Britain before the British firms could be notified. By signing these agreements Morris and Willing, like the other merchants, struck a blow at their own business.

There were many corollaries to the original resolutions. The committee imposed certain boycotts as well as suggesting constructive measures. No one was to eat lamb so that wool for clothing might be raised in the colonies (especially Pennsylvania and Delaware), and any butcher who violated this resolution was to be boycotted. A schedule of ceiling prices was drawn up and certain measures were taken to prevent or punish "black market" activities. Violators of the regulations had their names published in the newspapers and were depicted as "sordid vultures preying on the vitals of their country in a time of general distress."

Among the constructive measures was the establishment of a Philadelphia market for the sale of homemade linens and flannels. In connection with this project a factory was opened in which two hundred poor women spun flax. An advertising campaign was waged. "SAGE, SASSAFRAS AND BALM FAR SUPERIOR TO BOHEA AND OTHER FOREIGN TEAS" announced an advertisement. The ladies, however, were skeptical. Giving up tea struck at the very roots of their social structure. What was an afternoon without tea? Some real Bohea was hoarded against the arrival of extra-special company.

Partly as a result of the Non-Importation Resolutions and partly because of William Pitt's unremitting efforts in the British Parliament, the Stamp Act was repealed on March 4, 1766. A letter from Oxford, Maryland, brought the good news to Philadelphia. Bells pealed and bonfires flared. As an aftermath, in token of the gratitude of the colonies, pictures of William Pitt appeared in many homes and a medalet was struck in his honor.

In this, his first public service, Robert Morris won the confidence of his fellow townsmen through his firmness and tact in dealing with Hughes, his grasp of the political situation, his courage and altruism in considering the good of the entire group instead of his own prosperity, and his initiative and originality in suggesting methods of building up colonial industries. In the meantime Morris found time for relaxation and play.

CHAPTER III

LIFETIME PLEDGES

✤   ✤   ✤

PHILADELPHIA, Quaker City though it was, boasted the greatest prosperity and the gayest society of all American cities during the Colonial Period. Behind the sober red-brick fronts with their touch of white marble elegance, lights from crystal chandeliers sparkled nightly upon brilliant and merry companies. The dominant elements in that society were the merchants and lawyers. In that society Robert Morris took his place by virtue of his mercantile position and his own genial and dynamic personality. He was what is termed today a "good mixer."

Many evenings he visited the Willings in their dignified home, with the finest park in the city next door to it. Willing's small daughter Ann, later the dazzling Mrs. Bingham, considered Morris her "particular friend." His own boyishness and love of adventure and especially his ready laugh appealed to children. Sitting on his knee, she joked with him until her early bedtime. After her departure for bed, the two partners, so different in temperament, so alike in principles, sat discussing business plans or social events until, just at nine, glasses of claret or Madeira were served. After that Morris knew it was his friend's bedtime and so departed.

This friendship between the two men grew with the years. Later when they were separated during the Revolution, Willing wrote Morris: "I lament from my soul this cruel separation from the man I love"; and in another letter said: "I wish for nothing so much as to see you here before the last wine I have goes." Ordinarily cau-

22

tious in his statements as in every action of his life, he spoke in superlatives of his partner: "What you do will always be right, I'm sure, in this and everything else that concerns me. . . . I hope still to be happy in the esteem and friendship of the man in the world I love most and for whom I have every feeling of affection and regard."

As an eligible young bachelor and man-about-town Morris was invited everywhere. Since he had no home of his own at this time, he repaid his social debts by entertaining his friends at the city taverns or coffee houses. At this time he began to establish his reputation as the genial "host of America," a connoisseur of food and drinks.

One of his parties, beginning festively, ended sorrowfully, like his father's last party on shipboard. In fact, his father was connected with the incident. A friend had presented Morris with a fine large turtle. Not having the facilities to prepare it himself, he sent it to a tavern just outside the city, where he invited some friends to meet him. Turtle parties were more popular than clambakes in those days. Morris smilingly welcomed his guests and seated them at the table. When the festivities were in full swing and the turtle partly consumed, several naval officers entered the room. The talk and laughter continued. In a few minutes a friend at another table came over to Morris and whispered in his ear. His face blanched; his spirits seemed paralyzed. As his exuberance a few minutes before had dominated the party, his guests began whispering among themselves: "What is the matter with Morris?" "Why does he look so sad?" "He's like one in a dream."

Realizing that the company wondered at the change in his behavior and unable to explain the situation himself, he called a guest aside and told him: "I am this moment informed that the man who killed my father is in the house." Requesting his friend to present his excuses to the others, he left the tavern.

The most elegant and exclusive social events of the period were the Assembly dances, managed over a term of years by Thomas Willing. Only the socially elect were invited—such families as the Shippens, Dickinsons, Hopkinsons, and Whites. One evening Morris met there a charming, willowy girl in her later teens—Molly or Mary White. Her brown eyes, sparkling with pleasure or softening in response to the strains of the music; her curly brown hair and soft white skin; most of all her gracious manners, so sincere and unaffected, won Morris's heart almost before he was aware of what had happened. His heart beating a tattoo, Morris among other swains filled out her dance card. Even the older men admired Mary's poise, friendliness, and girlish sparkle. One evening in the Assembly Hall she blushed upon receiving these lines written by the elderly Colonel Shippen—lines improvised in the hall that evening:

> "In lovely White's most pleasing form,
>   What various graces meet!
> How blest with every striking charm!
> How languishingly sweet."

After the introduction to Mary White, Morris's affections did not wander. Many an evening he spent in the White's elegant home. Seated with her embroidery in the parlor, Mary welcomed Morris with a smile. Here was a little white needlebook he had brought. "How thoughtful!" Her brown eyes sparkled. Smile answered smile.

Her brother "Billy," a young man of twenty, with a B.A. from the College of Philadelphia, dropped in for a few words.

"I hear you were accessory to an elopement, William," Morris teased. It had been whispered around Philadelphia that William White, while still a student, had aided his friend Benjamin West in eloping with Betsey Shetwell.

"They were deeply in love," William replied blushing.

Morris threw back his head and burst into a roar of laughter. "That does seem sufficient reason for an elopement," he chuckled when his laughter had subsided. "What do you think, Molly?" Morris asked.

"Settle this between yourselves," Mary replied, smiling archly. "I'm a notorious lover of peace and law and order. Usually I don't approve of elopements."

"More seriously, William," Morris continued. "Have you decided upon law or the ministry?"

ROBERT MORRIS, FATHER OF THE FINANCIER

"Father would like me to follow in his footsteps and read law, but I favor the church. I hope to sail for England soon for study and ordination." William White's fine, aristocratic face brightened as his thin lips parted in a smile.

There is a spiritual quality about the boy, Morris thought.

Colonel White, Mary's father, came in for a chat on his way to bed. Thomas White, English by birth, lawyer and surveyor by profession, was an aristocrat without snobbery. He liked Morris. Here was a substantial man of business with whom he could talk on equal terms. There were, moreover, important political events in these days for men to discuss.

"These Non-Importation Resolutions, Mr. Morris, just what do they imply?" asked the Colonel.

Morris, full of fire, explained the necessity for them. "The three great ports, Philadelphia, New York, and Boston, are united, sir, in carrying out these measures. All the merchants refuse to receive British goods. This is being enforced remarkably except for the baser sort, unworthy the name of merchant."

The Colonel shook his head. He feared the repercussions of this act.

"The British will be forced to yield to our just demand for no taxation without representation," Morris continued earnestly. "The British Empire is founded upon the rock of mercantile prosperity."

In the back parlor sat Mary's mother, the Colonel's second wife, Esther Hewlings Newman White, knitting as she chaperoned her daughter. This charming woman, from whom Mary inherited some of her most winsome traits, apparently paid no attention to the young lovers while Mary played the clavichord or Robert made love.

When Morris not long after asked Colonel White for his daughter's hand, the father readily gave his consent. Although Morris had no "family," Philadelphia's passport to society, he had won his own position through his business ability and personal charm. At this time Molly was nineteen, being born on April 13, 1749, whereas Morris was thirty-three.

On March 2, 1769, the bells of Christ Church chimed for the

wedding of Robert Morris and Mary White. As the wedding procession marched down the aisle, the white interior of the church, under its crystal chandeliers sparkling with candles, shone like sunlight on snow. At the altar, waiting to perform the ceremony, was the Reverend Richard Peters, rector of the church, whose body now rests below the steps to the chancel. Here vows were made in accordance with the church of England.

"I, Mary, take thee, Robert, to my wedded husband, for better for worse, for richer for poorer—till death do us part. And thereto I give thee my troth."

The chimes pealed a paean of happiness that marriage day—the bells that so often in later years were muffled and tolled. About that brick church with its white steeple centered much of the Morrises' life together: their children's christenings, their brother's installation as rector of the church. They heard the bells ring from its belfry when the Stamp Act was repealed and when the glad news came of the British surrender at Yorktown.

In this Patriot's Sanctuary worshiped most of the great men and women in Philadelphia during Colonial and Revolutionary days. Near the rear, by the center aisle, sat Benjamin Franklin, watching with philosophic calm the pageant of Philadelphia society at church. Not far away, with a hymnal in his hand, was Francis Hopkinson, poet, musician, judge, and signer of the Declaration of Independence. In a pew on a side aisle knelt Betsy Ross. Number 58 on the main aisle, near the center of the church, was the President's pew when Philadelphia became briefly the capital of the United States. Here sat George and Martha Washington, prayer books in hand, the pillars of religion as well as of society and the state. A large, square pew at the very front, directly below the pulpit, was occupied by the Morrises. There in later years came a rather corpulent man in a handsome dark silk suit with satin waistcoat. Beside him down the aisle walked a lady, slight and willowy, with soft brown eyes and powdered hair piled high under her gray silk bonnet. Robert Morris's buoyant stride was somewhat moderated in keeping with the place and the occasion. After them trooped their large family of boys and girls—their real reason for renting so spacious a pew. But that was all very far in the future on that joyous marriage day—a day that marked for Robert Morris the beginning of a life-long companionship that heightened his joys, brightened his successes, and lightened the gloom of his last years. In all the vicissitudes of his life, so filled with fortunes and misfortunes, this union might well be considered the greatest of life's blessings.

No sooner were the Morrises married and established in their home on Front Street, facing the river, than that waterway became the scene of tremendous activity and dramatic events. A short time before their marriage, in 1767, the British Parliament, taking advantage of Pitt's illness and absence, passed a colonial tax on tea among other objectionable measures sponsored by Charles Townshend, leader of the House of Commons and for a brief period Prime Minister of England. When word reached Pennsylvania that the ship *Polly* with a cargo of the detested tea was sighted off the coast of Maryland, feeling ran high. Handbills addressed to tradesmen, mechanics, and artisans asked them to "reject every proposal but a repealing act." Another more threatening handbill was circulated among the Delaware River pilots. "We need not point out to you," thundered the bulletin, "what steps you ought to take if the tea-ship falls in your way." The conclusion was even more menacing, especially toward any pilot bringing up the *Polly*, who would "be hung as a spectacle to all nations and be forever recorded as *the damned traitorous pilot who brought up the tea-ship.*"

There was a Committee for Tarring and Feathering, which the more sober citizens like Morris tried to hold in check, but whose zeal was restrained with difficulty. The amiable patriots on this committee sent the following gentle hints to Captain Ayres of the *Polly:* "You are sent out on a diabolical service, and if you are so foolish and obstinate as to complete your voyage by bringing your Ship to Anchor in this Port you may run such a gauntlet as will induce you in your last moments most heartily to curse those who have made you the dupe of their avarice and ambition. What think you, Captain, of a Halter round your Neck, ten gallons of liquid tar decanted on your Pate, with the Feathers of a dozen wild Geese laid over to enliven your appearance?"

At Gloucester Point the vessel was hailed and the captain came on shore, probably to be handed the gentle hints recorded above. Through the lane in the jeering, threatening crowd he passed to meet a committee of more reasonable but equally determined citizens. In the meantime, on December 27, 1773, an orderly crowd of eight thousand Philadelphians held a meeting at the State House and drew up the resolutions against the landing of the *Polly*. It was resolved that Captain Ayres should carry back the tea immediately. The captain on his arrival met the committee and afterward embarked on a pilot ship for his own ill-fated vessel. Perhaps the letter from the Tarring and Feathering Committee, who were despoiled of their prey, carried as much weight as the more sober resolutions. Although this defiance seemed less spectacular than the Boston Tea Party, it denoted equally strong determination.

Not long after this event, Paul Revere, famed later for his midnight ride, brought news to Philadelphia of the closing of the Port of Boston, the quartering of troops in that city, and the revocation of the Massachusetts charter. Pennsylvania, wishing to express its sympathy and cooperation, held a meeting at City Tavern. There a committee was organized to correspond with the other colonies and call meetings of delegates. On the first of June most of the business houses in Philadelphia were closed to show sympathy for the closing of the Boston Port. Flags on the river vessels hung at half mast. Muffled church bells tolled.

After this, events of great historic moment occurred in swift succession. On June 18, 1774, a meeting was held at the Pennsylvania State House, at which Thomas Willing presided. There a resolution was passed that the Boston Port Bill was unconstitutional and that the cause of Massachusetts was the common cause of all the colonies. It was at that historic meeting that a Congress of all the colonies was suggested and a Committee of Correspondence chosen to make the arrangements.

On September 5, 1774, the fifty-five delegates to this Continental Congress met at City Tavern and walked over to Carpenter's Hall, where they began their deliberations. Although all the delegates agreed upon their common grievance, there were two divergent views concerning methods of achieving their ends: one, advocated by Joseph Galloway, looked to a closer union with Great Britain; the other, sponsored by Sam Adams, advised independence. Owing to the efforts of Galloway, Dickinson, and others from the middle colonies, the New England group was finally muzzled. A petition to the King was drawn up asserting the loyalty of the colonies, but insisting upon their fundamental English rights. The repeal of eleven objectionable acts was urged. The New Englanders must have signed this document with their fingers crossed.

On September 16 the leading men of Philadelphia gave a banquet to the delegates. The hosts escorted their five hundred guests to the State House from the tavern, to the accompaniment of a band and the distant boom of cannon. At the banquet thirty-two toasts were offered—among others one to "the free and independent States of America." This first Continental Congress, during its two months' session, not merely drew up the well-known memorials to King George and the people of Great Britain but also appointed a new Committee of Correspondence. It established the first "meatless days" for all the colonies as it advised citizens to abstain from the use of mutton and lamb between the first of January and May, 1775.

Before the Second Congress met in May, another historic banquet had been celebrated. It was an old well-established custom that on April 23, St. George's Day, a meeting of one hundred of the leading citizens of Philadelphia should be held to pledge their loyalty to king and country. It was probably at one of these meetings in 1772 that Robert Morris and others had planned the organization of the St. George's Society for Assistance of Englishmen in Distress, a benevolent society of which Morris was at first vice-president and later president (from 1789 to 1796).

On this memorable St. George's Day in 1775, one hundred men met as usual at City Tavern. Robert Morris presided. After they had toasted the king and St. George, they discussed the increasing difficulties with the mother country. Heated debates ensued, but in the end moderate counsels prevailed, the members deciding that reconciliation was the wisest course. While the banquet festivities were at their height, at about five o'clock in the evening, a messenger dashed into the hall with news of the Battle of Lexington. The men, gathered about the banquet table, gazed at one another with open mouths.

"This means war," someone shouted; "war with the mother country!"

"It is treason!" cried another.

"Britain is responsible!"

"What news to hear—and on St. George's Day!"

Members of the group, tight-lipped, sprang to their feet and rushed out. Others followed, overturning the seats as they ran from the hall. The tables were almost deserted. Among the handful remaining was Robert Morris, who with Richard Peters and a few others tried to determine what course to pursue.

"The massacre at Lexington can only be deplored," said one.

"After this," another lamented, "there is no chance of reconciliation. Let us chant its requiem."

Upon this they were all agreed, that it was too late for conciliatory measures. This was war. Solemnly they raised their glasses in a final toast "To the Colonies," each man pledging himself to his country's defense.

Robert Morris in earnest, ringing tones cried, "I pledge myself and all that I possess to the cause of my adopted country."

This vow, the acid test of his patriotism, marked the real turning point in Morris's life. Before this he had been a successful merchant, a genial host, an affectionate husband and father. Now he had acquired a goal—a motive larger than business or family.

The most difficult result of his decision was announcing it to his wife with her pro-British attitude. It was characteristic of Morris that he did not resort to subterfuge in business or at home. With his wife he shared all his joys and sorrows, successes and failures. "For better, for worse," in the marriage ceremony he had taken quite literally.

"Molly," he questioned that evening after the children had been put to bed, "have you heard the news of Lexington? You know what that means, my dear. It's war."

Mary nodded silently, reserving comment.

"And we are all in it," he continued earnestly, "not just Massachusetts; but Pennsylvania and all the Colonies. We're in it up to our pocketbooks," he smiled faintly, "or perhaps up to our necks."

Mary could not smile at that, but bent her head over her sewing. This was no time for jesting.

"Today those of us who remained at the banquet," he stated in firm, ringing tones, "made certain vows—vows to defend the country. I pledged myself and my possessions to this sacred cause. Perhaps this was not fair to you and our children."

Tears were in Mary Morris's brown eyes as she raised them to meet the blue ones gazing at her so pleadingly. "What else could you do, my dear?" She tried to smile through her tears. "We are partners, aren't we?"

"You are indeed my dearest partner," he replied as he kissed her.

Ample opportunities presented themselves for testing the vow Morris had so solemnly made. Soon two thousand men were under arms in Philadelphia. Two troops of light horse, two companies of riflemen, and two of artillery drilled daily. The Third Battalion, dubbed the "Silk Stocking Company" because of their breeding and sartorial elegance, began target practice on Race Street, where one over-zealous, incautious member shot a child. On May 27 the troops in the city were reviewed on the commons by Generals Washington, Lee, and Mifflin. In May a mass meeting was held in the rain, and another in June, followed by a dinner at the Indian Queen, where "Liberty" was toasted.

The Pennsylvania Assembly at this time appointed a Committee of Safety to succeed the Committee of Correspondence, with Benjamin Franklin as chairman and Robert Morris, vice-chairman. At six o'clock every morning the committee met, beginning on July 3, 1775. Franklin and Morris were notoriously early risers. "Poor Richard" obeyed his own injunctions, whereas Morris had been forced by business to appear in his office soon after sunrise. Their task, the supervision of military supplies and powers in the province, taxed Franklin's wisdom and Morris's resourcefulness. In those meetings at dawn they devised plans for the organization of the militia and fortification of the Delaware River, quite open to attack from the enemy. In fact, the committee took charge of all municipal and provincial matters connected with the conduct of the war. It issued bills of credit, amounting to £35,000, to pay its own drafts—a device preventing squabbles between conflicting boards and bureaucrats. It purchased arms and ammunition on favorable terms since Morris, a practical businessman, knew how and where to purchase such supplies. It created defenses for the city and port of Philadelphia —thirteen galleys and a floating battery of fire rafts—and it built a fleet of gunboats.

As a result of his successful labors for defense, Morris was elected to Congress on November 3, 1775, one of seven members from Pennsylvania. In December of that year he was chosen one of a committee to establish a colonial navy. This was a mammoth assignment, to create a navy without supplies or men or any real authority. This group recommended that five ships of twenty-eight guns, five of twenty-two guns, and three of twenty-four guns be constructed. When the recommendations were presented to Congress, Morris was placed on the committee to carry out the plan, a task on which he was engaged long after the committee itself was dissolved. Eight armed vessels were built, the nucleus of a national navy. Previously Congress had authorised a regular marine of seventeen cruisers, carrying from ten to thirty-two guns. Four of these ships, the *Washington*, the *Randolph*, the *Effingham*, and the *Delaware*, were being constructed in the Philadelphia shipyards. These were designed to destroy convoys and to capture transports and troopships. They were to be sent out on cruises to intercept supplies for the British. Of this projected fleet, a large part of which existed on paper, Ezekial (or Esek) Hopkins was commissioned the first Commander-in-Chief with the title Commodore or Admiral. The first ship to set sail on a long cruise was the *Lexington*, Captain Barry commanding. Soon after, a squadron of eight vessels under Commodore Hopkins was directed to proceed southward, arranging for a rendezvous in the Bahamas.

Morris received word of an amazing occurrence. The *Providence*, one of the squadron sent to the Bahamas, conquered the island of New Providence, capturing the governor and other notables. When

British ships appeared to rescue the beleaguered island, the American crews turned the guns of the fort against the would-be rescuers. The triumph was short-lived. While the ships, for others had joined the *Providence*, remained in port at New Providence, smallpox broke out. When Hopkins returned from his cruise, he was censured, despite his phenomenal success, and was later dismissed.

On another trip, the *Lexington* with Captain Hallock in command was captured on its return from the West Indies by a British frigate, the *Pearl*. The American vessel, manned by a prize crew, was ordered to follow the British ship. In the dead of night the Americans overpowered the English crew and carried the *Lexington* with its captives to Baltimore in triumph.

One of the greatest difficulties experienced by Morris and his committee was that of obtaining crews to man the new navy. The privateers offered sailors tremendous inducements in prize money and treasure, counterattractions which Morris and his committee could not hope to match. Morris was puzzled. What methods could he use to induce them to enlist? There must be military fanfare, some spectacular appeal to patriotism. There was a touch of P. T. Barnum in Morris. He realized the strong appeals to eye and ear.

Soon a recruiting officer, bearing a flag and attended by a band, paraded the streets of Philadelphia. The band blared martial music. The jolly officer sang:

> "All you that have bad masters
> And cannot get your due,
> Come, come, my brave boys,
> And join our ship's crew."

There was more such doggerel, followed by shouts and huzzahs from husky followers in the crowd. Some joined under the spell of the music and the shouting, especially as the parade led them straight to the recruiting office. Even then the ships were short-handed.

At the time Robert Morris entered Congress and began his work on the Maritime Committee (in November, 1775), a law was passed placing a marine corps, infantry soldiers to serve afloat, on all American vessels. These marines were to furnish guards and sentinels, to maintain discipline, to suppress the turbulence of ill-assorted crews, and, in short, to protect the ship. From the first, these soldiers were noted for their gallantry.

One day, soon after Morris had assumed these burdens, a great crowd gathered on the docks along the river front in Philadelphia. News had been buzzed about that some spectacular event would occur. All eyes were centered on the *Alfred*, the scene of the most intense activity. The crowd became restive.

"What is occurring?"

"I can't see."

"Make way there."

Soon martial music sounded. To its strains a young lieutenant stepped forward and hoisted a flag to the masthead—a pine tree on a white ground.

"What are the words below?" cried one onlooker.

"Liberty Tree," answered one.

"Appeal to God," said another.

The crowd surged backward as the thirty-six guns of the *Alfred* fired a salute to the new standard. The young lieutenant, his eyes upon the flag, stood at salute.

"Who is this officer?" asked one.

"He's called John Paul Jones," replied an old man, "but I've heard tell he was born John Paul—just added the Jones himself."

"A Scot, isn't he?" questioned another.

"Yes," said the old man. "He was a slaver's mate, I heard, and a privateersman. Joined up recently with our navy."

In the meantime John Paul Jones dropped his hand to his side and with the step of a conqueror paced the deck. When he had rejoined his companions, he again looked up proudly at the ensign floating above the *Alfred*.

By October, 1776, there were twenty-six vessels listed in the American navy, most of which never set sail. The *Reprisal* was the first American man-of-war to appear in European waters. With Benjamin Franklin as passenger it sailed for France. On its return voyage it took several prizes and otherwise distinguished itself; but unfortunately was finally lost on the banks of Newfoundland.

Robert Morris and his fellow commissioners had ordered a large frigate built at Amsterdam; but since the British objected, the neutral Dutch were unwilling to finish the *Indien* for the rebellious colonies. Thus Congress offered the ship to Louis XVI.

On the home front other difficulties loomed—difficulties in securing supplies, in obtaining shipbuilders and crews. Thus by the end of the year none of the vessels ordered had been launched. Every available cruiser, every privateersman that could be requisitioned, was placed in the service of the colonies. At these tasks Morris labored with tireless energy. The more he accomplished, the more Congress imposed upon him.

Early in 1776 he was appointed chairman of a Secret Committee to import arms and gunpowder for the army. Since the firm of Willing & Morris handled the contract, this matter rested almost wholly upon Morris's broad shoulders. Other merchants became jealous of the power and influence of the firm, especially when, in order to protect these much-needed supplies, a guard was placed over the ships and stores of Congress at the wharves of Willing & Morris. Jealousy, thus born and nourished with the years, grew apace until eventually it burst in full fury upon Robert Morris.

PART TWO

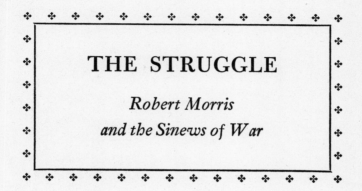

THE STRUGGLE

Robert Morris
and the Sinews of War

CHAPTER IV

DOORBELL RINGER

❖   ❖   ❖

IN the State House on June 7, 1776, there rose a storm of conflicting currents of opinion. Richard Henry Lee of Virginia introduced the resolution: "These united Colonies are and of right ought to be free and independent States, that they are absolved from all allegiance to the British Crown, and that all political connection between them and the State of Great Britain is and ought to be totally dissolved."

John Adams hastened to second the motion. Members from Massachusetts, New Hampshire, and South Carolina applauded. These provinces had already established administrative systems independent of England. The New York delegation frowned and whispered.

John Dickinson of Pennsylvania, the "Penman of the Revolution," rose to speak in opposition to the motion. With logical precision he stated his objections to independence as twofold: the lack of unity among the Colonies, and the lack of foreign allies. "The dangers of dissension" formed the burden of his speech. His colleagues from Pennsylvania nodded their approval. Action on the motion was postponed until July 1. In the meantime two committees were appointed: one to prepare a declaration, the other to draw up a plan of confederation. On the first committee were placed Thomas Jefferson, brilliant aristocrat and legal light from Virginia; Benjamin Franklin, wise writer and philosopher from Pennsylvania; John Adams, astute lawyer and politician from Massachusetts; Roger Sherman, also a lawyer, from Connecticut; and Robert R. Livingston, a jurist and army captain from New York. The final draft of the Declaration of Independence drawn up by this committee was primarily the work of Jefferson.

On July 1 when Lee's motion was again considered, the now famous document was read. "When in the course of human events," it began solemnly,—"We hold these truths to be self-evident," it continued, in an impassioned statement of democratic faith, "that all men are created equal, that they are endowed by their Creator with certain Unalienable Rights, that among these are Life, Liberty and the pursuit of Happiness." The members of Congress listened breathless. Nine hours of stormy debate followed the reading.

John Dickinson again rose to express his vehement opposition: "The Declaration will not strengthen us by one man or by the least supply. On the contrary it may inflame the calamities of the contest and expose our soldiers and inhabitants in general to additional cruelties and outrages. It may unite the different parties there [in England] against us. And it may occasion disunion among ourselves. It may rather injure than avail us."

Robert Morris in a white silk suit (according to the famous painting) turned in his seat to discuss the Declaration with his colleagues. "In my opinion it is premature," he stated. "It will neither promote the interest nor redound to the honor of America."

At the end of nine hours of torrid oratory, the meeting adjourned without a vote having been taken on the motion to accept the Declaration of Independence.

The next day both Morris and Dickinson remained away, unwilling to vote against their better judgment. When the roll was called on July 4, the motion to adopt the Declaration passed unanimously, as Morris, Dickinson, and Willing did not appear, and the New York delegates, still uninstructed by the state, did not cast their votes. That same day the dapper John Hancock, President of Congress, affixed his signature to the document with a flourish, thereby making his name synonymous with any signature.

On August 2 Robert Morris, among the fifty-three members of Congress then present, signed the Declaration of Independence since he felt that nothing would be gained by his failure to sign. His views, however, had not altered. Ever since voting against Lee's resolution he had confidently expected not to be reelected to Congress. Indeed he looked forward with satisfaction to the time when he would be freed from his burdens and be able to attend to his mercantile business. John Dickinson and James Wilson, Thomas Willing, too, to some degree, paid the price of opposing independence and not signing the Declaration. Morris, however, was not punished despite his candor in stating his views and principles. The country, profiting by his initiative and efficiency, deemed him too valuable for dismissal.

Very frankly he wrote Joseph Reed, President of Congress: "I have uniformly voted against and opposed the Declaration of Independence, for it has caused division where we wanted union, and will be ascribed to very different principles than those which ought to give rise to such an important measure. I did expect my conduct on this great occasion would have procured my dismission from the Great Council but find myself disappointed, for the Convention has thought it proper to retain me in the new delegation, and although my interest and inclination prompt me to decline the service, yet I cannot depart from the point which first induced me to enter the public line—I mean the opinion that *it is the duty of every individual to act his part in whatever station his country may call him to in hours of difficulty, danger, and distress.*" This is the keynote to the public life of Robert Morris: the duty to act for his country in hours of danger.

The hours of danger and distress were at hand. Early in December, 1776, riders galloped into Philadelphia announcing that an advance guard of Hessians and Highlanders were in possession of Burlington, New Jersey, pushing on toward Cooper's Ferry, opposite the city. Thereupon Congress fled to Baltimore, appointing Robert Morris, George Clymer of Pennsylvania, and George Walton of Georgia to assume charge of governmental affairs in Philadelphia. With the disappearance of his two colleagues, who remained long enough to sign a few letters, Morris was left with the entire responsibility of directing the business of Congress in the deserted capital —a duty which he did not seek but would not shirk. He was authorized to borrow $10,000 for the use of the Marine Committee, to strengthen the defenses on the Delaware, and to execute such Continental business as might be proper and necessary. Thus during the absence of Congress from Philadelphia, a period of about three months, Morris represented the government.

"I am well aware," wrote William Hooper, member of Congress, "of the burden of publick business with which our removal has encumbered you. When in Philadelphia when we took a small share of it to ourselves, I have been amazed how you waded thro' it, and found the leisure for your own private concerns and the enjoyment of your friends. Congress seems unanimously sensible of the obligations which they owe you, and you may boast of being the only man whom they all agree to speak & I really believe think well of."

John Hancock, "ambitious of being reckoned among the list" of Morris's real friends, assured him that his continuance in Philadelphia atoned for the flight of Congress.

Fortunately Morris, placed in this unique position of trust, was not the stuff of which dictators are made. He might easily at this time have become a Hitler, but he modestly considered himself merely the steward of the nation. He served as an intelligence officer, among numerous other duties, trying to secure correct information concerning the movement of Howe's troops—an exceedingly difficult task in those days.

"Howe's forces are coming down the river."

"Howe's forces are sailing up Chesapeake Bay."

"Howe is being reinforced at Brunswick."

"British soldiers are encamped at Cooper's Ferry."

These conflicting rumors Morris weighed and sifted. Daily he sent swift messengers to John Hancock, President of Congress, who replied (in January, 1777): "Without the least appearance of Flattery I can assure you your whole Conduct since our Flight is highly approved, and happy I am that you remained, many agreeable Consequences have Resulted from it, and your continu'd Exertions will be productive of great good. I must therefore beg you will continue as long as you can, tho' I sincerely wish you a happy Sight of good

Mrs. Morris, but I fear your departure from Philadelphia might occasion a Relaxation that would be prejudicial. I know however that you will put things in a proper way, indeed all depends upon you, and you have my hearty thanks for your unremitting Labours."

At the first word of the British approach Robert Morris had packed off his wife and four children to Harford County, Maryland, to visit Mrs. Sophia Hall, Mary Morris's step-sister, at Sophia's Dairy, an old family estate. These four children already revealed marked differences in personality and character. Robert, or Bob, the oldest child, resembled his father in many ways: in his physical strength and a certain sturdiness of character. Thomas (Tom), the second son, in his youth was not nearly so robust as his brother. On this journey he suffered from a "boil of an uncommon nature." At this early period he showed little of the initiative of his more mature life. Hetty, "darling daughter," had inherited her mother's poise and social charm. William, or Bill, the third son, remains a shadowy figure until spotlighted just before his death many years later.

On her flight Mary Morris found the inn at Tuscanah Ferry so crowded with delegates to Congress that there was no room for her and the children. Mr. Hudson, a friend of Robert Morris, came to see them at the inn and placed his house in Baltimore at their disposal. At Head of Elk another friend, a Mr. Alexander, invited Mrs. Morris to lodge at his house. When she declined the invitation, he offered to send teams to carry her goods to the Halls'. This service she gratefully accepted since she constantly feared the loss of their personal property. At Sophia's Dairy, which she finally reached after a trying journey, Mary Morris's parents soon joined her.

Her letters to her husband from Maryland contained a wealth of family news, the minute domestic details in which she knew he was interested. She spoke of Tom's being thin and remaining under the doctor's care. Bill, however, was "stout," and Hetty, very hearty. Bob, the oldest son, must have been well also as he walked three miles to school with his cousins. One family scene she describes graphically—the arrival of a letter from her husband. As she opened it, Bob began to dance around the room. "Read it out loud, Mamma.

Will you? Do, Mamma," he pleaded. At this insistence she read parts of the letter aloud, to the children's great delight.

His wife was concerned very naturally about Morris's living arrangements. She wondered where he was living and whether he was comfortable. In one letter she requested "news of the mercantile world," revealing that her husband must have confided some of his business affairs to her. She reported to him that on her way to Maryland she had heard that a pipe of wine which was supposed to belong to him was in danger of being confiscated by a certain skipper and his crew, who swore they would knock in one of the heads and drink the wine.

A housewifely touch was added in her request for needles from the white needle-book in a certain drawer in the back parlor at home.

While his family remained in Maryland, Morris feared for the safety of his household goods, which he kept packed, ready to send out of the city. He was too busy, however, to devote much thought to his own privations. Engaged in borrowing and spending, in hurrying defenses, in urging shipyard workers to hasten the construction and repair of vessels, he labored night and day. His robust figure in its long cloak, cane in hand, appeared wherever Congressional business demanded his personal supervision.

Mutiny on shipboard. Morris must take a hand.

"No carpenters available, sir." Morris must provide them somehow.

"The crews will desert unless they are paid." No money from Congress. Morris must find it somewhere.

To the outskirts of Philadelphia he rode on horseback to inspect the galleys and fire-rafts protecting the city. Here he had an interview with Commodore Hazlewood, in charge of the river fleet.

"The men are deserting in droves, Mr. Morris. Privateering strikes a blow at their patriotism."

Morris nodded thoughtfully. "This passion for privateering is so strong," he said, "even agriculture is abandoned to pursue it." By tact Morris helped the Commodore placate the deserters. Back to the offices of Willing & Morris rode the most indefatigable man in America.

The fleet, which was subject to his order, Morris held in readiness for departure down the bay at the approach of the British. He intended to prevent the few American ships from falling into the hands of the enemy. When Howe's army at Brunswick began to move, Morris ordered six ships in the Philadelphia harbor to try to escape, but upon receiving more favorable news, he recalled them.

"I exceedingly approve your conduct with respect to the Ships in your River," wrote Hancock appreciatively. "I dare say your dispositions of the several Arm'd Vessels after you are fully convinc'd of the Removal of the Ships from your Capes, will fully meet the approbation of Congress."

Another Howe, the Admiral, was now threatening Philadelphia by sea as was the General by land. The situation was a perilous one. There occurred a few strokes of fortune. The *Andrew Doria*, having captured a prize, the *Racehorse*, ran the blockade and slipped into port from St. Eustatia to increase the navy. Every ship was worth its weight in Spanish dollars. Just as valuable was its cargo of stockings, jackets, blankets, muskets, and powder. The ammunition was distributed at once to the army; the clothing was stored for the future. The time was not far off when no clothing would be available for soldier or civilian, when bare bleeding feet would mark the road to Valley Forge.

During these perilous days, Morris, acting as Secretary of the Treasury without title, was concerned chiefly with the Continental finances. In a letter to Congress he stated: "Continental currency keeps losing its credit. Many people refuse openly to receive it" (although there was a penalty attached to such a refusal). Again he warned: "Nothing can be got for your money." Characteristically he sought a suitable substitute for the worthless paper. "Some effectual remedy should be applied to this evil or the game will be up," he wrote Congress solicitously. Within five years the "game was up." It then required one thousand paper dollars to equal one silver dollar. Paper money was used to light fires or decorate rooms. But Congress, deaf to Morris's plea at this time, would not even use an ear trumpet. Had Morris been given full authority over finances at this time, much suffering might have been saved the Continental Army.

In the various financial crises, Robert Morris had already advanced funds from his own fortune and made use of his credit. He had kept his vow, pledging himself and all his possessions to his country. Now he felt it necessary to resort to other methods of raising funds. While he remained in Philadelphia, most of his wealthy friends had left the city. Only the Quakers, many of whom were disaffected or strongly Loyalist, could be solicited for loans. Morris's commanding figure ringing the doorbells of the Quaker merchants became one of the familiar sights in Philadelphia that winter. Although often quietly rebuffed by these pacifists, the great optimist refused to accept defeat. Robert Morris, the War Bond salesman *par excellence* of his day, sometimes made sales through his sheer buoyancy of spirit and integrity of character. A demand for extra funds, however, made even Morris's stout heart quail.

On December 31, 1776, Washington sent a fleet messenger to Morris with a request for $50,000, a large sum for that period. Washington needed an Intelligence Service to keep him informed of enemy movements. Without receiving their arrears of pay, moreover, the troops whose term of service had expired would not reenlist. Mutiny threatened. The Commander-in-Chief had also learned of the enemy's design to take Philadelphia and attack his battalions early in January when the Delaware River would be frozen over. By his own influence Washington had persuaded the troops to remain six weeks longer with a promise of a bonus or "bounty" of $10 per soldier in addition to their regular pay. Then he wrote Robert Morris for money to fulfill his promise, so great was his confidence in Morris's ability.

Before the war had ended, the Financier had become accustomed to such requests, but this first big demand seemed staggering. A short time before this, Morris had sent Washington a communication in which he stated: "I had long since parted with very considerable sums of hard money to Congress, and therefore must collect from others, and as matters now stand, it is no easy thing. I mean to borrow silver and promise payment in gold, and then will collect the

gold in the best manner I can. . . . Whatever I can do shall be done
for the good of the cause."

After he had received Washington's request, his fertile brain began to evolve plans and methods for meeting it. He never thought
of refusing any demand his Chief made upon him throughout the
war. After a troubled sleep, Robert Morris rose that New Year's
Day in 1777, and with furrowed brow started on an early morning walk toward the Quaker residential section. Fortunately, the
wealthy Quaker, Abel James, answered his ring at the doorbell.

"What news so early, Robert?" asked the Quaker.

"The news is just this, my friend," replied Morris. "General Washington needs a certain sum of hard money and I must send it to
him immediately. I would like you to lend me $50,000."

"But what is thy security, Robert, for this large sum?"

"My word and my honor," replied Morris.

"Thee shall have it," said the Quaker. Such was the trust everyone
placed in the integrity of Robert Morris.

An hour after sunrise a messenger galloped off to Washington's
headquarters with the money and this message from Morris:

"Sir,

"I was honored with your favor of yesterday by Mr. Howell late
last night and ever solicitous to comply with your requisitions, I
am up very early this morning to despatch a supply of $50,000 to
your Excellency."

As a result the troops reenlisted. The next day, on January 3,
Washington with his army crept up to Princeton in the night and
defeated the enemy. Thus Robert Morris played an important part
in this American victory. When the news of this battle reached
Mary Morris, a pacifist like most mothers, she wrote her husband
from Maryland:

"I have received five of your letters since my last, besides Mr.
Hall's, the contents of which almost petrified us; happy had we
been had the petrifaction reached our hearts and made them proof
against our feelings in this day of Triall. I suppressed mine all in my
power, as I wish to make myself as agreeable as possible to this

family, and as they had invited a party of young folks to a Twelfth Cake, I tryed to be cheerful; how could I be really so when hourly in expectation of hearing the determination of so important a Battle, and when the express arrived and pronounced Washington victorious, would you believe it, your Molly could not join in the general rejoicing? No! Nor never can at a victory so dearly bought."

Morris's task in Philadelphia continued to be one of almost insuperable difficulties. Not the least trying factor was Congress itself, often unwilling to act but equally unwilling to relinquish any of its authority. This tendency hampered Morris in his negotiations, especially with the French commissioners. Several of his correspondents deplored the lack of serious investigation of subjects considered by the Congress.

A letter from William Hooper spoke most sarcastically of such snap judgments: "We have been holding forth new lines to France by offering what we have not to give & provided they will conquer the whole of Newfoundland and secure the fishing, that we will give them one half for their trouble. We have found out that the Duke of Tuscany is a potentate of much consequence, while some of us are such Ignoramuses as to think him very insignificant in the naval and military line and in this respect not worthy attention. . . . But I anticipate an amusement which you have to come, the Picture of our follies will be more pleasing from being viewed at full length."

Morris probably smiled at the description of the ill-advised actions of Congress as he continued reading Hooper's letter:

"A plan is in agitation to appoint exclusive powers out of doors, and resolved the business of Treasury, Board of War and of Commerce into the hands of persons not members of Congress. A Committee appointed for that purpose and you are a member of it. You will be much wanted. I wish if your attendance is impossible that you will reduce a few tho'ts to paper upon the subject of a Chamber of Commerce which is the Hobby Horse & for which I fancy we are indebted to the abilities of Mr. P—e."

This was the first thinly veiled allusion to Thomas Paine so soon to play an important part in Morris's life as well as in that of the nation.

During these days of intense activity, Morris's friends who had left Philadelphia did not hesitate to make personal demands upon his time, energy, and pocketbook. He was delegated to carry out various commissions, some of them amusing for a man who was at that time virtual head of the government. One such commission was a request by Samuel Griffin that Morris purchase to order a set of curls for Betsey Griffin and curls and stays for Miss Braxton. Benjamin Harrison requested him to demand "a chariot with 4 harness" from Bringhurst of Germantown, a chariot maker, and pay for it, charging the amount to Harrison himself or his son Ben, then employed in the counting room of Willing & Morris. Silas Deane, one of the Commissioners in Paris, wished Morris to send him a phaeton and a pair of bay horses. He also commended his wife and son to his friend to "make decent provision" for their passage to France. At this time, too, Morris bought some coral for Martha Washington, who begged that it might be "mounted neatly without bells."

Complaints were as numerous as commissions, especially complaints of conditions in Baltimore. Benjamin Harrison, Morris's most gossipy correspondent, had a dozen epithets for that unpaved and otherwise unimproved city. Among other names he called it "the Damdest Hole in the World." William Hooper wrote: "This dirty boggy hole beggars all description. We are obliged except when the weather paves the streets to go to Congress on Horseback, the way so miry that Carriages almost stall on the sides of them." Harrison felt so keenly on the subject that he devoted one entire letter to it. "I most sincerely thank you for your kind wishes to see me again at the Hills," he said in part. "I generally appropriate some moments on Sunday to that Place let me be where I will, but in this infernal sink I scarcely think of anything else, there is not even a Tavern that we can Ride to for Exercise and amusement within 15 miles of the place. I mean such as a Gentn. can dine in with comfort."

Robert Morris also thought longingly of his country estate, "The Hills," just outside the city. Although he had little opportunity to find rest there during that distressing period, it was sweet to dream of that haven above the Schuylkill with its cool gardens and spacious rooms and porches. Whenever possible, he escaped there from Philadelphia.

The city at that time presented "the greatest scene of distress that you can conceive," he wrote his friends in Baltimore, perhaps to reconcile them to their stay in that uncomfortable town. "Philadelphia," he continued, "is a city on wheels, everyone who can do so fleeing from it." All day long over the cobblestones jogged the carts of the refugees, their vehicles loaded with household furniture and crying children. They were on their way to Maryland or Delaware, or perhaps even to Virginia—anywhere away from the advancing British troops. Into Philadelphia from New Jersey rumbled and creaked the wagons bearing sick soldiers to rapidly improvised hospitals. Smallpox was rife. Two thousand victims of this plague were buried in narrow trenches in Washington Square. Every day came more alarming reports of the approach of the enemy. All who could do so fled from these multiplying dangers—danger of the loss of property and family, danger of disease, danger of attack from Howe's forces. Only the peace-loving Quakers, a small body of troops, and Robert Morris remained in the city to guard it.

During this bleak winter of 1777 the river fortunately was full of ice. Nevertheless, the Philadelphians experienced many a scare when Howe was reported to be at their very gates. Although apprehensive, Morris preserved his poise and his wit. His letters to Congress sparkled with similes and epithets. That body, he knew, was as "hungry as hawks after news." He made merry at Howe's expense; if he would only "keep his myrmidons away," he promised to send six ships down to the bay. He wished to finish the work in Philadelphia "with General Howe's permission," but "if he advances," he continued, "I shall push off and leave him to finish the business in his own way." Although Morris was prepared to depart at a moment's notice, his possessions all packed, his horses and carriages ready, he was "determined not to quit until fairly done off."

Luckily for the country he did not have to leave the city. Still he did not consider it safe for Congress to return. The letters between Morris and Hancock flew by swiftest messengers. Toward the end of February the latter wrote: "In Consequence of yours by Express respecting the State of our Army" [which was appalling still], "& y'r opinion that at present it would not be prudent for Congress to Return to Philadelphia, the Congress have determin'd to suspend their Remove for Some Days, at least until we hear from you which I hope will be soon, and that the way is clear for us to pursue our own course. We must give these fellows a trimming, if we can but subdue the present force in the Jerseys, I think the day is ours, one noble Exertion by a large Body flying to the support of the General with a determination to oppose Howe's Army at all Events, would effect the Business and before any Reinforcements could arrive from Europe we should be in such Readiness as soon to give a good Acco't of them. Tho' I believe they will soon be tir'd of their game. We have got the Trumps. Let us play the Game well." Thus this American optimist believed the war would soon end.

Not so Morris, realistically facing the problems of the conflict. At last, however, he sent Congress the long-awaited word that they might safely return to Philadelphia. Hancock, who had grown impatient at the long delay, jubilantly wrote him:

"I send Mr. Tailor my Sec'y to Philada to procure a suitable house well furnish'd for me, and I have taken the liberty to desire him to apply to you for your advise in this instance, not doubting your good offices. Congress will adjourn on Tuesday next to that day week to meet in Philada, and I hope on Saturday or Sunday to take you by the hand; my Friend, it will give me pleasure to see you, & I hope our coming there will in some degree Relieve you from the great Burden that has laid upon you. I assure you I have felt for you. No money, constant application for it, and a steady succession of Business to attend to, has made yr. Scituation hard indeed, however you gave up all pro Bono Publico, & I know you will persevere & you are as well calculated to go thro' Business as any Gentleman I know."

Hancock, however, was not destined to take Morris by the hand the next Saturday or Sunday or the week following. Another scare occurred: "Howe's reinforced Army is sailing down the river." Again

Morris sent Congress a hasty message advising a postponement of their return, but a few weeks later, feeling that immediate danger was past, with a sigh of relief he sent word that Congress might again convene in Philadelphia.

CHAPTER V

FLIGHT FROM PARADISE

❖   ❖   ❖

WITH the return of Congress in March, 1777, Robert Morris gladly resigned his responsibility into their hands. Power and office were never of his seeking. To his great joy that same month brought his wife and family back to him.

On March 15 Mary Morris sent her mother a letter announcing her arrival: "Last Wednesday noon I had the pleasure to arrive safe in dear Philadelphia, after a much pleasanter journey than I expected from our setting off, and it made me very happy to find myself at home after so long an absence, with the terrible apprehensions we fled with of never seeing it again."

A month later Mrs. Morris felt somewhat less settled as the British again menaced the city. Nevertheless she wrote her mother optimistically: "We are preparing for another flight in packing up our furniture and removing them to another purchase Mr. Morris has made ten miles from Lancaster, no other than the famous House that belonged to Stedman and Steigel at the Iron Works, where you know I spent six weeks; so am perfectly well acquainted with the goodness of the House and situation. The reason Mr. Morris made this purchase, he looks upon the other not secure if they come by water. I think myself very lucky in having this Asylum, it being but 8 miles, fine road, from Lancaster, where I expect Mr. Morris will be if he quits this, besides many of my friends and acquaintances. So I now solicit the pleasure of your company at this once famous place."

When two weeks afterward the British had not yet arrived, Mary

Morris began to feel hopeful of spending the summer at "The Hills," just outside the city. "I am yet on dear Philadelphia ground," she told her mother, "but expect soon to inhabit the Hills, where we shall remain, if possible, in the enjoyment of all that's beautiful to the eye and grateful to the taste: for, as if to add to our mortification, are we obliged to leave, nature never appeared there so lovely, nor promised such a profusion of her gifts. We intend sending off our best furniture to Lancaster, with all the linen we can spare, and stores of all kinds, that our flight may be attended with as few incumbrances as possible."

Through froth of apple and pear blossoms the family chariot wound its way up the slopes of "The Hills." With eager eyes Mary Morris and the children gazed at the springtime beauty of their far-spreading lands: three hundred acres of woods and fields and gardens above the Schuylkill River. This estate, once the manor of Springetsbury in the Northern Liberties, Robert Morris had purchased from Tench Francis in 1770. At first it comprised only eighty acres, but subsequent purchases had increased it to three hundred acres or more.

As the carriage ascended the hill which gave the estate its name, the occupants feasted their eyes upon the waving grass, the flowering shrubs, the chestnut and tulip trees, the cattle and merino sheep that roamed the slopes. How good it was to be at home again at "The Hills" in the spring! Here were familiar landmarks. Here was the springhouse with the granary above, there the hog pen of stone, the brewhouse, and the icehouse [the first to be owned privately in America]. At the two farm houses, one of brick and one of stone, the tenants bobbed their curtseys and waved a welcome to the mistress and the laughing, chattering children. Now appeared the gardener's house, the coachhouse and stables, and finally, crowning the hill, the greenhouses and the mansion itself.

A royal welcome greeted them from the domestic staff of "The Hills," who were always ready to receive the family and guests. After a fatiguing week of business the weary master often sought relaxation there on Sundays and holidays. It was a refuge for him—at first from the cares of business and of public life and at the last from the attacks of a hostile world.

The glorious spring and summer days of 1777, the Morrises spent at this country home. From the spacious tree-shaded porches at the sides of the house they caught glimpses of the river or watched the ripening grain undulate in the breeze. The handsome two-storied house was built for comfort and hospitality. It had a high basement above the ground, in which there were a small dining room and servants' quarters. The high hipped roof afforded garret space. This was a commodious dwelling, capable of accommodating others besides the family. Many distinguished guests that summer enjoyed the hospitality of that delightful home with its large high-ceilinged rooms and bay windows.

At this time there arrived in America a young French marquis, destined to become a great American hero. He came highly recommended by Silas Deane, one of the Commissioners in Paris, to the care and oversight of Robert Morris, who, Deane knew, "would be a father to him on every occasion." "I have advised him to place the utmost confidence in you," the Commissioner concluded. So the Marquis de Lafayette became a frequent visitor at the Morrises' home that summer and in the years following.

In the large upstairs dining room at "The Hills" four men sat in Chippendale chairs sipping Madeira. The table, immaculate in snowy linen, shone with crystal and silver.

"This is Paradise, Mr. Morris, after the horrors of Baltimore," sighed the elegant, fastidious John Hancock.

"It reminds me of the charms of Paris, sir," said Lafayette with a bow.

"It's heaven upon earth," ejaculated the old Virginian, Benjamin Harrison. "We can even forget how short-lived this happiness promises to be."

"Let us forget the war," smiled Morris genially, "and remember only the verities and realities of existence—friendship, beauty, the growth of crops. Gentlemen, shall we inspect the gardens?"

Morris's guests nodded their assent as they rose from the table. Through French windows they stepped onto a veranda overlooking the flower gardens with their rare, vari-colored roses, peonies, and poppies. Beyond the palette of rich colors the trees sloped down to the Schuylkill River. Peace reigned over the broad acres of "The Hills." War and the threat of invasion seemed to belong to another country and another age. The men's faces relaxed.

"No wonder, Morris, you can keep your equilibrium under most distressing circumstances when you have this haven awaiting you," Harrison remarked with feeling in his voice.

"That does solve the mystery of your poise last winter when you had to attend to the affairs of Congress," agreed Hancock as he leaned on the balustrade drinking in the beauty of the scene.

"It is a refuge, especially when Mrs. Morris is here," Morris answered in deep, earnest tones. "But come," he continued, smiling boyishly, "I would like you to see my new orange trees and my pineapples."

On their way to the hot houses, they passed a fishpond gay with tropical fish. As they entered the long, glass-enclosed greenhouses, the fragrance of orange and lemon blossoms greeted them. They passed delicate, exotic flowers like butterflies impaled upon a stalk. At the farther end grew the pineapples imported from Madeira with the wine now stocking Morris's cellar.

"Return in a few weeks when they are ripe and you shall share them with me," said Morris beaming. These hothouses were one of his pet hobbies which he hospitably enjoyed sharing with his friends.

As they left the greenhouses and circled back toward the house, they passed a small marble pavilion.

"Charming! This is like Versailles—the Temple of Love," Lafayette smiled reminiscently.

"What do you call it, Morris?" asked Harrison.

"The Temple to Hospitality," replied Morris.

"Very appropriate," exclaimed Hancock. "You are, I believe, the most hospitable man in America."

"The Host of America," chimed in Harrison laughing, "that should be your title."

"You're also an Aladdin with his magic lamp," cried Hancock. "These grounds form an 'Arabian Nights' setting."

Morris threw back his head, his sides shaking with laughter. "Enough epithets for one afternoon, gentlemen. Shall we return to the house? The chairs on the verandas should prove more comfortable than this marble bench."

On the balustraded porches and in the garden the children played those summer days. That summer was made happier, too, by the birth on July 11 of the Morrises' fifth child, the ill-fated Charles. Mary Morris seemed supremely happy to rest at "The Hills." Here were peace and beauty after the discomfort and terror of flight. Whenever he could escape from the cares of business, Robert Morris spent days of joyous companionship with his family. He was essentially domestic—never so happy as when with his beloved Molly and the children. Like another Robert with his Mary, he recited:

"There oft as mild evening weeps over the lea,
The sweet-scented birk shades my Mary and me."

Much of the summer, especially during her pregnancy, Mrs. Morris spent in correspondence with her mother, who still remained in the South. Two family honors delighted Mary Morris: Reverend William White, her brother "Billy," was appointed Chaplain to Congress, and her husband was offered the presidency of Congress—an honor which he declined as "private affairs would not permit him to give more freely of his time and abilities to the public service."

"Don't you feel quite important?" she asked her mother. "I assure you I do, and begin to be reconciled to independence."

Her letters were full of news, domestic and political. Tom, she wrote, was still sick, under Dr. Shippen's care. He had apparently not recovered from the illness from which he had suffered in Maryland. Mr. Morris feared for her health, too, she told her mother, and insisted on her taking a daily walk. "I can hardly convince him," she said, "that my health is not declining." She also spoke of the stream of British deserters constantly pouring into the city and of "the general defection between the Hessians and the British soldiery." A naval item concerned the American ship *Morris*, laden with a valuable cargo of arms, ammunition, and dry goods. Beset by three other ships, she defended herself bravely. The captain, however, realizing the inequality of the struggle, ran her on shore and blew her up. "He perished himself," she concluded, "in his anxiety to do it effectively."

Unfortunately Robert Morris was too busy to spend much time with his family at "The Hills." That was a period of great agitation in Pennsylvania. The State Assembly seemed unable to organize a government which the people would obey. The State Constitution, Utopian and impractical in the opinion of many leading Philadelphians, needed revision. Morris among others signed a petition urging the Assembly to call a convention to revise and amend the constitution. Enthusiastic over this reform, he personally distributed copies of a memorial for the people to sign, requesting that such a convention be called. Opposing these policies were the "Furious Whigs" or Constitutionalists, Thomas Paine and David Rittenhouse among them, who soon unleashed political war in all its Blitzkrieg fury.

Other great events occurred that summer of 1777. On June 14 Congress looked at a design for a flag which Washington had helped create. After some discussion that august body passed a resolution: "That the flag of the 13 United States be 13 stripes, alternate red and white; that the union be 13 stars, white in a blue field, presenting a new constellation."

A committee thereupon was appointed to arrange for the manufacture of the flag. This committee comprised George Washington (whose coat of arms had probably suggested the design), George Ross of Pennsylvania, and Robert Morris. A short time later the three men rang the doorbell of Betsy Ross on Arch Street. Young Mrs. Ross, who had helped with the design and making of the flag presented to Congress, received the committee with pleasure and ushered them into a rear room overlooking the garden.

"The Congress has accepted the design, Mrs. Ross," they told her. "Now we should like you to make the flags for us."

Washington in a blue and buff uniform sat in a straight-backed chair facing Betsy Ross, with Morris in a brown suit seated beside him. George Ross remained standing, his eyes upon his Chief's face.

"So they approved?" Mrs. Ross smiled. "I have been thinking," she went on shyly, "that perhaps five-pointed stars might look better than the six-pointed ones."

Morris and Ross looked questioningly at Washington.

"I agree," he nodded slowly. "What do you think, gentlemen?"

Morris and Ross smiled their assent.

Drawing from his pocket a contract for her to make all government flags, Morris presented it for her signature.

There was one flag, however, that Betsy Ross did not make.

That same day, the first Flag Day in United States history, John Paul Jones received a commission to command the 18-gun *Ranger*. He had heard of the new flag and had seen the proposed design. In order to be the first to raise the new standard, the Stars and Stripes, he had prepared a flag in accordance with the plans. He felt reasonably sure that Congress would adopt the banner. If they didn't, there was no harm done. Jones, like Morris, was a good gambler.

Not stopping for breath or a salute, a messenger dashed on board the *Ranger*, shouting to the new Commander: "They've done it, sir."

"Adopted the new flag? You're sure?" asked Jones.

The messenger nodded.

Taking the new flag from its hiding place, Jones ran it to the masthead while the *Ranger*'s cannon thundered its greeting to Old Glory. That was a memorable day in the annals of John Paul Jones.

All that summer there were threats of a British invasion. To protect the city and prevent an attacking force from approaching Philadelphia, the Americans had effectually obstructed navigation of the Delaware. Howe, informed of these conditions, instead of sailing up that river, set sail for Chesapeake Bay. On August 27, 1777, the British landed at Head of Elk. To allay the fears of the Philadelphians, the American army marched through the city on its way to meet the enemy and encamped behind White Clay Creek. Later Washington retired behind the Brandywine on rising ground above Chadds Ford. There the British army advanced upon the Americans. Washington's army put up a valorous defense. The flank, however, attacked by Lord Cornwallis, who had made a wide detour for the purpose, was thrown into confusion and routed. The army thereupon retreated to Chester and next day to Philadelphia. In this action Lafayette was wounded. The British seized the government of Delaware and a quantity of coined money, a commodity that the Americans could not afford to lose. Washington, wise and calm, encouraged his troops and gave them a day for refreshment in Germantown.

Then began a series of river crossings and other maneuvers. On September 15 when the army crossed from the left to the right bank of the Schuylkill, the bridge over the river was loosened from its moorings to swing on the Philadelphia side. General Armstrong with the Philadelphia militia was directed to guard the river passes. General Howe, sending a detachment to Chester as though marching on the city, hurried with the main body of his troops toward Goshen. When he heard that Washington was approaching to give him battle, he started the action in a heavy rainstorm. The powder of the Americans, unprotected by badly constructed cartridge boxes, became wet and useless. While the storm raged, Washington withdrew and, recrossing the Schuylkill, encamped at Perkomy Creek. Thus on September 23 Howe was between Washington's army and Philadelphia.

For days preparations for evacuating the city had been in progress. Vessels at the wharves were moved up the Delaware. The public magazines and archives were evacuated. The Liberty Bell and the bells of Christ Church were taken farther inland for safe keeping. In an attempt to thwart "Fifth Column" activities, many Quakers, who refused to take the oath of allegiance to the new government, were arrested and sent to concentration camps in Staunton, Virginia. Washington was invested with dictatorial powers. (How familiar this pattern!) Just before Cornwallis entered Philadelphia on September 26, Congress once more fled, this time to Lancaster and later to York. Robert Morris went with them, although he would probably have preferred remaining in Philadelphia with Willing, had it not been for his family.

In preparation for such a contingency he had purchased in April of that year a home in Manheim, near Lancaster, the house previously mentioned by Mary Morris in a letter to her mother. The new home was a brick mansion formerly owned by self-styled "Baron" Stiegel, the glass manufacturer. There the Morrises had enjoyed the Baron's hospitality at one, at least, of his famous houseparties, at which his factory workers' orchestra played for the guests to dance. These gay,

MRS. ROBERT MORRIS
Portrait by Gilbert Stuart

luxurious parties often lasted for weeks. Mary Morris had visited there for six weeks at one such merry-making.

"The Castle," so-called, stood at the corner of Prussian (now Main) and East High streets in the center of Manheim. As its name indicates, it was a magnificent mansion with massive wainscotings and mantelpieces, the fireplace being constructed of porcelain tiles. On the parlor walls hung Arras tapestry reminiscent of medieval castles. Around the house in the spacious gardens grew flowers as rare and exquisite as Stiegel's glass; under the shade trees on the lawn squirrels frisked, while in the branches partridges grew plump. Behind the mansion rose the Lutheran Church, for which the Baron had donated the land and which then paid and still pays its yearly rental in red roses—one red rose each year.

At Manheim, as at "The Hills," the Morrises entertained lavishly. Their best furniture, china, linen, and silver had been sent from Philadelphia well in advance of their arrival. There the hospitable host and hostess entertained among others General Gates and John Hancock. Shortly after his visit Hancock sent Morris a gold-headed walkingcane "as a small token of real regard and friendship." This Robert Morris treasured to the end of his days and willed his son Thomas. He invited Richard Peters, the nephew of their former rector, to spend Christmas with them as "an act of charity," so eager was he to have his friends around him.

To Manheim, too, came John Brown, formerly an employee of Willing & Morris—not to be confused with John Brown of the Admiralty Board. He brought a message from General Howe, British commander in Philadelphia—a peace proposal first made to Thomas Willing and sent by the latter to Morris. Refusing to deliver this important message to anyone else, Brown waited at the Manheim home from Tuesday until Saturday for Morris to return. The substance of the peace offer was this: Willing had received a note from Howe, desiring to settle the differences with the colonies and prevent further bloodshed, and stating that he (Howe) had full authority to treat with Congress if they would renounce their independence. When Morris presented this proposal to Congress, they ordered John Brown arrested and placed in Lancaster jail, for to that body of pa-

triots this savored of treason. Oddly enough, Morris escaped all suspicion of complicity. Robert Morris found Brown there, and with
another member of Congress, William Duer, bailed him out. Almost
immediately he was re-arrested in York and returned to the jail in
Lancaster "for aiding the enemy of this Commonwealth and forming
combinations with them for betraying the United States into their
hands." Again Morris interceded for him, writing a letter requesting
his discharge and stating that he believed Brown to be "innocent in
his intentions." He asked that the prisoner be allowed to leave on
parole and pledged himself for his messenger's good behavior. Consequently John Brown was released by the Council on January 23
and allowed to live in Manheim. In April he was tried and discharged.
To the good offices of his former employer he owed his liberty and
probably his life.

In December, 1777, Morris was reelected to Congress for the
fourth time. The Secret Committee of which he was a member became the Committee of Foreign Affairs or Committee of Commerce
that arranged for exports of tobacco, indigo, and other products in
exchange for arms. Throughout this period of service to the nation,
even before his appointment as Financier, he was the fiscal agent for
Congress. He made contracts for arms, rations, and war supplies. His
ships were privateers, capturing British merchantmen and dividing
their proceeds among owners and crews. Theoretically Robert Morris
disapproved of this licensed buccaneering, but practically he considered it defensible because the Colonies lacked a strong navy, or any
navy worthy of the name. These privateers harassed the enemy, captured valuable merchant ships as prizes, kept the sailors satisfied with
their prize money, and enriched the merchant owners. As a matter of
fact, Morris himself owned a fleet of these privateers, which aug-
mented his fortune by a million dollars. Thus, despite his theoretical
disapproval, Morris's broad face wore a contented smile when captains brought in their booty. Whether this belonged to him or to the
United States, it was welcome and eventually served the struggling
young nation.

While Congress was in session at Lancaster, Morris was granted a
six-months' leave of absence to settle his private affairs. These had

been neglected while he transacted the business of Congress in Philadelphia. At one time he had planned to resign in order to carry on his own business but had been dissuaded. "It is rumoured here," wrote Benjamin Rush, Philadelphia physician and one-time Congressman, "that you do not intend to serve in Congress. . . . For God's sake do not desert them!" Thus Morris contented himself with a leave of absence. During that time, however, he occasionally attended meetings, and signed the Articles of Confederation at York, to which Congress had moved from Lancaster.

A great disappointment confronted Morris at this period. For many years he had assumed responsibility for his half brother Thomas, his father's illegitimate son. Robert Morris had always treated him as a son of his own or a younger brother. He had educated him at the best schools in Philadelphia and in every way had provided for him liberally. Although Thomas was known as a spendthrift and a scapegrace, his brother felt that a position of responsibility and confidence would reform him. Consequently, despite Thomas's repeated betrayal of the faith placed in him, Morris appointed him commercial agent at Nantes, France, where he represented both the United States and the firm of Willing & Morris. Probably Morris's greatest fault was his willingness to trust men, feeling because of his own integrity that others, too, must be essentially honest and trustworthy. This trait in later years proved his financial downfall. He should have been warned by the unhappy experience with his half brother.

Thomas Morris, instead of feeling a sense of responsibility and attending to business, squandered his brother's time and money. It was reported that while he was in England on his way to his post, he spent £1,000 (almost $5,000) in three weeks. He gambled and drank; he engaged in corrupt or at least dubious business transactions. His brother had advised him to learn French and Spanish that he might be of more value in his post. But he merely indulged in further dissipations and extravagances. Those who knew him at that time termed his behavior "a disgrace to America." Still Robert Morris believed in him and trusted him, refusing at first to credit the reports of his friends abroad although he spoke of his own annoyance at not hearing from him. Tolerantly he thought Thomas was merely "infatuated with the pleasures of that city [Paris], and that he would settle down after he had had his fling."

Silas Deane, a friend of Morris, wrote him very fully from Paris about his brother's scandalous behavior. He thought his friend should understand the situation before placing further trust in the young man. Morris, indignant at what he considered unjust criticism, inadvertently sent a letter to Thomas censuring Deane, so fully did he trust his scoundrel of a brother. This communication Thomas unwisely showed his friends and eventually word reached Deane that his friend Morris, as he (Deane) viewed the matter, had betrayed his confidence. Thereupon he wrote Robert Morris a sad and reproachful letter.

"It is hard for me acting as I have done from the most disinterested motives," chided Deane, "and from those Principles of Friendship which shall be ever sacred with me, to be thus censured by you unheard & that you should still confide so far in your Brother as to put the Censure in his hands, not to be shown to me but to others, when I wrote 5th January you wou'd almost think with a Presentment of what was to happen. I said then, that I would not be angry, so I assure you I am not, but I am extremely hurt, not on acct of any Prejudice your Brothers Conduct will in the End do me particularly, but on your Acct more immediately, for myself I know you will justify and thank me for the Part I have acted when you know the whole Circumstances of the affair, I say on your acct immediately, for let me inform you of what is probable others will not, it is reported that your Brothers excesses tho' no way comparable to the Present, were known to you several years before he left America. The Friends of America in France, as well as the Americans themselves, are surprized to find him still continued in the most important as well as the most delicate Trust of being at the Head as it were of American Commerce at this Critical Period, and at the same time are grieved to see the Effects this Confidence has on him."

At last, partly as a result of this letter no doubt, Robert Morris was convinced of his brother's unworthiness and treachery. Always eager to make amends for an injustice, Morris apologized for censuring Deane and the other Commissioners and deplored the fact that "in the midst of the most arduous exertions to promote the welfare of his country" he had introduced "a worthless wretch to disgrace and discredit it." He recommended that Congress dismiss Thomas. This proved unnecessary, however, since before the matter was brought to the attention of the Great Council, the wastrel had died of dissipation.

These were dark days for George Washington. After the British entrance into Philadelphia and their welcome by the loyalists in that city, Washington planned an attack upon the British troops in Germantown. Hearing that three British regiments had been detailed to Chester, the Commander-in-Chief thought this an opportune time to fall unexpectedly upon the enemy. That battle at sunrise in the fog has become a matter of history. The Americans at last took to flight despite General Greene's brilliant drive. The failure of this attack resulted from the haziness of the weather, the inequalities of the ground, and the unexpected resistance of Lieutenant Colonel Musgrove, who, occupying a large stone house with six companies of the enemy, poured volleys of musketry upon the American troops, stopping their advance.

After receiving reinforcements and engaging in a skirmish at Chestnut Hill, Washington went into winter quarters at Valley Forge. The privations and ravages of that winter have become legendary. The troops, tattered, half-naked, without shoes or blankets, were rendered incapable of bearing arms. Four thousand lacked clothing; three thousand lay ill in a pestilential den called a hospital. Out of seventeen thousand men, no more than five thousand were fit for service. Famine stalked the camp and the land. Money was virtually non-existent. Officers resigned their commissions; soldiers failed to re-enlist. Mutiny seemed inevitable.

It was at this critical period that anonymous letters sent Congress made dastardly attacks upon the Commander-in-Chief. A network of intrigues and machinations was woven around him, largely engineered by General Charles Lee, who aspired to supplant him. There were other plots in behalf of General Horatio Gates, who may or may not have directly inspired them.

During these troubled times Robert Morris's loyalty, sincerity, and tolerance were sadly needed. Colonel Tench Tilghman, Aide-de-Camp and Private Secretary to Washington, wrote Morris in great perturbation from Headquarters:

"I am sorry," so the letter ran, "that your private concerns should oblige you to attend to them at a time when in my opinion the assistance of men of abilities actuated solely by patriotic principles was never more wanted. . . . Liberal yourself, you can think and act liberally towards other people. . . .

"You must have seen and heard something of a party forming against him [Washington]. Publications under the signature of Delisle point out plainly his successor, and the unaccountable behaviour of the late Q^r M^r G [Conway] does not leave a doubt in my mind that he is at the bottom of it. What are his inducements God only knows, but I am sure no man stood higher in the General's good opinion. Our Enemies have already heard of and exult at this appearance of division and faction among ourselves, and the Officers of the Army who have been all of them at one time or another under his command are exasperated to the highest degree, at a thought of displacing him. I have never seen any stroke of ill fortune affect the Gen'l in the manner that this dirty underhand dealing has done. It hurts him the more because he cannot take notice of it without publishing to the world that the spirit of faction begins to work among us. It therefore behoves his Friends to support him against the malicious attacks of those who can have no reason to wish his removal but a desire to fill his place.

"Altho' your Business may not admit of your constant attendance upon Congress," Colonel Tilghman urged in concluding this long letter, "I hope you will have an Eye towards what is doing there. If the Gen'l's conduct is reprehensible let those who think so make the charge and call him to account publicly before that Body to whom he is amenable. But this rascally method of calumniating behind the Curtain ought to be held in detestation by all good men."

Benjamin Harrison now at Williamsburg, Virginia, also wrote Morris several letters on the subject of Conway's Cabal against Washington. In fact, many of his friends in Congress confided in him concerning this matter and wished him to use his influence against

Washington's enemies. In Harrison's first communication, written December 18, 1777, he said:

"We have a story circulating here that there has been a motion made in Congress to divide the command of the army and that R. H. Lee was at the bottom of it. It makes much noise, and if true, will effectively do his business, we are also informed that Genl Washington's character has been attack'd publicly by S. & J. Adams, and that the Genl. has been so informed. Your being sent to camp gives me some reason to fear that these reports may be true, and that my worthy Friend resents such treatment. I know his value & would not loose him, if we do America will repent it by the loss of her Liberty."

A few months later, in February, 1778, Harrison wrote Morris again on the same topic—one of paramount interest to everyone that cruel winter. "The General is fully informed of these Cabals," Harrison stated, "they pray on his Constitution, sink his Spirits and will in the end I fear prove fatal to him, if this should be the case, excuse me for once more repeating it, America will lose perhaps her only prop. He well knows bad consequences would follow his resignation or he would not leave it in the power of the wicked and designing, thus to insult him, with a few words more I shall finish this painful Subject, Beware of your Board of War."

At this period when unity was sorely needed by the new nation, the country was torn by dissensions, petty jealousies, and political machinations. After Washington's rebuke to General Charles Lee at the Battle of Monmouth where his retreat seemed treacherous, this temperamental general wrote his Chief an insolent letter and apparently began plotting against him. Since Robert Morris had, at the request of Congress, advanced him money toward the purchase of his Virginia estate, Lee sent Morris an explanation of events at Monmouth from his viewpoint. Washington, he insinuated, was jealous of his achievements and wished to detract from his successes by publicly rebuking him. Fortunately for Washington and the army, Lee as a result of the court-martial he demanded was found guilty on several counts, among others of disrespect to the Commander-in-Chief, and was suspended from the army for a year. Naturally these plots and quarrels annoyed Washington although with his usual dignity and courtesy he tried to ignore them. Morris also felt keenly the distressing situation that faced his friend, and with the full might of his influence attempted to suppress the calumnies. By this time, however, he himself had become a victim of venomous tongues. The political war was moving into his territory.

CHAPTER VI

THE FURIES

❖   ❖   ❖

"PENN gave me a hint of evil intended you by a certain great man," the gossipy Benjamin Harrison wrote Morris in June, 1778; and added, "If he ever makes his attack, I am sure it will end in his own confusion and prove him to be an empty, envious, conceited—" The epithet was left to his correspondent's imagination.

If the identity of the enemy was at first unknown to Morris, he did not have to wait long to discover the secret. Newspaper attacks and innuendos revealed the virulent pen of the gifted Tom Paine, author of *Common Sense*, whose calumnies were inspired by Arthur Lee, one of the three Commissioners in Paris. The motive behind this unexpected and unmerited attack seemed to be the quarrel between Silas Deane and Arthur Lee. Benjamin Franklin, the third envoy to France, refused to become embroiled in the feud despite slanders circulated about him by Lee, but eventually John Paul Jones as well as Robert Morris became involved in the fracas.

In 1776 Silas Deane, a member of Congress, had been sent to France as a merchant to obtain military supplies for this country. Before he arrived, however, Pierre Augustin Caron de Beaumarchais, the noted author of *The Barber of Seville* and *The Marriage of Figaro*, had begun secret mercantile negotiations in behalf of the United States. He was in reality a secret agent of Vergennes, the Foreign Minister of France, who from the first sympathized with the American cause. Through Vergennes's influence France and Spain furnished Beaumarchais with one million livres each, which he used in the purchase of munitions and other supplies to send the Americans. With his strong dramatic instinct, Beaumarchais established a fictitious firm, Roderique Hortalez and Company, to carry on this trade with the United States, and shrouded all his transactions in an atmosphere of mystery. At one time there were presumably forty vessels engaged in an enormous traffic with the new nation. When Deane arrived, authorized by Congress to pay for the military supplies in American products, largely tobacco, he made a contract with Beaumarchais on that basis. The two men carried on this enterprise enthusiastically, shipping munitions from Marseilles to America usually by way of Haiti and Martinique, where American agents received and reshipped them. This indirect method of transacting business was deemed necessary since France was presumably a neutral nation. Occasionally, however, a ship was sent directly to an American port. A letter from Beaumarchais to Morris, written in Marseilles, November 17, 1777, reveals the French author's enthusiasm for the American cause, his confidence in Silas Deane, and his high regard for Robert Morris.

"I embrace this opportunity to renew the assurance of my esteem for you," wrote Beaumarchais, "and to inform you that if you have not heard from us by the Ship *Flamand* which left Marseilles loaded with articles of the greatest value to the Republick, I hope it will not be long before you receive accounts of her arrival at Boston. Notwithstanding the difficulties of every kind surrounding me, I let slip no opportunity of giving you undoubted proofs of my real attachment to your cause. . . . Your friend Mr. Deane is the most useful man in all your French affairs, and whom the Republic ought the most to rely on. . . .

"They tell me here that Philadelphia is taken, that Mr. Washington is beat. We do not believe it, for we know that at a meeting of Parliament it is necessary such reports, whether true or false, should be spread to silence the cries of the people and the violent attacks of the minority. At any rate, if Mr. Howe has taken that city, he would in my opinion only have gained from America the ground Philadelphia is built upon. It would be some Acres well built over, lost and liable to be regained, but what effect could it have on the Grand Cause of Liberty? None, while there are men with courage & virtue left."

Everything was proceeding satisfactorily to the firm of Hortalez et Cie. and to the United States until Arthur Lee arrived in France to sow dissension. His motives were doubtless highly honorable. When he heard of the donations (as he considered them) by France and Spain to America, and then of the contract made between Deane and Beaumarchais, he became suspicious of the firm's transactions and thought both men had been stealing the public funds. Lee represented to the Committee of Secret Correspondence that money for the munitions had been granted as a gift by France and Spain. Consequently when the firm presented its bills and expected payment in shipments of tobacco, Congress refused to acknowledge the debt, thinking that Deane and Beaumarchais were merely lining their own pockets. Through the continued machinations of Arthur Lee, working through his brother, Richard Henry Lee, and Samuel Adams, Congress suspected that it was being defrauded and ordered Deane home to report on "the state of affairs in Europe." To Robert Morris, Deane confided his distrust of the Lee brothers (for William Lee had joined Arthur in Paris). This letter reflects Silas Deane's misery and misgivings:

"I am ignorant of what kind of complaint the two Brothers here will prefer against me. I know they are implacable and indefatigable, whatever their complaints may be, I pray I may not be condemned unheard, I cannot live with these men or do business with them, nor can I find the man in the World who can. These Characters cannot be unknown to you in some Degree, permit me once more to refer you, and the Honorable Congress to Doctor Franklin who knows me, and who to his sorrow & Vexation, knows them. This Confidence I have the Honor of enjoying at Court is the unhappy ground of our Difficulties, for the Minister has the most distrustful opinion of A. L., Esq. nor will he see him but when obliged to. . . .

"Permit me my dear Sir," the letter continues, "to give you candidly my opinion on the having Ambassadors, Agents or Commissioners at Foreign Courts, as soon as our Independence is confirmed and Peace is established, I would advise you to have none in any Part of the World. Consuls in the Ports are all that will be wanted and they will cost little or nothing. I would wish America to have as little connection as possible with Europe except what arises from Commerce & the exchanging of mutual good offices. At any rate never appoint more than one Man at one Court, nor send one Man at the same time to Two."

Since Deane had been summoned home hastily, merely to report on conditions abroad, as he thought, he neglected to bring with him accounts of his expenditures or those of Beaumarchais. Expecting to be reimbursed, he had advanced his own money; but Congress was unwilling to pay without more definite proof of indebtedness than he offered. A year of investigation followed. At last Deane, his patience exhausted, published a newspaper appeal to the people, as a result of which Congress considered itself insulted. A newspaper war followed, waged primarily by Paine at the instigation of Lee, Deane's implacable foe. Everyone took sides in the quarrel. Harrison, writing to Morris from Virginia in June, 1778, expressed his opinion very strongly.

"The characters he [Deane] has drawn of the two Bros. [Arthur and William Lee] in my opinion are just ones," said Harrison. "You who know them not can form but an imperfect Idea of those on that side the water by what you have seen on this, they being much more designing, vindictive and overbearing, perhaps you may think this impossible, but be assured it is a fact, and that they are no more fit for the characters they bear, than any man that can be thought on, however they are fixed and I suppose America must suffer them for a season longer, as the Cabal is at present too powerful to afford us the least prospect of their removal."

After more than a year of these altercations, Deane returned to Paris to have his accounts audited, and Lee returned to America, where as a member of Congress he continued his machinations.

As Robert Morris was a friend of Deane's and had engaged in commercial transactions with him, he too was drawn into the controversy. It was alleged that he had not settled his accounts with Congress. To some degree this charge was true. During those early years of the war, Congress had provided certain individuals and firms with funds to purchase commodities for export. The recipients were to account for the money either by proceeds to be paid agents of Congress in France or in the West Indies, or by a return cargo of supplies needed by Congress. Transactions were extremely complicated. There were in some instances no invoices. Trans-shipments were made to avoid the enemy's cruisers. Sometimes goods were placed in warehouses in France or the West Indies, where they remained for many months. Sometimes cargoes were seized. Receipts were often unobtainable since there was frequently no agent at the port where the ship was forced to land, and mails were slow and uncertain. Complete transactions often took years. Unquestionably such business methods afforded opportunities for dishonest practices. Just as certainly it would be almost impossible for any merchant to prove his honesty.

Moreover, Morris had conducted his private business as well, exporting, importing, dealing in bills of exchange. As secrecy was essential for many government operations, he carried on the public commerce under his own name to deceive the British and secure more favorable terms for Congress. Thus extensive transactions, private and public, were inextricably interlinked. In settling the accounts of his firm, however, he found that instead of his being indebted to Congress, that body owed him a balance, which he made no attempt to collect.

In reply to repeated attacks of profiteering at the expense of the government, Morris requested an investigation of his official conduct. The committee appointed for the purpose reported that "Robert Morris has clearly and fully vindicated himself, that he has acted with fidelity and integrity and an honorable zeal for the happiness of the country." The committee stated further with regard to the transactions of Willing & Morris: "The purchases made by them for the public account were done on the best terms. The invoices will show their attention and prove how useful their names and measures were in keeping down the prices as long as possible." In fact during the time Willing & Morris were employed in making purchases for the public, they neglected their own business, wishing to avoid censure or suspicion. During this period they delivered cargoes of provisions and ammunition—three hundred pounds of gunpowder, in addition to saltpetre, sulphur, and sailcloth—and dealt in bills of exchange. An

Act of Congress acquitted Morris personally, as well as the firm, of any dishonest transactions and expressed approbation of his conduct. Hurt as he was by these attacks, Morris did not let them interfere with his business for the government.

It was gratifying, however, to realize that his friends had confidence in him and rallied to his support. General Mifflin declared himself "surprised and provoked at the rascally and ill-managed attack" against Morris's character, adding, "The attention you have given to public business for the three last years and the commercial sacrifices you have made to your country, I believed would have placed you out of the reach at least of the attempts of every censorious scoundrel." The General spoke of Paine as meeting only contempt for his slanders. "Like the enthusiastic madman of the East," wrote Mifflin in a grand peroration, "he sallied forth, stabbed three or four slightly, met with you, but missing his aim, fell a victim to his own stroke."

While this political war was raging, the war with Britain came near ending. After hearing of the treaty of amity between France and the United States, England was willing to make great concessions in order to end the struggle. Three commissioners, the Earl of Carlisle, William Eden, and George Johnstone, were sent on a peace mission to America. Early in June they arrived, eager to make every concession except independence. A few years earlier their conditions might have been accepted. Now it was too late. Independence had been declared and seemed to the Americans worth fighting for. Discussions in Congress lasted many days, but since independence was deemed "inadmissible" by England, Congress voted to continue the war.

In the meantime, however, George Johnstone, formerly Governor of West Florida, was using whatever influence he possessed to achieve the ends of the commission by fair means or foul. Indeed Johnstone's private correspondence and attempts at bribery greatly embarrassed the other commissioners in their negotiations. Among the many "feelers" Johnstone sent out was a letter to Robert Morris, whom some thought lukewarm in his desire for independence since he had voted against the Declaration of Independence. So Johnstone, already acquainted with Morris, wrote him wishing that they might cooperate in working for reconciliation. That wish might seem quite legitimate. The letter continued, however: "I believe the men who have conducted the affairs of America incapable of being influenced by improper motives. *But in all such transactions there is risk, and I think whoever ventures should be secured; that honour and emoluments should naturally follow the fortune of those who have steered the vessel in the storm and brought her safely to port. . . .* I wish, above all other things, to see you, and I hope you will so contrive it." If there was any doubt in anyone's mind about Morris's loyalty to the new nation, it was quickly dispelled. Without any delay or hesitation and with righteous indignation he placed this paradoxical missive in the hands of Congress.

While these negotiations were pending, the British forces in Philadelphia, fearing an attack by the French fleet, evacuated the city. This seemed an incredible bit of good fortune: the arrival of the French fleet, so long expected, and the evacuation of Philadelphia. Upon the return of Congress, Morris resumed his duties in that body, his leave having expired. There he raised his voice in protest against the artificial devices used to give value to worthless currency, to fix prices, and to prevent free exchange of goods by embargoes. But his was a voice crying in the wilderness. More paper money was issued, the value of which was maintained by artificial means. Citizens were even penalized for not receiving it in exchange for commodities and debts. The price of necessities was also kept down artificially. Price schedules (or ceilings) attempted to prevent any person or firm from "forestalling" or "engrossing"; that is, buying goods before they were brought into the general market and selling them in that market for a much higher price. Monopolists and other offenders were tarred and feathered. An embargo, moreover, was laid upon products sent from one state to another. This led to jealousy and distrust among the different states and paralyzed commerce. All these measures Morris fought since he considered them a menace to the trade of the nation. Truly capitalistic in his viewpoint, he believed that commerce and industry should be free from government interference.

At the end of his fourth term Morris did not run again for Congress. He had been chosen once by the Proprietary Assembly of Pennsylvania, once by the Constitutional Convention, and twice by the State

Legislature. After leaving Congress, he again became a member of the Pennsylvania Legislature on the Anti-Constitution ticket. Thus he made enemies among those who favored the State Constitution. The "Furious Whigs," advocates of the weak state organization with its hydra-headed executive branch and its unicameral legislature, began a series of venomous attacks upon Morris, which lasted for almost twelve years. When he entered the legislature, Morris suspected what the result would be. He did not flinch from the battle; but he did deplore the necessity for fighting and the methods used by his enemies.

"Morris the monopolist!" "Morris the speculator!" These were some of the epithets flung at him. "The same Morris who cornered the flour market!" They forgot that that had occurred almost thirty years before. "Morris rolling in wealth while mothers and babes starve!" Although he tried to ignore these virulent attacks, his sensitive nature was wounded by them.

Here was an anonymous letter on the floor of his office speaking of him as a monster of selfishness. Here a jeering word as he passed on the street. He became afraid to appear in the city streets after dark.

Civil war was rampant in Philadelphia. Men carried their muskets; ladies remained indoors. The mob, roving with an eye to mischief, assaulted anyone of wealth and power. Men were clubbed on the streets. Morris, as the wealthiest and most influential merchant of the city, was in imminent danger of assault. He and James Wilson headed the so-called "Republican Party," opposed to the Utopian theories of such men as Tom Paine, the writer, Charles Wilson Peale, the artist, and David Rittenhouse, the scientist and natural philosopher, who led the Constitutionalists. These "Furious Whigs" of course deplored the physical violence of the mobs, but made their attacks in speeches and newspaper articles.

This verbal bombardment reached a climax with the arrival of a French vessel, the *Polaire*, containing flour and other "dry goods." Word sped from mouth to mouth that Morris had purchased the cargo. At once the price of flour rose. Morris was accused of conducting a "black market" in flour. Men with clubs threatened him on the street. Women knocked on his office door begging with tears in their eyes, "Give us flour. Our children are starving!" Such an appeal was hardest of all for Morris to bear. His heart, always sympathetic toward distress, was deeply touched; but he sadly shook his head. "There is some mistake. I have no flour to sell."

Bitter over the soaring prices, the citizens of Philadelphia, inspired by the Constitutionalists, held a public meeting on May 25, 1779, in the State House yard. Paine and others made inflammatory speeches accusing Morris and a few other merchants of price boosting and monopolizing.

"Banish all monopolists!" someone shouted.

"Banish Robert Morris from the city!" cried another.

"He's a monopolist! He's a price booster!"

"We and our children will starve!" ran the refrain.

Indignation soared like the price of flour.

On the outskirts of the crowd a few Republicans tried to heckle the speakers but were quickly silenced. Resolutions were drawn up that a committee be appointed to fix prices (serving as the O.P.A. of that day), and that another, the Committee of Inspection (or Complaints) should investigate all cases of monopolizing or those suspected of monopolizing.

A few days later this investigating committee, headed by Rittenhouse, called upon Morris, who was charged specifically with buying the cargo of the *Polaire* and selling it retail at a higher price. As Morris, due to overwork, was suffering from a "painful inflammation of the eyes," he begged to be excused from seeing them but promised to communicate with them within a few days.

Brows were arched. "Afraid to meet the committee, eh? This will teach him!"

As soon as the condition of his eyes permitted, Morris sent the committee an explanation of his transactions with regard to the *Polaire*'s cargo of flour.

He explained that he had made no effort to procure the cargo but was approached on the subject by the agents of the consigners, in this instance, His Most Christian Majesty, the King of France. He had concluded the bargain on his own terms: that he sell reasonably and leave those concerned a moderate profit. The contract unfortunately was written in the French language, which he could not understand, but he was told that it was conformable to his terms. Thus he received the cargo and immediately sent for the purchasing agents of Congress and offered them whatever they wanted for the army on moderate terms. It developed, however, that the parties to the original contract had not understood each other because of linguistic difficulties. Thereupon Robert Morris stopped all proceedings and held a meeting to clarify the matter. The former agreement was rendered void, but Morris consented to act as agent in the sale of the cargo if the consigners or their agents would ratify the sales already made. Thus Congress had gained supplies more reasonably than they otherwise could have done. Since he was acting as agent for the King of France, he had not felt free to give information concerning this transaction, he told them.

The committee was satisfied by his explanatory letter, but not so the Constitutionalists. The "Furious Whigs" spread the report that he had large quantities of flour stored in his warehouses, which he was hoarding there. When women besieged him in his office begging for flour, he sent the Committee of Complaints a reproachful note, saying, "Four or five poor women with sacks under their arms came to me this morning, demanding supplies of flour, alleging they were directed by the Committee to me for that purpose and informed by them that I had received two wagon loads of flour from the country yesterday. I confess this surprised me a good deal at first, but on reflecting a little, it seems highly improper the Committee or any of their members could be capable of giving such directions, because some of them had before been informed by my clerks that the flour under my care belonged to His Most Christian Majesty, and my letter to Capt. Heysham yesterday confirmed it; consequently it must be known I could not deliver it to any person, but by orders of my employers."

Ever more bitter grew the attacks on Robert Morris despite his clear, candid explanations and the complete vindication of his conduct. He disliked to walk through the streets since he was the victim of pleas, threats, and assaults whenever he appeared in public. Even his friends shared this ill treatment at the hands of the populace. At a town meeting in July, 1779, General Cadwallader began a speech in

Morris's defense. He was booed and hissed. Hoodlums with clubs (the most popular weapon of the day) set upon him and injured him. Friends at last rescued him and spirited him away.

Most of Morris's friends eventually became involved in the altercation. Richard Peters, a judge and nephew of Morris's rector at Christ Church, was attacked, at least verbally. "The enemy," Peters prophesied, "will prevail more by our animosities than they have yet been able to do by their arms. If the jealousies which seem to exist continue to rage much longer, I don't see how any man of feeling or sentiment can continue in a public department where every measure is looked upon with a jaundiced eye and of course all mistakes are magnified into sins political or moral."

Sometimes the radical Whigs' enmity expressed itself in bullets instead of billets. One day getting wind of a threatened attack on Wilson's house at Third and Walnut, Robert Morris, General Mifflin, Samuel Morris, Captain Campbell, and others rang his doorbell.

"We have come to help defend you if defense is needed," Mifflin told Wilson upon his arrival.

The house resembled an armed camp or arsenal. The doors and downstairs windows were barricaded. The defenders, armed with guns, took their stations at upstairs windows, where they peered through closed shutters at the crowds below. The mob began shouting oaths at "Jamie Wilson." Some threw stones. Captain Campbell, standing boldly at an open window, called out threateningly to the besiegers. A gunshot replied. Campbell crumpled where he stood at the window and died a few minutes later. Rapid-fire shots were exchanged by besiegers and defenders. Bullets penetrated the shutters wounding Mifflin and Samuel Morris. In the street a man and a boy were killed. Robert Morris and Wilson miraculously escaped injury.

Marching down the street almost simultaneously from opposite directions came two groups of militia. The defenders gasped with relief. The mob, hurling a few last oaths and missiles, scurried away. As the bands met in front of Wilson's home, they halted glaring at each other. One band had recently expressed its approval of the Constitutionalists and had promised to protect them. The other favored the Anti-Constitutionalists.

"See the aristocrats," one militiaman of the first company sneered.

"How much do Morris and Wilson pay you?" another yelled.

"You rabble rouser," shouted a member of the second company, "you like to see citizens murdered!"

The guardians of public safety began hurling stones as well as words until their captains subdued them. The bodies of the man and boy were removed. Before midnight the street was quiet and Wilson's friends were free to return home. The fracas, known as the Fort Wilson Riot, was ended.

Not so the personal attacks on Morris. Despite his honorable acquittal and praise by Congress, he continued to be the victim of slanders. His friends were indignant. The conservatives organized a meeting, to be held in the yard of the College of Philadelphia to be free from the attacks of hoodlums. Morris was elected chairman. As he took his seat on the platform, his eyes and brow showed the strain of the civil war upon him. With his usual poise and good humor, however, he called the meeting to order. Indignantly the members discussed the virulent attacks by the Constitutionalists, especially upon their chairman. A resolution was proposed stating that "Robert Morris be acquitted of the charge of unpatriotic action." This was adopted in the midst of cheers for Morris.

With tears in his eyes he rose to thank them. "Friends," there was a catch in his voice, "I am profoundly grateful for your loyalty and confidence." He paused trying to choke back the surging emotions, failed, and took his seat. The arrows of attack he could withstand smilingly, but the rays of sympathy melted his courage.

In an effort to silence his enemies, Morris wrote a letter and a public reply. The letter was addressed to Joseph Reed, the extremely sensitive President of Pennsylvania, who accused Morris of obstructing the operations of the state government and of opposing Reed himself. In answer to his charge, Morris sent him the following letter, written March 29, 1779:

"In justice to you and myself I cannot refrain from telling you, that you are entirely deceived in the opinions you seem to have formed respecting my conduct. . . . As a private gentleman I ever entertained as much regard for your Person and respect for your character as you could possibly expect our acquaintance to have laid foundation for. . . .

"As to political connections I never sought them, in that line all advances came from you, but every engagement I made, has been most faithfully observed. It is well known to the company I generally associate with that I was your firm and steady Friend on all occasions where your Public Character and Conduct was the Subject of Conversation in my presence, that I did invariably advocate your measures and express without reserve my opinion of expectations of an honourable performance of your engagements and in this belief my feeble efforts were made on all suitable occasions to support the dignity of Government. . . .

"Believe me Sir, I never came forth into Public Life on any other ground than a desire to promote and support the just and necessary opposition to the Tyranny of Great Britain. That is still my principal object. Next to the establishment of our Independence I wish the establishment of a good Constitution in Pennsylvania, but the latter I trust will yet become a consequence of the former and as I have not a doubt but the virtue and good sense of the citizens of this State will accomplish it at some early period, without violence, I am content to wait that happy event, having neither ambition, inclination, or leisure sufficient to induce me to form plans for obstructing the operations of this present Government. On the contrary I am withdrawing myself from public business and shall get entirely clear of it as soon as possible, but whilst I have a share in the Public Councils you may depend that my Voice will always speak the dictates of my own mind, and whether that happens to promote or oppose your measures will depend on the nature of the questions and not on the person or party they come from. . . . Wherein I have opposed any measures of Council I do assure you it has been from a sense of duty and not because they were yours or the Council's measures."

In addition to this fearless statement of his policies, Morris, on July 7, 1779, made a public reply to his detractors in an *Address to the Citizens of Pennsylvania*, which concluded with this defense: "While I was your servant, it was my pride to serve you faithfully, to serve you cheerfully. I have done so near four years and made as great sacrifices of private interest as any man among you. I made them with alacrity. I had and still retain a proper sense of the honour of sacrificing my property, my labour and my ease to the voice of my country."

"What right has he to speak of 'sacrificing' his property or his ease for 'his' country?" asked the "Furious Whigs," whose bitterness curled their lips and envenomed their tongues. From the treatment accorded him one might have thought Morris Public Enemy No. 1 instead of a self-sacrificing public servant.

Friends and acquaintances, however, continued to rally to his support. George Walton of Georgia, formerly a Congressional colleague of Morris, defended him. John Langdon of New Hampshire denounced Morris's detractors. "I have full evidence of your candour and great exertions in public business," he wrote Morris, "and I do know that it never was done better than when under your care."

In addition to defending himself, Morris was engaged in helping others out of political difficulties. His trusted clerk, John Swanwick, was accused of being a Tory and corresponding with the enemy. Morris was instrumental in saving him from prison when he explained the situation to the authorities. Swanwick's parents and sister, it developed, were Tories, who wished passes for themselves and their servants and permits to take their household goods into the English lines. The rest of their estate they bequeathed to their son John, who was loyal to the American cause. Swanwick was writing with regard to this matter when he was accused of corresponding with the enemy. Morris's efforts to vindicate his clerk proved successful. Several years later Swanwick became a member of the firm, Willing, Morris & Swanwick.

Morris's well-known kindness and generosity caused friends and even mere acquaintances to impose upon him. James Duane wrote him to use his influence in behalf of General Schuyler, who was being court-martialed. Although he was one of the most faithful patriots and most skilful generals in the American army, he faced trial on the charge of accepting pay for evacuating Ticonderoga upon the advance of Burgoyne. This rumor, set in motion and kept in circulation through the machinations of Philip Skene, a political enemy, gained momentum. Schuyler himself demanded a trial in order to clear his name. The worst feature of the case was the postponement of this trial for eight months while the General remained under a cloud of suspicion. So Duane wrote Morris: "You, my dear Sir, who have an abundant portion of sensibility, who know how precious a jewel is a good name, who would advocate innocence as you abhor guilt, will I trust with manly freedom press forward the trial of General Schuyler without further delay." Results indicate that he used his influence in the general's behalf. Schuyler was tried and acquitted in October, 1778.

Morris was also petitioned by some of the Tories who remained in Philadelphia after the evacuation by the British. The city was demoralized upon the return of the Continental Army. A large number of the Tories tried to join the British in their withdrawal. Howe discouraged their attempts, however, since they would present too many economic problems, and advised them to make their peace with the Americans. The most hot-headed patriots sought vengeance on the Tories. In a miniature Reign of Terror they condemned to death a miller and a carpenter. Morris and other saner patriots tried to calm the populace and prevent further destruction. Violence threatened daily. Tory-hunting became the chief sport of over-zealous citizens. To the merry music of the "Rogue's March" all those who were accused of sympathizing with the British were carted away to prison or to concentration camps.

Among others Benjamin Chew, at one time Attorney General and at another Chief Justice of Pennsylvania, was found guilty of pro-British sympathies and was imprisoned. (His daughter Peggy, one of the most popular belles of Philadelphia, was engaged to the ill-starred Major André.) From a concentration camp at the Union Iron Works in New Jersey, Chew sent a pathetic letter to Morris, requesting him to use his influence to have him released. Despairingly he wrote:

"I take the Liberty of requesting the Favour of your friendly assistance and the interposition of your Influence and good Offices for me in a Point, on the Success of which not only my Happiness

& that of my Family, but it is more than probable, my very life may depend. Bless'd as I was with every Domestic Felicity, the being separated at all from my numerous Family, you, who have the tender feelings of an affectionate husband and Father will easily conceive to be one of the severest Strokes that could befall them or me."

After stating that he had kept his parole most strictly without any prospect of release, he pled that his health demanded his discharge, as for years he had not been well. "In this State of Ignorance and Uncertainty" (concerning the advisability of presenting his petition directly to Congress), he concluded, "instead of forwarding the Letter directly to the President I have taken the Liberty of inclosing it to you, with my most earnest request that you will be so good as either to make Use of it, as you can do from your thorough knowledge of the Gentlemen with whom the matter must be negociated, or of the Propriety of the Application. . . . I am ready with the utmost Cheerfulness & Sincerity of Heart, to sign any Parole that may be thought necessary to tie up my Tongue & hands from saying or doing anything injurious to the Cause of America."

To this plea Morris replied that the former Chief Justice would be released if he took the oath of fealty to the United States. With native kindliness Morris rejoiced in aiding his opponents as well as his friends.

Upon their return to Philadelphia Robert and Mary Morris were saddened by the ruin wrought at "The Hills," which had been occupied by British soldiers during their absence. They were more fortunate than John Dickinson and others whose homes had been burned. Sometime during the next few years Morris repaired the damage to the house and estate, making it again a place of beauty. The children did not at first return to Philadelphia but remained in Manheim for safety, under the care of Joseph Shippen, Junior. At least, Charles and Hetty were with him, Charles contented and quiet, Hetty happy with a little friend. Bob spent the time with John Brown, Secretary of the Admiralty, in New York. When he forwarded Morris's mail to him, Brown sent him news of "Master Bobby," who appeared to be satisfied and well-behaved. A letter from Richard Bache, Franklin's son-in-law, spoke of the neighbors bemoaning the loss of Robert Morris and "drowning their sorrow in drink." Three years later Morris sold his Manheim properties to James Jenkins for £1,200. "The Castle" had served its purpose and justified its purchase.

As he had written Joseph Reed, Morris most eagerly sought release from the cares and calumnies attendant upon office holding. It was not until 1780, however, that he was out of office. In the meantime he secured some relief from his burdens through domestic and social pleasures.

In 1778 Lady Washington, as she was called, visited Philadelphia and stayed as usual with the Morrises in their home on Front Street. A ball in her honor was held at City Tavern, with all the élite of the city there. A few days later Washington arrived to join her. With military pageantry, the militia and leading citizens, Morris among them, rode out to welcome him. As the cavalcade advanced, crowds along the roadside cheered, and as he entered Front Street, cannon thundered from the ships in the harbor. Washington, exhausted by the privations and problems of the preceding year, might have welcomed a more quiet entrance. Rest he always found, however, in Morris's home. There all ran smoothly under Mary Morris's expert superintendence. Her graciousness and Morris's geniality made their guests feel themselves a part of the family. The boys, Bob, Tom, and Bill, who had just returned from Manheim, bowed to Washington and his lady; Hetty dropped a curtsey; two-year-old Charles toddled away out of sight; Morris smiled contentedly.

The social season was very gay despite the war, especially while Benedict Arnold was in command of Philadelphia. One brilliant social event followed another in swift succession. Mary Morris wrote her mother: "We have a great many balls and entertainments and soon the Assemblys will begin. Tell Mr. Hall even our military gentlemen here are too liberal to make any distinction between Whig and Tory ladyes—if they make any, it's in favor of the latter, such, strange as it may seem, is the way those things are conducted at present in this city. It originates at Headquarters, and that I may make some apology for such strange conduct, I must tell you that Cupid has given our little General [Benedict Arnold] a more mortal wound than all the hosts of Britons could, unless his present conduct can expiate for his past—Miss Peggy Shippen is the fair one."

Neither his political troubles nor his social pleasures interfered with Morris's service to his country. One evening Richard Peters, head of the Board of War, and Robert Morris met at an entertainment given by Don Mirailles (or Morales), the Spanish Minister. During the evening Morris, always sensitive to the moods of others, observed that Peters was worried. Taking him aside, Morris said: "I see some clouds passing over that sunny countenance you assume. What is the matter?"

Peters hesitated for a few minutes, then drew from his pocket Washington's letter giving an alarming account of the military stores and stating that there were no musket cartridges except those in the boxes of the soldiers and that those were wet. "Lead is exhausted," Peters remarked bitterly, "none to be found in the city."

A little later that evening Morris called Peters aside and told him that the *Holker*, one of his privateers, had just arrived with ninety tons of lead on board as ballast. "You shall have my half," Morris exclaimed, and pointing to others in the room, "there are the owners of the other half. If I give them my guarantee, they will certainly agree to give you their share."

After their permission had been obtained somewhat grudgingly, Morris beckoned Peters. "It is all arranged," he assured his friend. "Now to secure some workmen. Do you care to come with me?"

Together they took leave of their host, found idle men on the streets and on the wharves, who followed them to the *Holker*. There, assisted by the crew of the vessel and supervised by Morris, they began to mold cartridges from the lead. All night fires burned and metal clanked. All night Morris remained superintending the work. He believed with "Poor Richard" that "we must oversee our own affairs with our own eyes and not trust too much to others." In the morning, tired as he was, he beamed as he looked at the supply of cartridges ready to be dispatched to the army. By sunrise the wagons he had engaged were being loaded, and the boxes of much-needed cartridges were on their way to Washington. What did sleep matter to Morris when the country needed munitions?

CHAPTER VII

FINANCIAL WIZARD

❖   ❖   ❖

ROBERT MORRIS had long had a dream—a dream he shared with Thomas Willing and James Wilson: the establishment of a state bank. At the Merchants' Coffee House on June 8, 1780, Morris, Willing, Wilson, and other influential citizens met and agreed to raise a fund for "bounties" or bonuses to new army recruits as soldiers refused to enlist or reenlist without these sums.

"Men are deserting daily. All is lost unless we supply the needful," exclaimed Morris, using his favorite epithet for money.

Enthusiasm at the meeting ran high. Little of the "needful," only £400 hard money (£1,360 in Continental currency) was subscribed, however, on that occasion. Another meeting was held on June 17, this time at City Tavern. A subscription by security bonds to the amount of £300,000 (Pennsylvania currency) was proposed, to form the capital of a state bank to furnish supplies for state troops and for the United States Army. Members of the group gathered there vied with each other. Ninety-seven subscribers bonded themselves for £315,000 before adjournment— £15,000 more than the quota agreed upon. Even ladies became subscribers: Mrs. Morris, of course, Mrs. Wilson, the Countess de la Luzerne, wife of the French minister, and the Marchioness de Lafayette among others.

Thus the Bank of Pennsylvania, located on Front Street near Walnut, opened its doors December 1, 1780, with Thomas Willing as president, and Robert Morris the chief of five inspectors. This institution pumped new life into the tottering finances of the state.

Our republic probably owes its very existence to this bank. It took the place of lackadaisical states and a bickering, inefficient Congress.

The public looked with a new respect at the founders of this institution—Willing with his poise and his calm judgment; Wilson with his superior education and profound mind; Morris with his insight, daring, and resourcefulness. All of these leaders, moreover, had an unusual grasp of the problems connected with national institutions. Thus it was natural that the country should turn to one of this group in a period of financial stress.

This was just such a period. By the Act of March 18, 1880, Congress had declared the country bankrupt. The public treasury was empty. The currency had collapsed. Continental money was valued at $500 to $1,000 for one silver dollar. Men marched through the streets with paper notes fastened in their hats as cockades. Continental bills were buried with dirges at mock funerals. A dog, covered with tar and plastered with Continentals, paraded the streets. At least the Yankee sense of humor survived even in these tragic times.

Commodities rocketed skyward. Samuel Adams has become famous in song and story for paying $400 for a hat and $125 for a pair of shoes. Four months' pay of a private would not procure a single bushel of wheat; the pay of a colonel would not purchase oats for his horse. Taxes were paid (if paid at all) in notes or in commodities—flour, corn, cattle, meat, or tobacco. Consequently great stores of perishable materials spoiled before they could be distributed for use. Speculation and peculation flourished. Fortunes were won and lost over-night. Debtors, eager to settle their accounts in the depreciated bills, "triumphantly pursued their creditors, paying them without mercy." In different localities and from week to week prices varied so widely that gamblers rapidly enriched themselves. State laws, attempting to regulate the sale prices of goods, failed to stem the torrent of price soaring and gambling. Citizens, disgusted, concealed their commodities, refusing to sell.

Congress, driven by necessity, had issued paper money based on public credit and pledged taxes or on land security. There was not one-tenth enough gold in the country to meet the paper issues of the government. The states had complicated matters by issuing almost as many millions as the federal government. Those who depended upon life incomes, fixed salaries, or rents were ruined.

To increase these difficulties, counterfeiters, finding it easy to copy the crude designs and signatures on the notes, added tremendously to the bulk of the paper. The British did not scruple to use this device of counterfeiting to hasten the financial ruin of America. They proclaimed joyfully: "Their [the Americans'] paper money hangs like a mill-stone about their necks and is ready to sink them." This was not mere wishful thinking or propaganda but a literal fact.

The condition of the army was deplorable. Repositories were without supplies; arsenals without arms. Muskets were collected from house to house as were clothes and blankets. There was not enough powder in the thirteen states for one week's military resistance. Recruits refused to join the army; veterans deserted it. America, it seemed at this crisis in her history, was weighed in the balance and found wanting. After having made tremendous strides towards freedom, the country was on the verge of collapse. The nation, utterly unable to wage an offensive war, could not even protect its own homes.

There was mutiny in the army. Fifteen hundred men, regular troops of the Pennsylvania line, decided to march on Congress to collect their arrears of pay and to arrange different terms of enlistment. In vain officers endeavored to quell the insurgents. In the ensuing riots several soldiers and an officer were killed. General Anthony Wayne, fearless and determined as always, advanced upon them pistol in hand. With their bayonets against his breast, they warned him to take care or he would be cut to pieces. Washington, fearing perhaps that his authority might be defied, failed to intervene. The seditious troops began their march with all the baggage, wagons, and artillery belonging to their division. A small army, they encamped at Princeton.

In the meantime news of the insurrection had reached Philadelphia. Congress, alarmed, dispatched commissioners—Generals Reed and Sullivan among others—to restore tranquillity. The soldiers refused to be placated. They stated arrogantly that they would no longer be put off with empty promises. They demanded that all soldiers who had served three years should be discharged and those remaining in the service should have full arrears of pay, clothing, and provisions, and that in the future they should be paid punctually.

While negotiations were still pending, General Clinton sent a delegation of three American Tories with a proposal that the insurgents seek the protection of the British government, with free pardon for past offenses, with full payment for their past military service, and no further demands upon them. The only conditions were that they lay down their arms and return to their allegiance to England. The insurgents gave no answer but detained the British emissaries. In this grave crisis a committee of Congress and delegates from the rebel camp met and, after exasperating debates and delays, reached an agreement. Soldiers who had enlisted for three years were granted discharges. All were promised certificates for sums lost by depreciation of the paper money and were assured the earliest possible payment of arrears and immediate delivery of clothing. Thereupon the insurgents delivered Clinton's emissaries into the hands of the Congressional commissioners, who had them hanged as traitors.

The soldiers' demands must be met without delay. Congress had exhausted its resources. It issued new bills of credit as worthless as the old. It increased the taxes but lacked the authority to collect them. Congress had in reality no right to impose taxes since that was the cherished prerogative of the state legislatures. The individual states, fearing to increase the power of Congress and distrusting other states, would not part with their authority. Even a successful system of taxation in full swing would not have produced the enormous revenue needed. War expenditures totaled twenty million dollars a year, an enormous sum for that era, although a mere bagatelle today. All resources had failed. All but one.

In the midst of its dilemma Congress had one of its rare inspirations. It turned hopefully and confidently to a man who had never failed his country—Robert Morris of Philadelphia. The demands upon him were merely, as Redwood Fisher states them in his *Revolutionary Reminiscences:* "to bring order out of chaos, to provide means where none existed and to give a new tone and spirit to languishing and fast failing hopes." His alert mind, his resourcefulness, his extensive knowledge and experience in commercial and financial affairs, his zeal for independence, and his high reputation made him the natural choice as a financial administrator. Consequently he was appointed Superintendent of Finance, a position created for him and held by no one else. He was "authorized to oversee and direct the receipt and disbursement of public money, to investigate the state of the public debt and to report a new plan of administration." This was a tremendous and discouraging task. But Robert Morris was probably the one man in America with suitable talents and character to meet the demands of the situation.

The other members of the triumvirate, Willing and Wilson, urged the reluctant Morris to accept this position of Financier General or Superintendent of Finance. Yielding to the pressure of his friends and of Congress, he consented against his personal wishes. He felt that here was an opportunity to serve his country in "hours of difficulty, danger and distress." This opinion he gave as his reason for acceptance. "I think the individual who declines the service of his country because its Councils are not conformable to his ideas, makes but a bad subject," he stated. No doubt he was here referring to the fact that Congress and he had never agreed on financial policies. For years he had attempted to warn the nation against inflation, which had now swept the country, bringing ruin in its wake.

In a letter to Washington he expressed a desire to keep his seat in the Pennsylvania Assembly until the Tender and Penal Laws were put to vote. This would mean a postponement of his taking oath as Financier. In the Assembly he spoke for the repeal of the old, outmoded tender and penal laws in order to increase the value of the state's paper money. His efforts succeeded at last. In February, 1781, the Assembly repealed these laws and laid a tax to help redeem their notes. State lands were sold to establish a fund for taking up the issue of paper money. Continental bills were outlawed— not received as legal tender. Fines and public salaries were to be determined in gold and silver instead of in wheat as heretofore. These measures resulted in an immense rise in the value of Pennsylvania paper money. After assisting in this financial stabilization in the state Morris was ready to tackle a larger task, that of stabilizing finances in the nation.

On February 20, 1781, Morris was unanimously elected Superintendent. He remained reluctant to accept this office, desiring relaxation instead of added burdens. In agreeing to serve he made certain stipulations: he must be released from responsibility for previously contracted Continental debts; he must be permitted time in which to make arrangements for the continuance of his commercial enterprises; and he must be free to select and dismiss clerks and officers in his department.

This last stipulation perturbed Congress as it seemed to vest too much authority in the Financier. Finally after spirited debate Congress agreed to all these conditions, with the proviso that the superintendent's extensive powers should last only for the duration of the war. Military officers, secret service agents, and the Commander-in-Chief of the armies were considered not subject to his jurisdiction.

On May 14, 1781, Morris informed Congress of his acceptance of the office. In a previous communication to that body he had stated that he sacrificed his interest, ease, domestic enjoyments, and tranquillity for the service of his country since he considered it his duty. "The United States may command everything I have," he assured them, "except my integrity and the loss of that would effectually disable me from serving them more."

The task that confronted him was staggering. In a letter to General Schuyler he stated that he had been induced to accept the position although he trembled when he thought of it. (And well he might!) The letter continued: "I am led by a gleam of hope that my exertions may possibly retrieve the poor distressed country from the ruin with which it is now threatened merely for want of system and economy in expending and vigor in raising the public monies." System, economy, vigor—these characterized the business life of the Financier; these were the roots of his success. Confronted with an empty treasury and exhausted credit as well as an enormous debt, he needed, as he expressed it, "the support of all good citizens willing to promote the service of their country."

A business friend, Peter Whiteside, described the difficulties facing the Financier. "The finances of the country are in perfect chaos (if chaos can be called perfect)," he wrote, and enumerated other evils: "prejudices of people, some in favor of paper money, some against it, the violence of party feeling, the effects of envy and malice to combat—at the immense sacrifice of private fortune and ease." Whiteside considered Morris "the chosen person for this employ." . . . "It has frequently been in the power of one or a few men to save a country," he added. "Although the labor will be immense, yet in case of success the reward will be immense."

Other friends were equally enthusiastic over his election. James Wilson in his note of congratulation, said: "The Intelligence that you have accepted of the Office of Superintendent of Finance gives great and very general satisfaction. The minds of people seem now open to the Necessity of adopting a system very different from that which has been so long injudiciously pursued. They seem sensible that the War cannot be carried on by a depreciating Medium."

In more caustic vein, the embittered Charles Lee wrote Morris: "You are, I find, placed at the head of the finances; it is an office I cannot wish you joy of; the Labour is more than Herculean. The filth and dung of that Augean stable is, in my opinion, too great to be clear'd away even by your skill and industry,—but however you succeed in this I do assure you that you are almost the only man on the whole Continent in whose hand the management of my personal finances I cou'd wish shou'd be deposited."

A letter from General Gates expressed his confidence in Morris and pleasure in his election: "If you can place public credit upon a solid formation, let the operation be ever so slow,—your fame will be immortal, and your services the most eminent to your country. Your hand I know to be equal to everything official, your heart I will not say anything about, lest you think me a flatterer."

Alexander Hamilton, himself an able financier, wrote enthusiastically: "I am happy in believing you will not easily be discouraged from undertaking an office by which you may render America and the whole world no less a service than the establishment of American Independence. 'Tis by introducing order in our finances, by restoring public credit, not by winning battles, that we are finally to gain our object." Hamilton saw the problem in perspective and accurately gauged the worth of Morris's services and the difficulties confronting him.

Especially heartwarming to Robert Morris was the following from George Washington: "My hand and my heart shall be with you and as far as my assistance can go, command it. We have, I am persuaded, but one object in view, the public good, to effect which I will aid your endeavor to the extent of my abilities and with all the powers I am vested with."

Sustained by such messages of encouragement and support, Morris assumed his new duties as Superintendent of Finance. In his letter of acceptance of this office, he stated that his sole motive was the public good. "As my ambition was entirely satisfied by my present situation and character in life, no motive of that kind can stimulate me to acceptance," he assured Congress. The whole business of finance, as he interpreted it in this same letter, was "to raise public revenues by the easiest and fairest possible modes, and to expend them in the most frugal, fair and honest manner." How ironic that statement must have seemed to Morris within a few months' time!

With extreme modesty he was "filled with apprehension" that his "small abilities supported by application and attention may be inadequate." He feared the public would be disappointed in expectations based on his election and entreated that "no flattering prospect of immediate relief may be raised." "Honest industry" was all he promised. His own private business he placed in the hands of others to avoid "illiberal reflections" by his fellow countrymen, and to enable him to devote his entire time and attention to the business of his department. In fact he postponed taking office until his private affairs could be adjusted, lest he might become involved "in a labyrinth of confusion."

His avowed object was to rescue and restore the country financially. What plans had the Financier to offer in the face of apparently insuperable obstacles? First of all he had a system, a carefully defined plan of attack, a financial strategy. His business had inculcated habits of exactness and punctuality; he was naturally energetic and resourceful. His large objectives he stated as follows: "to reduce public expenditures; to obtain revenues in our own country to meet these expenses; to show foreign nations engaged in the war we must look to them for the balance." The immediate objects of his attention he placed in the following order of importance: (1) feeding the army, (2) clothing the army, (3) equipping the army, (4) caring for the sick and wounded, (5) paying the army. By retrenching in all other expenditures he hoped to meet these essential demands. His most energetic efforts were concentrated on trying to stimulate the states to action; to induce foreign governments—France, Spain, and Holland—to make loans to the United States, and by various and devious devices, especially by making regular business contracts, to feed and clothe the army.

As the historian Botta says in his *History of the War of Independence of the United States of America:* "If the charge imposed on Morris was ponderous, the talent and firmness with which he sustained it, were not less astonishing. He was not slow in substituting regularity for disorder and good faith in the room of fraud. . . . To him it was principally owing that the armies of America did not disband and that the Congress instead of yielding to an inevitable necessity, recovered the means not only of resisting the efforts of the enemy, but even of resuming the offensive with vigor and success. *Certainly the Americans owed and still owe as much acknowledgment to the financial operations of Robert Morris as to the negotiations of Benjamin Franklin or even to the arms of Washington.*"

Even before his induction into office, the Financier made specific recommendations to Congress for placing the financial structure of the country upon a more stable foundation. He advised Congress to appoint a committee to examine into the management of his and other great offices, as he wished "to lay the whole of the proceedings and management before Congress" as frequently as possible. He urged the establishment of a national bank—the Bank of North America—to succeed the Bank of Pennsylvania, which in its year and a half of existence had given great assistance to the army. A few days after his acceptance of office, Morris sent plans designed to clear away constitutional obstacles in establishing the bank. He asked Congress "to make immediate application to the several states to invest them with powers of incorporating a bank and prohibiting all other banks or bankers in these states." The Financier also advocated the establishment of a mint for coining United States money since a maze of confusion existed with regard to the value of foreign coins. This plan, however, did not materialize for several years.

The vision of Robert Morris extended beyond the boundaries of this new country. He planned a system of international banking as well as national banking, and requested Benjamin Franklin to name a Paris banker to handle the finances of the United States in France. With this banker he wished all money from the French and other European governments, available for the use of the United States, deposited and made subject to the drafts of the Financier. At first he engaged the banking firm of Le Couteulx et Cie. to attend to his business in France. Later Franklin suggested Le Grand, a banker in hearty sympathy with America, to conduct the financial operations in Europe. This marked the beginning of a system of international finance that saved the United States from ruin.

On June 27, 1781, Robert Morris took the oath of office before the Chief Justice of Pennsylvania. In order to conserve his time, he established the Office of Finance next to his home on Front Street. Gouverneur Morris, his friend, who for many years made his home with him, was appointed his assistant.

This younger Morris, not related to the Financier, was a handsome, aristocratic, able, and fearless man, with just the degree of daring and lofty disinterestedness to enable him to collaborate most effectually with his chief. A highly educated, cultured man of the world, he was also an alert, clear-sighted, cool-headed business man and an able financier driven almost frantic by Revolutionary financial economy (or lack of it). Before he assumed the office of Assistant Superintendent of Finance, he had already drawn up an excellent plan of taxation and had been chairman of the committee that conferred with the British Commissioners on Lord North's conciliatory bills. After retiring from Congress he had practiced law and had written a series of thought-provoking essays on finance. He was, moreover, an accomplished French scholar since his mother was of Huguenot descent, and he had also studied the language at a school in New Rochelle and at King's College (Columbia). In 1780 just prior to his assumption of this office he had suffered an accident, which resulted in the loss of a leg.

The Financier was always most appreciative of his assistant's talents and efforts. To John Jay in France, Morris wrote: "Your friend Gouverneur writes you political letters, but as he tells you nothing of himself, it is just that I tell you how industrious, how useful he is. . . . I could do nothing without him." This association marked the beginning of a life-long friendship between the two men. Gouverneur Morris was one of the few persons whom Robert Morris addressed by name in his letters. Even in writing his life-long business partner, Thomas Willing, he began "My dear Sir," as he did in addressing his own son-in-law and his closest friends, but the salutation to the younger Morris was always "My dear Gouverneur."

The work of the Superintendent of Finance required unremitting diligence. It seems incredible that one man could supervise the numerous and varied tasks that devolved upon him. Morris, however, not content with mere supervision, attended to many of the details personally. He assumed charge of hospital activities: the procuring of supplies, such as sheets and bedcases, as well as money. He arranged to send "putrid patients from the new gaol to the bettering-house" and those less putrid to the Pennsylvania Hospital, whose fastidious managers refused to receive the filthiest and most objectionable prisoners. To the delegates from the Carolinas and Georgia, who had come to him with complaints concerning conditions in those states, he sent a plan for a lottery to relieve the unhappy sufferers and to provide funds so that the states might meet their quotas to the United States war fund. He made provision for the Oneida Indian boys, the wards of the nation, who had been sent to college in New Jersey.

His life was brimming with activity. Over venison at Byrn's Coffee House he discussed "interesting business" with John Penn, proba-

bly concerning state collections of taxes. To Morris all business per-
taining to the war or the government proved interesting. Meetings
of the Board of War, headed by Richard Peters, were held at Morris's office, to discuss the clothing and supplies for the army. The
needs were imperative. How could they be met without money or
any reasonable prospect of it? Morris's resourcefulness and ingenuity
were taxed to the breaking point. He himself had been a ringer of
doorbells in order to secure money for Washington in 1777. Now
he advocated the same method of procuring other supplies—muskets,
stockings, shoes. Bell ringing became the chief patriotic service—
that and the resultant donations made by the citizens at Morris's
suggestion. The Post Office Committee also met with the Financier
to consider abolishing the franking privilege for members of Congress and others. This was not a question of privilege but of need,
Morris thought—the need of hard money to win the war.

Every Monday and Friday evening a dignified group assembled
in the Finance Office: the Commander-in-Chief, weighed down by
his military problems and saddened by the wretched condition of
his troops, the Secretary of Foreign Affairs, the Secretary of Congress, Gouverneur Morris, and Robert Morris. The Financier grasped
his chief's hand warmly.

"Oh, Robert," said Washington sadly, "the country has failed
me. If I am not now extricated by you, all is lost."

"You shall be extricated," Morris replied earnestly. His faith and
optimism buoyed the spirits of all.

But the gigantic problems of his office often kept him awake.
Where could he secure the money for the successful prosecution
of the war? How could he procure supplies without funds? The
burdens of his office affected his rugged health. The painful eye
inflammation returned. Asthma attacked him, leaving him gasping
for breath. Despite these handicaps he labored on night and day.
Pitted against him were forces stronger than any man—worthless
paper money, the indifference and disaffection of individuals and
states, threatened mutiny in the army unless pay was forthcoming,
venomous criticism by all those whose pocketbooks were tapped.
"A tax gatherer will always be an unwelcome guest," Morris said,

"because his demand must necessarily interfere with some pleasurable or profitable pursuit." How deaf and blind the country seemed to him! Did it not realize that this was war, and that the war must be won in order to secure any individual rights? The issue seemed to Morris so clear. With cooperation he knew that he could accomplish his aims—could at least feed and clothe the soldiers, supply them with ammunition, and pay them a part of the large sums due them.

His mind was filled with plans for increasing the supply of hard money. He proposed new taxes—a poll tax, a land tax, and an excise tax. Although Paine had long been a bitter political enemy, a suggestion of his met with Morris's approval: the collection of a quarter's rent from all houses in Philadelphia to defray municipal expenses, especially those involved in the defense of the city. Over a few oysters, "a crust of bread and some cheese" at Paine's lodgings, Washington and Morris discussed the plan with their host. Morris tried to be fair even to political enemies and those distasteful to him personally.

One serious problem involved in financial stabilization concerned state certificates, which had been received as money. These he attempted to liquidate by accepting them for taxes and retiring them. He prohibited the issuance of any more Loan Office certificates— certificates offered by an insolvent government for loans of money or property. All these efforts were designed to get rid of superfluous paper money, most of it worthless, in order that the new government notes might be honored.

Above all other measures, Morris brought pressure to bear upon American ministers abroad, urging them to induce the governments to which they were accredited to grant loans to the United States. "The matter is urgent!" Morris wrote Franklin again and again. Fortunately Franklin was highly successful since France saw an opportunity through these loans of hampering the efforts of her ancient enemy, England. The French loans—those from the nation itself, from the Farmers General and the King—saved the United States from utter ruin. As soon as he assumed his duties as Superintendent of Finance, the sum of a million livres granted by King

Louis XVI was placed under the Financier's direction, to be expended by him. Five hundred thousand livres was deposited at once with the banking house of Le Couteulx, subject to the Financier's drafts and orders. Unsold bills of exchange at Versailles, Madrid, and the Hague were also committed to his management. These were the "sinews of war" which the Financier stretched and flexed and manipulated.

To John Jay, minister to Spain, he sent a long list of logical reasons for Spain to contribute considerable sums, at least five million dollars, to the United States. This loan, Morris argued, would weaken the common enemy, would assist Spain in the reduction of the Floridas, the Bahamas, and Jamaica, would prevent contraband commerce destructive of the Spanish King's revenue, and would enable the United States to carry on commerce advantageous to Spain. Of course the debt would be repaid. The loan was needed just then, he told Jay, because *"in a democracy time is required to accustom the people by degrees to bear heavy burdens."* Jay, however, was unsuccessful in his negotiations.

Optimistically and persistently the Financier continued his attempts to negotiate loans, to raise taxes—to raise revenue somehow, using all his ingenuity and mental resourcefulness. His assets were the balance due from the states, "frozen assets" as Morris was soon to discover, and, more valuable, the French loans; his liabilities, the worthless Continental paper and the huge, ever-increasing national debt.

Washington, in winter quarters at Morristown, sent Morris the most urgent pleas for supplies of all sorts for his starving army. A serious situation threatened. The famishing troops in Pennsylvania and New Jersey planned to pillage the countryside, to seize provisions wherever they might be found, Morris heard. Such action would alienate the sympathies of many at home and abroad, he realized. In haste he wrote General Philip Schuyler in New York and Thomas Lowery in New Jersey, requesting each to procure one thousand barrels of flour, charge it to him, and forward it at once to Washington. Thus by using his own credit he supplied the famishing troops and prevented large-scale pillage.

In the meantime Morris was restoring regularity and order from the chaos of the five or six preceding years. His *Official Diary* and *Official Letter Book* reveal the system, the organization, the meticulous attention to detail that characterized all his business dealings. He made business contracts with the firms that supplied the army instead of leaving such provisions to chance or to the states as had been done previously. It was his task to choose from among the bidders the one offering the cheapest and most satisfactory terms, to hold the successful applicant to his contract, and to make cash payments in accordance with the terms agreed upon.

He kept a watchful eye on all expenditures. At one time he thought the Commander-in-Chief's table expenses excessive and requested that they be reduced, although Washington was a close personal friend. His economy measures would fill a volume. The war debt, which had risen to eighteen or twenty million dollars annually before his administration, was reduced to five million a year through his retrenchments. It was not then a question of how much could be spent, but how little would meet the demands of the army. This was not the wealthiest country in the world, voting billions for the conduct of the war, but the youngest of republics, lacking any organized resources. This chaos Morris attempted to systematize. Great organizer as he was, he found the task overwhelming.

In order to accomplish his purpose, he became a national merchant on a grand scale. He was empowered to export and import, to send tobacco and indigo abroad in exchange for munitions and other military supplies. The rice, tobacco, and other products which he received for taxes he shipped abroad. An agent of his in the South, George Abbott Hall (a relative of Mary Morris), was authorized to buy skins and furs if he could not obtain indigo. Although disapproving of the barter system, Morris was forced to use it since paper money was valueless and hard money (well named) virtually unobtainable.

Throughout this period of intense effort and stupendous operations, he was bombarded with pleas and supplications for money. Conductors and drivers of wagons made "teasing applications for pay." Captains, colonels, generals kept up a rapid-fire of demands

—demands which he was unfortunately forced to refuse but which he invariably answered. Usually he showed courtesy and genuine sympathy for the applicant, but occasionally he replied "with some warmth" if the criticism became too heated. After consultation with other officials Morris had made a rule that no partial payments should be made. Thus no charge of favoritism or injustice could be offered. Morris, as much as anyone else, deplored the suffering this rule often entailed, but he refused to deviate from it. When General St. Clair asked for money to send his family, who were in danger of starving, Morris was unable to pay him part of his salary but gave $320 of his own money to aid the general. For one of Morris's keen sensibilities and generous nature it was hard to steel himself against such requests. This added tremendously to the heavy toll laid upon him physically, mentally, and emotionally, so that he felt "hunted and fatigued to death."

These were not easy days for Mary Morris, constantly worried about her husband's health. His multifarious activities kept Robert Morris so busy, so closely confined that his robust constitution suffered. There was frequently recurring inflammation of the eyes. For the asthma that had begun to develop, a remedy seems to have been exercise at the pump. "On certain days," he wrote friends, "I have been pumping for dear life." (This expression, of course, might mean struggling for breath.) No consideration of health, however, interfered with his performance of duty. The demands of the war were paramount.

Some of the demands upon him were entirely unconnected with his office. He became confidential adviser even to military men. General Horatio Gates, for instance, consulted Morris about accepting command of the Southern army. Morris advised against it fearing there were "too complicated perplexities." Very frankly and unflatteringly Morris predicted, "I fear your laurels may wither if you accept the command." Gates, like so many who seek advice, ignored it. (He had probably sought only compliments.) The disastrous battle of Camden, South Carolina, proved Morris's foresight correct.

The most remarkable instance of foresight or insight was the

Financier's advice to Washington to attack Yorktown instead of New York. Authorities have doubted Morris's part in the mapping of this campaign, but the following is the story as reported by Robert Morris to his son, Thomas, and by the latter related to Redwood Fisher, who told it in his *Revolutionary Reminiscences*.

In July, 1781, Judge Peters of the War Board and Robert Morris went together to Washington's Headquarters "for the express purpose of dissuading the Commander-in-Chief from his meditated attack on New York and representing to him the immense advantages that must flow from his leading his army to Yorktown." After a tedious journey made by a devious route in order to avoid the enemy, they were met by Colonel Blaine, Commissioner General, at Princetown (Princeton), reached Dobbs Ferry on Friday night and Headquarters, Saturday morning, August 11. General Washington, returning to the camp at one o'clock, gave them a hearty welcome and held his levee as usual from 1:30 to 2:30 P.M. There the guests met the officers of the American and French armies and the heads of the various departments, all of whom made demands upon the Financier for money. He was never free from business cares and solicitations for pay, even in society. The two guests remained in camp several days in long conferences with Washington in regard to reducing the number of officers and augmenting the number of privates, and also in regard to the expenditures for the army and the transportation of supplies.

One morning at one o'clock, "at beat of reveille," Morris and Peters, who occupied the same marquee, were aroused by a messenger with the word that Washington wished to see them immediately. When they reached headquarters, they found the general in a rage, as he had just received information that the French were entering Chesapeake Bay, not New York Harbor, as previously agreed.

This gave Morris the opportunity he had been seeking. "An attack on New York, even if successful, would be a barren triumph," he told his chief. "The enemy, having command of the sea, could easily retake the city."

Washington, becoming calmer, assented, but inquired: "What am I to do? The country calls on me for action; and, moreover, my army cannot be kept together unless some bold enterprise is under-taken."

To this Morris rejoined: "Why not lead your forces to York-town? There Cornwallis may be hemmed in by the French fleet by sea, and the American and French armies by land, and will ultimately be compelled to surrender."

"Lead my troops to Yorktown!" exclaimed Washington, appear-ing to be astonished at the suggestion. "How am I to get there? One of my difficulties about attacking New York arises from want of funds to transport my troops thither. How, then, can I muster the means that will be requisite to enable them to march to Yorktown?"

"You must look to me for funds," the Financier replied.

"And how are you to provide them?"

"That I am unable at this time to tell you, but I will answer with my head," said Morris, "that, if you put your army in motion, I will supply the means of their reaching Yorktown."

"On this assurance of yours," assented Washington, "such is my confidence in your ability to perform any engagement you are willing to make, I will adopt your suggestion."

At breakfast when they met again, Washington seemed com-posed—and later in the day stated his plan to attack Yorktown. Turn-ing to Peters, he asked, "Well, what can you do for us, under the present change of plan?"

"I can do everything with money," the Judge replied looking significantly at Morris, "nothing without it."

"I understand you," said the Financier. "I must have time to con-sider, to calculate." After a few minutes he stated that he had only "promised support but little tangible effects from it. If, however, anticipations of my personal credit succeed, I will supply the means," he promised.

After a vow of secrecy had been imposed upon them, Peters and Morris left the camp, and escorted by a corps of horse, took a short and dangerous route to Philadelphia.

Peters set to work at once, aided by an efficient staff, and within a few weeks provided sixty pieces of battering cannon and a large amount of field artillery. Morris's task was even more stupendous:

that of furnishing the financial "sinews of war and the mainsprings of transportation and supplies." He issued his own notes for $1,400,-000 (according to some authorities) and, by the evidence of his own accounts, advanced $12,000 for army supplies. His colleague voiced his appreciation of this valuable cooperation. "Who, knowing all these things," exclaimed Peters some years later, "can doubt of his having been among the most eminent and the most prominent saviours of his country?"

Undoubtedly without Morris's assistance Washington could not have carried out his plans. In addition to money for supplies, the Financier promised to provide transportation for six thousand to seven thousand men.

"How will you do it?" Washington queried.

Morris replied, "I don't know, but I pledge my head" (his favorite guarantee) "that when you get to Philadelphia, I will provide the transportation for you."

Robert Morris's head was safe although at first it may have seemed in danger. The requirements for conveying the army secretly to Yorktown and provisioning it were tremendous. At the beginning he had to provide three hundred barrels of flour, the same amount of salt, and ten hogsheads of rum for the army on its way down the bay. These provisions were to be waiting at Head of Elk. Other supplies were to be provided at certain points along the route. The Financier appealed to Virginia, Maryland, Delaware, and New Jersey for supplies—to Delaware and Maryland for fresh and salt beef, pork, and rum; to Virginia for flour, tobacco, corn, and forage. From Baltimore he requested boats to carry the troops to Yorktown, but an inadequate number was provided.

The desperate need was for money: "the douceur of a little hard money," as Washington expressed it, "to put the Northern Troops in the proper temper to go South." For this purpose the Financier needed more money than he had himself supplied. An appeal to the states he knew would be futile. Consequently he solicited a loan from the French. One day early in September he called upon the French minister, the Chevalier de la Luzerne, and the Count de Rochambeau, commander of the French army, at Luzerne's house in Shoemaker's

Place. The Chevalier was unwilling to make the loan since he had barely enough funds on hand to pay the French troops. "But the demands for Yorktown must be met," pleaded Morris. "A victory there might bring the war to a speedy conclusion." At last due to Morris's insistence, Luzerne grudgingly consented to a loan of $20,-000 in silver until October 1, on Morris's personal credit. At this time when the credit of the United States was nil, the credit of the Financier was accepted by a foreign power. This promised loan was naturally made contingent upon the arrival of silver in the French vessels commanded by the Count de Grasse; but this fleet was overdue, its fate uncertain although it was reported to be in Chesapeake Bay. Morris, always sanguine, trusting that the ships with their precious freight would arrive in time, continued with his plans for supplying and transporting the army. He was by nature an optimist, and also a gambler, a "dealer in Futures" when necessity demanded such faith.

Soon after this, Washington and the army entered Philadelphia on their way south. Robert Morris and other prominent citizens rode out on horseback to meet them and escorted them triumphantly into the city. The streets were lined with cheering crowds who threw up their hats and shouted. Morris led the weary general and his staff towards his home, since Mrs. Morris and the children had not yet returned from "The Hills." On the way they stopped at City Tavern for refreshments. The cheering crowds had followed the cavalcade and pressed forward as they alighted, not too close, however, for the comfort of the distinguished guests. That night Washington, Rochambeau, and Generals Chastellux, Knox, and Moultrie occupied Morris's comfortable, spacious home. The entire house was turned over to them, mattresses being placed upon the floor to accommodate Washington's aides. That evening Morris gave a feast for these military visitors, during the course of which salutes were fired by ships in the harbor. Between salvos the host and his guest drank toasts in Morris's best Madeira and whiskey: "To the United States," "To His Most Christian Majesty the King of France," "To the United Provinces" (Holland), and "To our Allied Armies." With the pageantry of victory Robert Morris and his fellow townsmen

bade farewell to their Commander-in-Chief as he set out for Yorktown.

Yet the French loan had not been received. Morris was gambling
on the arrival of the Count de Grasse at the last moment. The army
had already reached Head of Elk. The soldiers had been promised
their bonuses. No money was in sight. Morris made all arrangements
for their embarkation as if all the funds were in his hands. He had
unbounded, unswerving confidence in the ultimate success of the
campaign and of the war itself. The silver *must* come in time. If
Morris's faith wavered for an instant, no one knew it. He alone
seemed calm and confident. Beneath the surface, however, he must
have experienced many anxious moments.

As he was leaving for Head of Elk where the troops were waiting
to embark, he offered Luzerne and Rochambeau seats in his carriage.
Early in the morning they set out. They had not ridden far when
an express rider galloped towards them. Morris called to the messenger to stop.

Leaning his head out the carriage window, he asked, "To whom
are you bearing dispatches?"

"To Mr. Robert Morris, Superintendent of Finance," the messenger replied.

Making his identity known, the Financier eagerly grasped the dispatches and broke the seals. Here was good news indeed—news of
the arrival of the French fleet with the long-expected silver.

Morris, returning at once to the city, dispatched Audibert, Deputy
Paymaster General of the United States, to the Head of Elk to receive the French money and to carry it to Washington's army. In
making the plan for delivery, the Financier demonstrated his show-
manship and his knowledge of psychology. He ordered that the
heads of the kegs containing the silver halfcrowns should be knocked
in and that the kegs with silver rolling out should be paraded on
wagons before the army. This was done to the astonishment and
delight of the soldiers, who feasted their eyes on wagon-loads of
silver—a sight more heartening than millions of dollars in paper
money. One soldier in ecstasies cried out: "Look! Look, Jonathan!
By jingo! it is hard money!" So the soldiers were paid and con-

tentedly set sail for their Southern campaign. Well Morris knew the effect of a display of silver or gold to enhance the value of money, to revive drooping spirits, and to restore confidence. This device he used again in a later crisis.

Even with the French loan of 144,000 livres (about $20,000), the amount fell short of the sum required. This Morris had to supply on his own credit. He borrowed money from a friend and advanced a sum from the treasury really needed for use in Philadelphia. As he confided in the President of Pennsylvania, he was "left almost penniless to face obligations which cannot be violated." The treasury was empty. The Financier was faced with pressing demands. Yet instead of receiving assistance or relief, he was given new responsibilities.

CHAPTER VIII

FATHER OF THE FLEET

❖   ❖   ❖

TO add to Morris's other burdens, he was appointed early in September, 1781, Agent of Marine, to supersede the innumerable boards, committees, and agents previously charged with marine affairs. This care-infested office he did not wish to assume but felt obliged to accept. "They [Congress] thought proper," Morris wrote John Bradford, "to devolve the duties of that station on the Superintendent of Finance, who God knows, had already more to do than either his time or abilities permitted him to execute equal to his wishes." In his *Official Diary* he recorded: "I shall undertake the task, however contrary to my inclinations and inconsistent with the many duties which press heavily upon me, because it will at least save money to the public."

Economy—that was his chief refrain. As one method of economizing he consolidated his two offices, combining the functions of Marine Minister and Superintendent of Finance. In this way he saved at least $700 annual rent. No retrenchment was too small for him to consider.

His responsibilities were those of Secretary of the Treasury and Secretary of the Navy. Morris, well acquainted with the problems of shipping and of dealing with naval officers and seamen, felt an intense interest in naval matters. Now as these new duties devolved on him, he had more control over the affairs of the navy than any other civilian had had. His experience on the Marine Committee in 1776 had prepared him for this even more responsible office, as had his years as a merchant engaged in commerce with Europe and the islands of the Caribbean. Indeed he was the ideal choice for such a position.

Immediately after his appointment, he visited wharves in the harbor at Philadelphia to ascertain the number of vessels there and obtain information about those to be hired for transport. The fleet, which consisted of frigates, small merchant vessels, and privateers, was responsive to his call. He sent the frigates *Alliance* and *Deane* to sea with instructions to harass the enemy, to plan "places of rendezvous in case of separation," and to send prizes to the port that was most accessible. Private shipowners were authorized to fit out armed ships to prey on British commerce. In 1781, the peak year, when Robert Morris became the Agent of Marine, 449 of these ships, with 6,735 guns, were commissioned. These did not, of course, constitute the United States Navy, but they served as an effective substitute. These privateers, swarming like seagulls, distressed the enemy and captured rich cargoes. Sometimes one lone privateer took twenty-eight prizes. The owners of the vessel received a certain share of each prize; the remainder was divided among officers and crew in fixed proportions. Profits were enormous. Sometimes a common sailor received as much as $1,000. Some of the greatest American naval officers of the period were at one time privateersmen; for example, Jones, Decatur, Hopkins, Barry, and Barney. These ravages upon British commerce naturally distressed commercial England. If privateers were captured, the harshest punishment was inflicted upon officers and crew. The *Jersey*, a prison ship, was the fate of many a privateersman. This was a 74-gun vessel, moored on the Long Island shore—a loathsome prison, where living conditions were foul and the food damaged. Nevertheless privateering continued to roll up fortunes for shipowners, officers, and crew. Richard Peters once laughingly told Morris that he wished "to be admitted to the Privateers' Circle." Morris had greatly augmented his already large fortune by privateering.

Most of the officers knew Morris, loved and trusted him. John Paul Jones, who as a young lieutenant had first raised the flag of the United States over any vessel, had long been a friend and correspondent of his. Jones's achievements since that initial flag-raising had been truly amazing and spectacular. In the unseaworthy *Ranger* he had

alarmed the coasts of England and Scotland, had scuttled merchantmen and sent the crews ashore to spread the news that an American
man-of-war was ravaging the Irish Sea. He had captured ships, the
first of these the *Drake*, a capture constituting the first United States
naval success. Jones had many "firsts" to his credit. He had paralyzed
the British shipping trade and made incursions (commando raids)
into British territory. One of the most dramatic of these raids was
that in which he looted the castle of Lord Selkirk, in the shadow of
which he had lived as a boy. His excellent discipline over his men,
who waited outside the castle while the family silver was brought to
them, and Jones's purchase and return of the silver won from Lord
Selkirk a letter of appreciation and commendation—an unusual sequel
to a looting raid. The other inhabitants of the coast, however, had no
kind words for Jones; they trembled at the thought of his approach
and nicknamed him "the pirate."

Perhaps the most amazing of his exploits was the moonlight battle
between the *Bonhomme Richard*, a ship donated by the French and
commanded by Jones, and the British *Serapis*, Captain Richard Pearson commanding. The crippled *Richard*, shipping water, barked
defiance at the 44-gun two-decker. It was under those circumstances
that the *Richard* was called upon to surrender. And it was under
those circumstances that Jones flung back that world-famous challenge: "I have just begun to fight!" The final surrender of the *Serapis*
to the now utterly incapacitated *Richard* ranks among the miracles
of history.

At the time of that victory another ship of the French fleet under
Captain Landais stood by presumably to assist Jones. Landais, however, bitterly jealous of Jones's achievements and fame, fired upon the
disabled *Richard* and in every conceivable way hindered his commander's efforts in that bloody battle. That of course constituted in-
subordination of the first water. Jones reprimanded him and reported
his actions to the French authorities, who merely reproved Landais
and relieved him of his command. Later, seeking revenge, the Frenchman aligned himself with Arthur Lee, the chief trouble maker in
France (and later in America). With regard to this quarrel Jones had
written Morris, telling him how Landais had treacherously stolen

from Jones the command of the *Alliance* and sailed from France without orders, confining Jones's sailors and marines in the hold of the vessel.

"I found the *Alliance* at the entrance of Fort Lowis," wrote Jones to Morris in June, 1780, "and every necessary disposition was made to stop her from going out, but my Humanity would not suffer me to remain a silent Witness of Bloodshed between allied Subjects of France and America. My having prevented that Scene of Horror has been I am persuaded no small disappointment to the wicked Heart and Empty head of Captain Landais' two principal advisers [Arthur and William Lee]. . . . The one of these two would-be great men will now have his Carriage, Baggage, and Family transported from hence in the space on board the *Alliance*, that should have been occupied by the Soldiers Cloathing, while the Red-Ribboned Commodore has taken advantage of the Confusion and inveigled away from the Continental service a number of seamen that I have redeemed from English Dungeons, and fed for three months on board the *Alliance*. . . . The brave Men who so gloriously served with me in the *Bonhomme Richard*, are now confined as prisoners in the Hold of the *Alliance* and treated with every mark of indignity. . . . After Mr. Lee had made a written application to me as Commander of that Ship [the *Alliance*] for a passage to America, I am at a loss what name to give Mr. Lee's late conduct and duplicity in stirring up a mutiny in favor of the Man who was at first sent to America contrary to Mr. Lee's opinion . . . and who is actually under arrest by an order of his Sovereign. What gives me the greatest pain is that after I had obtained from Government the means of transporting to America under a good protection the arms and cloathing I have already mentioned, Mr. Lee should have found the means to defeat my intentions."

Upon his return to America, Commodore Jones found that efforts had been made to poison public opinion against him. These intrigues he ascribed to Arthur Lee, and wished to summon him to a duel. It must have been wormwood to Paul Jones after his great victory and the adulation he had received in France to be greeted upon his return to America with suspicion and neglect. It took the combined persuasive powers of Robert Morris, Robert Livingston, and Alexander Hamilton to pacify Jones and persuade him to request Congress to inquire into the causes of difference between Lee and himself. Becoming exasperated at questions evidently framed by Lee and sent Jones by the Board of Admiralty, the Commodore determined to publish his paper, "Arthur Lee in France," revealing his enemy's diplomatic treachery. He was so stubbornly determined upon this action that Morris and the other peacemakers called on Washington to help them dissuade Jones from publishing this treatise, as they felt its revelations might be prejudicial to the stability of the government. Washington, Morris, and the others employed strenuous measures to avert this calamity. When the Commodore demanded that his reports be handed over to Congress, he was snubbed by the Admiralty Board. Thereupon Jones appealed to Robert Morris for "protection against the chicanery of a packed Board," or for permission to handle the affair in his own way. An appeal to Robert Morris always brought results. That was one reason he was so harassed by complaints and pleas. The effect of this entreaty was the immediate reference of his papers to Congress, and, shortly afterward, the abolition of the so-called Board of Admiralty and the appointment of Morris as Agent of Marine. Intervention on his part had resulted in new responsibilities.

Before the new Minister of Marine had taken office, Commodore Jones was appointed by Congress to command the 74-gun ship, the *America*, in process of construction at Portsmouth, New Hampshire. This was the most important naval assignment at the disposal of Congress. Morris at once wrote the Commodore urging him to accept the post as "the most ample vindication of yourself from any wrongs of which you may have hitherto entertained a sense." The letter, striving to pacify Jones, added: "You should also view them as having placed you upon a plane of honor and dignity from which you could but derogate by further meditation of personal recourse in any direction whatsoever." Here spoke the peacemaker, adroitly suggesting through vague generalities the cessation of hostilities with Lee. The Commodore understood.

When Robert Morris entered upon his duties in the maritime office,

John Paul Jones was in charge of construction work on the *America*, with the task of getting her ready for launching and of rigging, arming, and outfitting her. Little progress had been made on this vessel although she was one of three line-of-battle ships authorized by Congress in November, 1776. The keel was laid in May, 1777. Until 1781 work had been impeded by lack of money for supplies and wages. With Morris as Agent of Marine and with Jones as supervising commander, the construction progressed. Unfortunately a sum appropriated by Morris for this purpose had to be diverted to aid the Yorktown expedition. In the meantime the Commodore gnashed his teeth and paced the docks at Portsmouth. He requested Morris to obtain three or four months' leave for him so that he might join Lafayette's Division in the Yorktown campaign. He preferred fighting to rotting. The Minister of Marine refused, however, as he considered the early completion of the *America* more important.

The sad sequel to this story came a year later. After months of disagreeable and arduous labor supervising the construction work and guarding the harbor, Jones felt jubilant that the *America*, his battleship, was almost ready to be launched. He had a crew of 380 enlisted men, 100 of them survivors of the *Ranger* and the *Bonhomme Richard*, who had answered his call. Just at that time, about September 1, 1782, when the Commodore was prepared to take possession of the finest ship—the only real American battleship he had ever commanded—Congress passed a resolution giving the *America* to the King of France to replace the lost *Magnifique*, wrecked at the entrance to Boston Harbor. It seemed like good economy as well as excellent diplomacy to make this gift; in fact, Morris advised it. But it struck a blow to the pride of the nation's greatest naval hero, who was now a commodore without a command. This was just one instance of the strange fatality that seemed to dog the steps of John Paul Jones. Robert Morris as head of the United States Navy had the unpleasant task of directing the Commodore to hand over the ship to the Chevalier de Martigne. Morris sent Congress the fine letter from Jones that he received in reply. With his warm heart and generous sympathies, the Financier understood better than anyone else, probably, how Jones's proud, ambitious, sensitive nature was stung by this crowning disappointment. Thus he appreciated the naval officer's sportsmanship and fine courtesy revealed in his letter.

Still later, in October, 1783, Paul Jones sent Robert Morris another letter, which shows his hurt pride and humiliation as well as his naval genius:

"I have many things to offer respecting the formation of our navy, but shall reserve my observations on that head until you have leisure to attend to them and require them of me. . . . It was my fortune as senior of the first lieutenants to hoist the flag of America the first time it was displayed. Though this was but a slight circumstance, yet I feel for its honour more than I think I should if it had not happened. . . . I hope I shall be pardoned in saying that it will not be expected after having fought and bled for the purpose of contributing to make millions happy and free, that I should remain miserable and dishonoured by being superseded without any just cause assigned.

"I have met other humiliations in the service that I have borne in silence. When the *America* was presented to His Most Christian Majesty, I presume it would not have been inconsistent with that act of my Sovereign if it had mentioned my name. . . . I appeal to yourself, sir, whether, after being unanimously elected to command the first and only American ship-of-line, my conduct after more than 16 months while inspecting and launching her had merited such cold neglect. When the *America* was taken from me I was deprived of my tenth command. Will posterity believe that out of this number the sloop-of-war *Ranger* was the best I was ever enabled by my country to bring into actual service? If I have been instrumental in giving the American Flag some reputation and making it respectable among European Nations, will you permit me to say that it is not because I have been Honoured by my country with either the proper means or proper encouragement."

It is small wonder that Jones, the greatest naval genius of that day, should feel so bitter concerning his treatment by the United States after his stupendous efforts and brilliant successes in European waters. Morris replied with sympathy. He was the real "trouble shooter" of that era because of his kind heart and tactful manner. Moreover, had he not also experienced the lack of appreciation and the carping criticism of his fellow countrymen? Unfortunately for the United States Navy, Morris evidently had not the leisure to study Jones's observations on the formation of the navy and consequently did not demand them of him. This plan lay buried for fifty years.

Another problem facing the Agent of Marine was the old one of defending the port of Philadelphia and its approaches. In March, 1782, the Delaware River was infested by barges and cruisers of the enemy. From those dwelling near the river Morris received word of frequent raids by these vessels and their crews. Other communications mentioned that American river craft was being captured as prizes by the British. Here was a new menace to be met. At Morris's suggestion Pennsylvania fitted out several cruisers, and the merchants of Philadelphia advanced funds for outfitting the *Hyder Ali,* under Captain Barney's command. The captain was ordered to keep open the navigation of the river and bay, and especially to drive off British privateers. The exploits of this river boat read like a fairy tale.

On one occasion Captain Barney used a clever ruse to deceive and decoy the enemy. An American convoy was sailing down the river to Chesapeake Bay, escorted by the *Hyder Ali.* In the bay British vessels were sighted. Thereupon the convoy turned and sailed back up the river, its retreat covered by the *Ali.* The enemy advanced. One ship Barney allowed to pass, determined to engage the other.

To his helmsman he gave private instructions: "When I give the word, pay no attention to my order, but put the helm hard-a-starboard."

A few minutes later on deck Captain Barney shouted in stentorian tones so that the enemy could not fail to hear him: "Port your helm. Hard-a-port."

The British captain, hearing the order, prepared to maneuver the *General Monk* into the proper position. Suddenly to his amazement, he saw the American ship lying athwart his bow, his bowsprit caught in the *Hyder Ali*'s rigging. This gave the American vessel an excellent raking position.

"Strike your flag!" called Captain Barney.

Shots were fired. Men fell on the decks of both ships—twenty in all. After half an hour the enemy flag was lowered.

Later that evening two battle-scarred vessels careened up to the Philadelphia wharf, with tattered sails and shattered hulls, cordage hanging loosely from their masts. On the decks lay twenty lifeless bodies. In this way the *Hyder Ali* returned with its prize, the *General Monk*—once the American privateer, *General Washington*—captured by the British and now restored to the Americans. Such dramatic events as this relieved the tedium of Morris's position as Marine Agent.

CHAPTER IX

THE NATION'S BANKER

❖   ❖   ❖

UPPERMOST in the Financier's mind since his induction into office were the larger financial issues, especially his favorite scheme, the establishment of a national bank. This project, in fact, was the foundation of his financial system. The Pennsylvania Bank had proved so valuable an asset to the finances of the state and to the army that Morris wished to enlarge its activities and give it a national character. From Congress he expected and for once received the fullest support in the establishment of this institution. In urging the matter upon them, he stated three specific benefits of a national bank: it could absorb worthless paper, replacing it with bank notes; it could lend large sums to the United States for the prosecution of the war; it could unite the states in a general financial connection to their advantage. Naturally all other banks and bankers would be prohibited, at least during the war. The bank notes were to be accepted as specie, to be payable on demand, and to be receivable for taxes by the states and the United States.

At a meeting of the stockholders of the Pennsylvania Bank, these patriotic citizens agreed to transfer their holdings to the Bank of North America. Capital stock of $400,000 was decided upon, the shares of $400 each to be paid in gold or silver. There were to be twelve directors and two inspectors to examine and control the business of the bank for the ensuing three months, when other inspectors would be appointed. To the Superintendent of Finance statements of the cash account and notes of the bank were to be delivered daily so that he might know the exact balance at any time. The Financier, moreover, was given the right to examine the affairs of the bank whenever he wished.

Robert Morris was jubilant over the initial success of his enterprise. In a letter written on June 11, 1781, he exclaimed: "This may prove the means of saving the liberties, lives and property of the virtuous part of America." Unfortunately others were less sanguine than the great optimist. The subscriptions languished. Morris, supersalesman as he was, issued appeals to governors, generals, and merchants—all those he thought might be induced to subscribe, but the response was disheartening. The public remained cold. States' rights men were opposed to the charter for a national bank. Others had no money or kept it hidden. Generals who might have purchased shares were unable to do so because their salaries had not been paid. There was indeed little hard money in the country.

The Financier was determined that the United States should own a large number of shares, but the treasury was empty. Robert Morris's determination and persistence, however, could overcome the strongest obstacles. As usual he looked abroad for money. At first he planned to transport it from Spain by way of Cuba.

Plans had been made in detail and with great secrecy. The *Trumbull*, with Captain Nicholson in command, was to be dispatched to Havana laden with flour—and bearing a bill of exchange for 500,000 livres on French bankers and approximately $120,000 worth of old bills on John Jay. These were to be sold on the best possible terms, preferably to the Governor of Havana. This voyage was shrouded in secrecy. The *Trumbull* was reported to be carrying flour to the French fleet in Rhode Island. The destination of the ship was to remain a secret even to its officers. Instructions to the Captain, in a sealed envelope, were to be opened after the pilot had left the vessel. Letters to the Governor of Havana and to William Smith, the continental agent there, were slung with proper weights so that they might be sunk if the ship were captured. Despite all these precautions the *Trumbull* was overtaken and seized by the British soon after leaving Delaware Bay. Captain Nicholson and Richard Dale were taken prisoner and later exchanged through Morris's negotiations. Only the letters escaped capture.

Although this attempt failed, at last through the Financier's enthusiasm and stubborn perseverance he was granted approximately $254,000 of $470,000 in specie, brought from France by Colonel Henry Laurens, formerly President of Congress. Because of severe storms off the coast, the ship *La Resolue,* containing the French silver, landed in Boston instead of in Philadelphia.

The task of transporting such a large amount of specie from Boston to Philadelphia through country occupied by the enemy was attended by the gravest difficulties. It was a task for a Titan, but Robert Morris was equal to it. This particular type of maneuver he most enjoyed. Difficulty and danger stimulated his imagination, setting free his ingenuity. The journey had to be carefully planned to the last detail; nothing could be left to chance. So the Financier himself arranged every minute detail of the journey.

On a certain evening toward the end of the summer, Morris requested Tench Francis, Willing's brother-in-law, and Samuel Nicholas, Major of Marines, to appear in his office. In preparation for their arrival he carefully closed all doors and windows. Morris felt a boyish delight in mystery and adventure.

"Gentlemen," he said when his guests were seated, "I am confiding certain instructions to you in the deepest secrecy. You know that you are to carry out this mission of bringing a large amount of French silver from Boston to Philadelphia through enemy territory. Mr. Francis, you, sir, are in charge of the expedition. It is your task, Major Nicholas, to act as guard and assistant."

The two men bowed, awaiting further instructions.

"Since it would be difficult to transport such a large amount of specie for so long a distance, invest a considerable part of it in good bills of exchange in Boston. Pack the remaining coin in small square boxes of strong oak. Each box should contain 500 to 1,000 crowns. Place twenty such boxes in a great oak chest and nail the lid down tightly." No detail was too minute for Morris's attention. "Each chest," he continued, "should next be set upon the axle and tongue of an ox cart, from which the body had been removed. Secure it by heavy iron straps. In the meantime, gentlemen, you should have purchased six-year-old oxen and seven- to ten-year-old horses. Now see that each cart is drawn by four oxen led by a horse. Of course you must also have obtained the services of honest, sober teamsters. Before starting on the journey, arm each man with a musket and a bayonet."

Early in September the expedition was on its way. Then began the long anxious period of waiting. September passed without news. Indeed Morris did not expect any word since the expedition was shrouded in mystery. Although sanguine by temperament, the Financier could not help fearing for the safety of the mission. Every precaution had been taken. A party of dragoons accompanied the teams, and at fixed points along the way infantrymen were detailed to act as a military escort. The circuitous route led from Boston through Worcester and Newburgh to Philadelphia. In order to complicate the itinerary and obscure the movements of the expedition, the secret instructions advised Francis to head toward a certain town, then veer sharply in another direction. October came and went—and still no news of Francis and the teams.

At last on November 6 the carts creaked and rumbled into Philadelphia. Immense relief and joy at the success of the mission shone on the face of the Financier. This was a masterly maneuver, revealing clever strategy on the part of Robert Morris and dauntless courage on the part of all members of the caravan. Tench Francis, the efficient leader, sold the cattle, horses, and wagons, then assisted Morris in the establishment of the Bank of North America. The money thus obtained from the French was used to purchase $250,000 worth of capital stock in this new institution, the specie being placed in the vaults of the bank to redeem its notes.

On December 31, 1781, Congress incorporated the Bank of North America. On January 7, 1782, the bank opened its doors. Thomas Willing was elected president, a position he retained until 1792. The capable, conscientious Tench Francis became the first cashier. The bank was located on the north side of Chestnut Street, west of Third. Its hours were from ten to one and from three to five daily except Sunday. Some business men set their watches by Willing's arrival and departure, so regular were his hours.

Many devices were used for keeping silver in the bank and for reassuring the depositors. Whenever silver was removed, secret agents of the bank were sent to persuade those withdrawing it to deposit it again. This practice continued for six weeks until the bank was well established. A clever device was the endless chain or belt with silver coins in boxes attached to it, which ran from the vaults into the bank behind the cashier's cage. The silver was hoisted, lowered, hoisted again, and finally strewn in glittering heaps upon the counters. Reflectors multiplied the coins, dazzling the eyes of the spectators. The public was properly impressed; the depositors, satisfied. This device, illustrative of Morris's ingenuity, revealed his clever showmanship and his knowledge of human nature.

The bank immediately proved its worth to the United States. In less than two weeks after it had opened its doors, the directors made the government a loan of $100,000 and of later sums totaling $400,000. This was $100,000 more than the national shares had cost. To Benjamin Franklin, Morris wrote enthusiastically and prophetically: "The bank will be the pillar of American credit. . . . It will exist in spite of calumny, operate in spite of opposition and do good in spite of malevolence." Thus one of Morris's most cherished dreams materialized. The bank formed the bulwark of his financial operations, without which he would have been forced to capitulate.

On October 23, 1781, two hours before sunrise, came the news of the surrender of Cornwallis on October 19 at Yorktown. Church bells rang and bonfires flared in the most approved patriotic fashion. On the heels of this first announcement the British colors arrived, brought by Colonel Humphreys to Chester, met there by Colonel Tilghman, and conducted by him to Philadelphia. Troops of light-horse rode out to escort the colors into the city. At the head of the procession were borne the American and the French colors; behind, the captured trophies. Down Market Street to the Coffee House on Front Street, down Front to Chestnut, and up Chestnut to the State House, the soldiers marched to the music of the fife and drum, the many-colored flags billowing in the breeze. Into the State House the standard bearers stepped with triumphant, martial stride and laid the trophies at the feet of Congress. The members, Morris said, "seemed impressed with solemn thoughts." He himself recalled the threats of Lord North that he would "bring America to England's feet." Here, ironically, lay the emblems of Britain's greatness at the feet of her rebellious colonies, now a nation—the United States of America. Robert Morris exulted in his *Official Diary* with a triumphant note, like that of a Psalmist: "Glory be unto thee, Oh Lord God, who hath vouchsafed to rescue from slavery and from death these Thy servants."

That evening the house of the Chevalier de la Luzerne was brilliantly illuminated. Under the crystal chandeliers a large company, Robert Morris among them, enjoyed a concert and oratorio, followed by a sumptuous supper. This was the French celebration of the military successes. Early in November, Morris at the invitation of the Chevalier attended a Te Deum in the Catholic Cathedral (St. Mary's Catholic Church) to render thanks for the victory.

On November 26 George and Martha Washington arrived in Philadelphia and as usual accepted an invitation to the Morrises' home. In the evening Morris conferred with Washington and Lafayette, another house guest, concerning "aids of money." A few days later the Morris coach carried Washington and Morris on a house-hunting expedition, to look over a house owned by Dr. Rendon. Morris's advice on such matters was much sought by his friends because of his innate good taste and practical experience with Philadelphia real estate. The two men, bound by warm, personal ties and by collaboration in the war effort, enjoyed the intimacy of the expedition as they examined the convenient features of the mansion. Washington, deliberate in his judgment, often depended upon Morris's more rapid decisions. Evidently the house proved satisfactory as Washington rented it for a winter, adding another roof to the hundreds that might proclaim, "Washington slept here."

December 13 that year was set aside by Congress as a special day of prayer and thanksgiving for the Yorktown victory. Services were held in the churches. Soldiers marched in reverently, and knelt in prayer. Fathers and mothers prayed, "Grant peace in our time, O

Lord." The great and the humble knelt side by side. Washington and
Morris attended, their hearts full of thankfulness as they thought of
the uncertainties and dangers of that campaign.

Many felt that this victory ended the war, but Robert Morris knew
that "the only moral surety for peace is a state of constant preparation for hostilities." He earnestly desired the army to follow up its
victory and establish national independence. Very wisely he felt it
necessary to strike the enemy at once before he had time to gather
reinforcements. Procrastination Morris could never understand. His
own ardent nature impelled him to rapid action; his decisions, partly
intuitive or inspirational, leaped toward a goal while others loitered.

The time had not yet come for relaxation, Morris realized. At least
there was no rest for him. His problems remained: the huge national
indebtedness, the arrearages of pay to the army, and countless other
demands upon the empty treasury. Thus, instead of relaxing, the
Financier redoubled his efforts. Paine brought him a demand from
the officers and men of the Pennsylvania Line and the New Jersey
troops for immediate pay. Morris agreed that their demands were
just but stated that due to unfortunate circumstances they would have
"to be satisfied temporarily with the interest."

One ray, however, shone upon Morris at this time, the feeble be-
ginnings of one of his pet projects: the establishment of a national
mint—a natural corollary to the founding of the bank. This was
sorely needed since foreign coins, the only specie in use, were not
standardized. In the different states even the Spanish dollar, the most
familiar of these coins, had a wide variety of values: in Georgia it was
worth five shillings; in Virginia, six; in North Carolina and New
York, eight; and in South Carolina, thirty-two shillings sixpence.
Thus there was need for standardization and uniformity if financial
order were to be restored. On January 15, 1782, Morris presented a
report on the currency and a plan for the establishment of a mint.
With this report Gouverneur Morris assisted him, so that it is difficult
to determine how much was the work of the Financier and how
much that of his assistant. Morris wished to establish a legal tender of
a definite value, based upon a silver standard and secure from debase-
ment and counterfeiting. The different coins were to be represented

by a number of pennyweight or grains for both the alloy and the pure metal. The price of coining should be defrayed by the coinage, Morris thought. He considered it right that money should acquire a value as money, distinct from that which it possesses as a commodity. He advised that the proportion of gold to silver should be too small rather than too large, because paper money already issued might supply the place of gold and because silver was always worth more at market than the mint price. Coinage to be intelligible must have an affinity to the former currency. For this reason the Spanish dollar seemed the best standard. The money unit, he felt, should be small and increased in a decimal ratio, the lowest coin to be a cent.

On February 21, 1782, Congress approved the establishment of a mint, and Benjamin Dudley of Boston was put in charge of this new national institution. In April, 1783, the first silver coin from the United States mint was received. The Financier had added another financial fortification to the defenses of the country. Morris was doomed to disappointment, however. Owing to lack of funds in the national Treasury, the mint could not be supported at this time and was not re-established until 1792.

Despite all these arduous labors, Robert Morris, of an intensely sociable nature, found time for receptions and other social activities and ceremonies. After the French Minister, on May 13, 1782, announced to Congress the birth of the Dauphin, great festivities celebrated the event. Appropriate ceremonies were held by Congress, during which Morris and the others stood for more than an hour. Later in the day Robert Morris, Robert Livingston, Gouverneur Morris, and General Lincoln called upon the French Minister, the Chevalier de la Luzerne, to pay their compliments. Congress, in order to honor France, ordered an entertainment at City Tavern. This was followed by fireworks at the State House and an entertainment given by the Secretary of Foreign Affairs.

During the summer, on July 15, came the magnificent Fête du Dauphin, at which the Chevalier entertained fifteen hundred guests. It was, perhaps, the most spectacular party ever given in America. For six weeks carpenters and decorators were busy constructing arches, colonnades, leafy bowers, glittering domes, and a dance hall with statues of Diana, Flora, Hebe, and Mars in four specially prepared niches. This miniature Versailles was lighted by hundreds of tapers. Amid all this magnificence the guests enjoyed a concert, fireworks, a ball, followed by a supper at one o'clock in the morning, prepared by thirty French army cooks.

Such social events as this relieved the tedium and distress of Morris's public life. Among friends, in the gaiety of social life, his worries vanished temporarily.

CHAPTER X

"PREACHING TO THE DEAD"

❖   ❖   ❖

EVEN before the Yorktown campaign the Financier had attempted to arouse the patriotic consciences of the state legislatures. His efforts seemed to him like "preaching to the dead." After the Yorktown victory the states, flattering themselves that peace would result, became more apathetic than ever. In despair Morris sent them urgent appeals almost daily, pleading for provisions for the troops and for money to meet the country's indebtedness. "The duty of the public to pay," he asserted in ringing tones, "is like the same duty in an individual." State governments demurred. Morris argued, pleaded, appealed to pride and patriotism. "States must give money or the army must disband," he thundered. "The army must be fed." This was the burden of his refrain. He began to sound the note of financial ruin. "Unless vigorous exertions are made to put money into the Treasury, we must be ruined," he exclaimed to the indifferent or bickering states, who had become absurdly jealous of one another. He wrote the governors angrily, threatening to resign; he wrote tactfully and appreciatively, eager to cooperate. Finally in desperation he appealed to George Washington, who sent out circulars to the states—without results.

Morris had a three-fold plan for which he needed the cooperation of all the states: (1) to burn the paper money, (2) to sell "specifics" (produce) previously received from the states, (3) to abolish this method of receiving products from the states and to substitute a business-like contract system for obtaining army supplies. Consequently he wished the quotas from the separate states paid in hard money. The amount of revenue required for the fiscal year 1782 was eight million dollars, the quota from each state depending upon the population. The payments were to be made quarterly. Robert Morris, always meticulous in business matters, sent the states certified statements of their indebtedness to the Union, and requested from them copies of their laws relating to tax collections and the execution of these laws. He also wished information concerning the amount and character of the paper currency and the sums in the state treasury. On his part he promised that accounts with the states would be settled promptly: "As I am determined," he said, "that justice and order shall rule my conduct of affairs." To all his requests the governors turned deaf ears. If they responded at all, they answered evasively.

In defense of the states it may be said that the Union was a very loose bond. It consisted of thirteen separate and proudly sovereign states, seeking individual independence, rather than an independent union with a strong central government. Consequently they resented what they considered any infringement of their sovereign rights. They permitted Congress only such of their powers as were deemed absolutely necessary for common defense. Evidently they did not consider in this category of essentials the money to meet expenses incurred by that defense. During the course of the war, moreover, the states became more jealous of the power and authority of Congress. They felt that each state should tax itself and regulate its own trade. These suspicious states objected to taxes laid by "King Congress" as heartily as they had to those levied by King George. It is difficult for us today to realize how intensely individualistic were the colonies and the states, how opposed to a strong union. This makes the miracle of Revolutionary victory even more amazing. It also made the tasks of the leaders of this infant, undisciplined republic far greater than they should have been.

Morris, like Washington and Hamilton, was an ardent Federalist, realizing that a strong central government was necessary for effective action. According to his political doctrine, the Senate should be composed of leaders, men of property and intelligence, elected for life;

the House of Representatives, chosen more democratically, to act as a check upon them. Because of this radical difference in their theories of government, the Financier and the governors could not reach an understanding.

Morris, in desperate need of money, having exhausted his foreign credit, turned to the states as a last resort. Patiently at first, later more insistently, he tried to show them the grim necessity for meeting their obligations to the nation so that it in turn might meet its own most urgent obligations. To the state governors, therefore, he sent eloquent circular letters that said in part: "Should the army disband and should scenes of distress be reiterated, I again repeat that I am guiltless; the fault is in the states; they have been deaf to the calls of Congress, to the clamors of the public creditors, to the just demands of the suffering army and even to the reproaches of the army, who scoffingly declare that the American army is fed, paid and clothed by France."

Rebukingly he replied to the evasive pomposity of some governors: "Dignity is in duty and in virtue, not in the sound of swelling expressions." This circular swept onward vehemently to the peroration: "I am now compelled to transgress the bounds of prudence by being forced to declare that unless vigorous exertions are made to put money into the Treasury we must be ruined." Nor were these idle threats. Morris knew whereof he spoke. This forceful circular was never sent, however, as Congress feared exposing the country's financial status to the enemy. Instead Commissioners were dispatched to the states to settle their accounts, to receive the Continental bills in state treasuries, and to count, examine and destroy the bills after crediting the amount to the states on their quotas.

When the first quarterly payment of $2,000,000 was due, not one shilling was paid except $5,500 by New Jersey. "The habitual inattention of the states has reduced us to the brink of ruin," Morris lamented, "and I cannot see a probability of relief from any of them. How long is a nation who will do nothing for itself to rely on the aid of others? The complaint by people of want of money to pay taxes is as old as taxation and will last as long. . . . That times are hard, that money is scarce, that taxes are heavy—are constant themes of declamation in all countries and will be so. But the very generality of the complaint shows it to be ill founded. Hundreds who cannot find money to pay taxes can find it to purchase useless gewgaws and expend much more in the gratification of vanity, luxury, drunkenness and debauchery than is necessary to establish the freedom of their country."

To the Governor of Rhode Island he sent a logical case for the necessity of taxation: "If we will not submit to Great Britain, we must carry on the war; and if we carry on the war, we must obtain means; and if we cannot get means abroad, we must provide them at home; and if we do not provide them by law, they must be taken by force."

Earnestly, persistently Morris tried to awaken in the governors a sense of responsibility, to inculcate an honorable, proud patriotism. This plea to the governors of New Jersey and Delaware is typical: "I hope, *entreat, expect* the utmost possible efforts on the part of your state and I confide in your Excellency's prudence and vigor to render those efforts effectual." At this point the Financier was still hopeful of results. In a Circular Letter to the governors of the states he urged the necessity of preparation for war: "It is necessary that we should be in a condition to prosecute the war with ease before we can expect to lay down our arms with security, before we can boast of peace honorably and before we can conclude it with advantage." Cooperation between the states and the Union he considered of paramount importance in restoring national and international confidence. A vital element in this cooperation was promptness in responding to appeals. "In matters of public credit," he warned the governors, "long delay is equivalent to direct refusal."

As the states became even more unresponsive and irresponsible, Robert Morris grew more caustic, as in the following remarks: "What monies the states may grant and when they may grant them is known only to Him who knoweth all things." Even more bitter was his reference to Congress's lack of power to enforce laws: "While it [the Confederation of States] confers on Congress the privilege of asking everything, it has secured to each state the prerogative of granting nothing."

Sometimes he delivered a blow straight from the shoulder; as in speaking of his apprehension of the continued negligence of the states and their boundless demands, he asserted: "All Europe gazed in astonishment at the umparalleled boldness and vastness of the claims blended with an unparalleled indolence and imbecility of conduct." Morris did not mince words in his righteous indignation, for he wished the United States to be rendered "truly independent—independent of the smiles of our friends and the frowns of our foes."

The resourceful Financier had definite plans for improving the situation. He made a number of specific recommendations. The states, he believed, should provide soldiers; otherwise, they, not the Federal government, should support their soldierless officers. He requested each state to send the War Office a list of all non-commissioned officers and privates from that state. By a system of debits and credits he sought to encourage the states to increase the number of recruits. Officers without men should retire to their own states and be supported at state expense.

At the suggestion of the Financier, Congress recommended (this seemed to be its chief "power") that the states impose a 5 per cent tax on imports. In favor of this impost Morris (although he had always been an advocate of free trade) advanced the following arguments: "Articles are either wanted or not wanted: if wanted they must be purchased at the price for which they can be had; if not wanted, people will not buy and thus will consume less of foreign superfluities." In this way, he reasoned, the tax was just, falling equally on all.

In a long letter to the President of Congress, written on February 11, 1782, the Financier stated that Massachusetts, Rhode Island, and Maryland had not passed these tax laws, and Virginia had suspended operations of the impost. Consequently the interest on the government debt could not be paid and those who trusted the country would be defrauded. This was a less advanced era than ours; then nations or their leaders naively felt a responsibility to pay a national debt. In fact Robert Morris thought that "the duty of the public to pay is like the same duty in an individual. Having benefited by the advances, they are bound to replace them to the party or his representatives." Robert Morris was innately honest and direct. He continued to expound his doctrine that it was folly to expect others to confide in a government which did not meet its obligations and which lacked credit with its own citizens.

In addition to his other specific recommendations, Morris advocated free trade among the states and with other countries. "Perfect freedom of exchange," he wrote the Governor of North Carolina, "makes people easy, happy, rich and able to pay taxes." For the payment of taxes was the burden of his song. The embargo law was repealed in Pennsylvania and the price of flour fell from 28 to 17 shillings. This gave a fresh impetus to trade. Vessels laden with West Indian produce, European goods, and Spanish dollars arrived in port. The majority of the states, however, remained apathetic to this as to the Financier's other suggestions.

His difficulties became more burdensome. In 1782 he could not command more than one twentieth the sum necessary for the current expenses of the year. To the President of Congress he wrote: "When I say that I cannot command more than one twentieth the sum necessary for the current services of the year, I am within the strictest bounds of truth." By September 1, payments had barely reached $125,000 of the required $8,000,000. Ten thousand suits of clothes were needed by the army at a cost of $20,000. These could not be supplied. To the Governor of Virginia, Morris sent an urgent appeal: "What in the name of Heaven can be expected by the people of America but absolute ruin if they are so inattentive to the public service. Not until December will Virginia give anything you say toward the service of the current year. How, then, are we to carry on those operations which are so necessary? How is our country to be defended? How is our army to be supported? Is this what is meant by the solemn declaration to support with life and fortune the independence of the United States?" To Morris this vow to support the new nation "with life and fortune" had been taken with profound seriousness, despite his reluctance to sign the Declaration of Independence. The evasion of obligations and responsibilities was entirely foreign to his nature. Moreover, such an attitude aroused his red-headed temper, usually held in check by his good humor.

He also tried to stimulate Maryland to meet its payments by writing its Governor: "Every operation is at present supported by credit, and that credit has long hung by a thread. Unless the states give speedy and effectual aid, that thread must break. It would long since have broken, and scenes of military pillage, waste, murmuring, extravagance and confusion would again have opened if I had not for some time declined all expenditures except what was necessary merely to feed the army." The five aims with which Morris had so hopefully entered office were now reduced to one—feeding the army. There was no money for clothing, for ammunition, or hospitalization; none for salaries, wages, or bonuses.

The problems facing the harassed Financier with his empty treasury were legion. The United States was not acknowledged by any European power except France. The misinformation concerning foreign loans had grown pernicious, as the states, counting on foreign aid, were all the more unwilling to pay their quotas. "Let Jacques [or Louis] do it" might have been their slogan. All bills consequently were referred to the Court of France for payment. The French ministry became alarmed as well as embarrassed, and Franklin wrote Morris warningly not to count on France for further loans. "No more pecuniary assistance can be expected from Europe," the Financier in turn warned the states. He announced that he could not pay public creditors until the states provided revenues for liquidating principal and interest of the public debt. There was a grave necessity, moreover, for providing a sinking fund for this debt. In the meantime funds were lacking for the immediate necessities of the army. In a letter to Washington Morris regretted that he had "little besides wishes to dispose of. There is [in the states]," he continued, "a degree of torpor and lukewarmness which nothing can justify."

Vainly the indefatigable, persevering Financier attempted to borrow abroad but finally realized that he could not expect more aid from France or any succor from Spain, Holland, or Russia, to which countries envoys had been sent. "Even the slightest anticipations of revenue are made on the personal credit of the minister," he told Congress. "Wherever the United States attempted to borrow, mouths were stopped by one word, *Security*."

Despairingly Morris lamented that he found "no solicitude anywhere for the support of arrangements on which the salvation of our country depends." All his hopes and those of the nation were frustrated. "I feel as an American for my country," he said, "as a public servant for the interest and honor of those whom I serve, and as a man that I cannot enjoy the ease and tranquility I have sought for through a life of continual care and unremitted labor." A touch of self pity unavoidably mingled with the larger issues.

All the retrenching was left to Robert Morris. The states continued to send officers but few soldiers, few supplies, no money, and wagonloads of complaints. "If complaints of difficulties were equivalent to cash," he wrote a friend, "I should not complain that the quotas are unpaid." Although the recalcitrant states paid nothing, they presumed to advise Morris and Congress just how the public money should be spent. State officers attempted to show that their state had done as much as others—in fact, a little more; that stupendous sacrifices had been made, outweighing benefits; that specie was out of circulation, the people poverty-stricken, and thus unable to pay taxes. The other states were jealous of Pennsylvania, which they felt received more favors than they.

This was the spirit against which Robert Morris had to contend. Of course again and again he became the target of personal attack. He, the saviour of the tottering financial structure, was considered the cause of the nation's pecuniary misfortunes. He was accused of robbing the eastern states of specie, of being partial to Pennsylvania because he was a Philadelphia merchant, of establishing the bank "for sinister purposes," of conspiring with Pennsylvania to keep Virginia poor, and (time-worn accusation) of engaging in speculation.

All these charges he refuted. In the first place he accused those who said these things of a wish to injure the public service and sow dissensions among the states. He met attack with counter-attack, reminding his accusers that he had not received from the eastern states one shilling of specie but had, on the contrary, sent aid to those states. In refutation of his being partial to Pennsylvania because he was a Philadelphia merchant, he stated that merchants are attached to no state, their place of residence being accidental. In defense of Pennsylvania he asserted that he had received $180,000 from the state and that the contracts given out there had not equalled that sum. He had, moreover, exhausted his credit and supplied every shilling from his private fortune to support the southern states. He wrote most eloquently of the function of the Bank of North America in saving the country. "About the affairs of a bank," he assured them, "there is nothing sinister—nothing of mystery, disguise or concealment." He could not refrain from moralizing a bit concerning his "conspiring to keep Virginia poor." It was the fault of Virginia herself, he said, if she was poor. "Prudence, diligence and economy promote national prosperity, and vice, indolence and prodigality involve national ruin," he preached. He had constantly labored to effect measures calculated to make Virginia wealthy and powerful, he informed the Governor of that state.

He appointed a representative to receive Continental taxes in each state. Many of these state "receivers," including Alexander Hamilton for New York and John Penn for North Carolina, resigned because their commissions were small, their duties unpleasant, their task unsuccessful. Only the General Receiver, the Superintendent of Finance, whose duties were the most unpleasant of all, continued in office until, later, conditions became intolerable. While the Financier was "driven to the *greatest* shifts to find the *smallest* sums for the *commonest* purposes," and while he was bombarded with complaints, advice, and personal attacks, he sent words of encouragement to the receivers and grateful acknowledgments to the governors whenever any money or supplies were received. On the other hand, he urged that the state dereliction be published in the newspapers, for as he knew too well, "Men are less ashamed to do wrong than vexed to be told of it."

A less staunch, sturdy, or determined character than Robert Morris would have sunk beneath the load of perplexities that pressed upon him. Even he faltered. To his friend George Washington he confided: "There is scarce a day passes in which I am not tempted to give back into the hands of Congress the powers they have delegated and lay down a burden which presses me to earth. Nothing prevents me but a knowledge of the difficulties I am obliged to struggle under.

What may be the success of my effort God only knows, but to leave my post at present would, I know, be ruinous." Consequently he remained.

Unremittingly his efforts continued in his warfare with the states. By July, 1783, he reported that all taxes received during his entire administration amounted to only $750,000. Only South Carolina had paid her quota for 1782—not in money but in men and supplies. New York and Maryland had paid approximately one-twentieth of their quotas, and New Hampshire less than one one-hundred-twentieth of hers. The Financier threatened military collections.

Since he had exhausted the resources of an unresponsive country and did not dare expect (although he continued to hope for) foreign loans, only one resource was left him—his own credit.

CHAPTER XI

"LONG BOBS" AND "SHORT BOBS"

❖ ❖ ❖

DESPITE the Financier's ingenuity and resourcefulness, despite his constant demands upon France, he lacked means even to repay the loans from the Bank of North America. Consequently no more credit was extended. The interest on the national debt was overdue. Of "moratoriums" and "token payments" he knew nothing. Bitterly he felt the financial stringency. In his private business Robert Morris was scrupulously honest. It hurt his conscience and his pride that he could not operate governmental business by the same methods. At least he had retrenched, economized, and organized to such a degree that the annual cost of the war was reduced from eighteen million dollars in 1780 to five million in 1782. He made constant pleas and demands that the Federal government and the army reduce their expenses. The national debt, however, had risen by 1782 to twenty-seven million dollars, a staggering sum in those days.

The loans negotiated in Paris and Amsterdam he expended wisely. By the end of 1781 he had borrowed six million livres from France (the livre was valued at about 19 cents) and had received six million as a gift from King Louis because of the King's satisfaction with Robert Morris's conduct of affairs. This account he overdrew by three and a half million livres, through a miscalculation or through grim necessity. Franklin protested. Money in France which he thought at his disposal had been appropriated without his order, Morris replied. "I rely upon you to honour my drafts," he wrote Franklin in desperation. If the bills were protested, he felt that both the Financier and the United States would be disgraced. To Franklin he made a candid statement concerning his financial embarrassments. "Imagine the situation of a man," he wrote, "who is to direct the finances of a country almost without revenue—surrounded by creditors whose distresses while they increase their clamor, render it more difficult to appease them; an army ready to disband or mutiny; a government whose sole authority consists in the power of framing recommendations. . . . The settlement of accounts long and intricate beyond comprehension becomes next to impossible from the want of that authority which is on the verge of annihilation from those confusions which nothing can dissipate except the complete settlement of accounts and an honest provision for payment." Here he revealed the squirrel cage in which he revolved. Hoping against hope that America's friends, especially France, would furnish money before his bills were presented, he sent them the long way around, through Havana and Cadiz. He constantly urged Franklin, Jay, and Adams to look after the United States accounts, as "a protest would reduce our affairs to infinite distress."

In order to negotiate further loans, he presented to European bankers glowing reports of America's wealth—a wealth in which he himself believed most enthusiastically. Philadelphia alone, he told them, was worth more than all the public and private debts of the United States. At last a public loan was secured through the Dutch bankers under the guarantee of France—a loan due in part to the bankers' "faith in a capable and honorable business man who pledged his private credit to the repayment." Although the loan was for only two million guilders (the guilder was valued at 40.2 cents) instead of the five million that had been expected, this amount served to save the country from bankruptcy. Due to some misunderstanding of the amount placed in the bank to his credit, Morris drew $530,000 in bills on Holland—a sum which was protested for non-acceptance. At last the bills were saved, however, by charging a higher rate of interest.

In response to a reproachful letter from Willink & Company, the Financier sent them an explanation of his financial policies: "I agree with you," he told them, "in the sentiment that there is danger in drawing before we know that the funds are placed, and I do believe that the protest of my drafts forced you into higher terms than might otherwise have been settled with the undertakers. But, gentlemen, it is no uncommon thing for a government to find itself in situations where nothing is left but a choice of evils, and where the smallest of these evils will be a very great one. When you see the public accounts of my administration, you will see that if bills had not been hazarded without a certainty of funds to answer them, we could not have made head against the enemy. . . . I do not, however, approve of risques, and if I were to continue longer in administration, I would pursue a conduct directly the reverse of that which I have hitherto observed, and without making a single anticipation either at home or abroad, wait quietly for the revenues, and in the meantime the service might suffer for want of the expenditure. This would in time of peace produce only a little murmuring and discontent, the consequences of which would prove beneficial. But when a country is at war for political existence and the life and fortune of every citizen dependent on the controversy, the stake played for is too great to mind a risque which may involve the loss of two or three hundred thousand guilders, when that risque is necessary to save the game."

Against his wishes and his better judgment, Robert Morris became an opportunist and a commercial speculator on a vast scale. His transactions on behalf of the government consisted of acts of dexterous juggling. He sent supplies to southern regiments and received tobacco and indigo in return. Rice, which he accepted for taxes in South Carolina, was exported to Amsterdam to pay interest on the Dutch loan. Salt was imported from Spain and silver from Havana. Fortunately Morris had had long and arduous training and years of experience as a merchant and banker dealing in bills of exchange, before he was called on to produce magic results without a cent in the Treasury. Like the Isrealites he was forced "to make bricks without straw," or like a magician to draw a rabbit from an empty hat.

One device that he used with great benefit to the nation and to himself as Financier was the issuance of his own notes or orders drawn on John Swanwick, payable at sight to the bearer. These were numbered, lettered, and signed in Morris's own handwriting for

$25, $50, $80, and larger sums, and were negotiable as money. Named for their endorser, they were known as "Long Bobs" or "Short Bobs" according to the length of time they ran. It is interesting to note that, as the historian Botta described the situation, "when the credit of the State was almost entirely annihilated, that of a single individual was stable and universal." Men had confidence in the integrity, responsibility, and efficiency of Robert Morris. In issuing these notes he became answerable personally for about half a million dollars.

Realizing the danger of counterfeiting these notes, he tried to prevent this evil by appointing an agent to carry the mould to the paper mill and to oversee the entire process of manufacture. It was this agent's duty to watch the workmen, to count the sheets, and in the evening to return the mould and sheets to a place of safekeeping in Philadelphia. Despite these precautions the notes were counterfeited. This lowered their value as the market became flooded with them. Morris warned the public to make sure that the notes were genuine before circulating them. The counterfeit bills, he explained, were yellower than the authentic. He finally caught the counterfeiters and placed them under lock and key. In July, 1783, he told a friend that "the knot of villains is pretty well broken up." Even then it required constant vigilance to prevent his notes from being sold at a discount. Because of his alertness and vigorous prosecution of offenders, the notes usually circulated at par and were always redeemed at face value.

The patriotic motives that animated him in issuing the "Long Bobs" and "Short Bobs" are revealed in a letter he sent to Benjamin Harrison: "My personal credit, which thank Heaven I have preserved throughout all the tempests of the war, has been substituted for that which the country has lost. I am now striving to transfer that credit to the public, and if I can, regain for the United States the confidence of individuals so that they will trust their property and exertions in the hands of government. Without that confidence we are nothing."

Besides these important demands upon his time and efforts, there were others as imperative despite their pettiness—constant, torturing requests for money from everyone. Although usually patient in listening to these demands and pleas, at last the Financier became intolerably vexed. "It seems as if every person connected in the public service entertains an opinion that I am full of money," he complained; "for they are constantly applying, even down to the common express riders, and give me infinite interruption, so that it is hardly possible to attend to business of more consequence." The greatest part of each day, he stated in one of his periodic circulars to the state governors, was consumed in hearing and answering "the most torturing solicitations from individuals whose claims are founded in justice and precluded by necessity."

In spite of his sympathy and willingness to help these applicants, he was forced to use every possible device to withstand attacks on the Treasury. Sometimes he made excuses. Sometimes, in violation of his rule against partial payments, he paid part of the amount and carried the balance as credit at regular rates of interest. Sometimes he met the demands from his own pocket as he did with General St. Clair. He refused salary increments; he preached frugality to the applicants—a most unwelcome sermon. "Every new demand for money," he wrote George Washington, "makes me shudder." Finally in desperation he insisted that applications to him for money be made in writing. This plan was exceedingly unpopular with creditors and proved unsuccessful. Yet it was necessary that he conserve his time for important business. Therefore, he decided to receive personal applications at certain hours three days a week: Monday, Wednesday, and Friday from 10 to 12 A.M. This system infuriated the applicants who refused to abide by these hours and pounded at his doors or approached him on the street at any time of day or night.

The most serious demand for arrearages of pay was made by eighty Continental soldiers of the Pennsylvania Line. Led by several sergeants, they broke from their camp at Lancaster and marched into Philadelphia to collect their back pay. Through the city they marched, the citizens fleeing before them. Finally they lined up in front of the State House, where Congress was in session. There they passed grog, threw stones at the windows, and vociferously demanded their pay. "We'll seize you and hold you hostage until we're paid," they shouted drunkenly at the trembling Congressmen, who shrank back from the windows. "We'll break into the bank and take what's due us," others blustered. Congress, thoroughly terrified, appealed to the state government of Pennsylvania, but the legislature did not summon the militia for fear they might side with the mutineers. The Philadelphia municipal government shrugged its shoulders. The soldiers became more insistent. Congress demanded that they submit to it before considering their proposals. They refused. Six sergeants at last submitted. Two others, Carberry and Sullivan, were arrested and impeached; the former was discovered to be deranged.

At dark the soldiers appeared before the house of John Dickinson, President of the Executive Council of Pennsylvania (an office corresponding to that of governor). There they renewed their demands for pay. Cool and calm as usual, Dickinson reasoned with them. "Return to your barracks, men; your demands will be considered," he told them. They followed his advice and for the day the mutiny was repressed.

The next morning, however, the Lancaster contingent renewed their demands and threats on the streets and before the State House. Congress, thoroughly alarmed, fled to Princeton. At first Robert Morris took refuge in a friend's house in Philadelphia, but he was advised by Congress to leave the city as they feared the Financier might be held as a hostage. Consequently both Robert Morris and Gouverneur Morris also fled with Congress. For several days all public business in Philadelphia was suspended. At last, however, their officers induced the insurgents to return to camp. But the repercussions of this minor incident reverberated through Europe. It was reported there that the American troops (presumably all of them) had mutinied and attacked Congress, and that Congress had fled. This destroyed all confidence abroad and the last shred of credit.

Had the states met the demands upon them, the situation need not have been helpless even then, but they repudiated all their obligations. Somehow the national debt, which in January, 1783, had grown to $35,327,769 had to be funded and the interest paid. This amount excluded arrearages to the army and indebtedness connected with the old Continental bills. The Financier was determined that the country should meet its obligations and that therefore the states should pay their quotas. To fail would render the nation "the reproach of all mankind." He could not understand their apathy in the face of such a situation.

Added to these never-ending troubles were the personal attacks upon Morris himself. Again he became the object of calumny and obloquy. He was publicly charged with ruining the credit of the United States, which he had tried desperately to sustain through his own fortune and reputation. "Speculator" was the title again flung at him. Worst of all, he was accused of speculating in his own notes. "Such a charge," he tried to show his detractors, "works an injury to those holding the notes."

"He fails to provide for the soldiers." "He fails to pay them." "Our soldiers suffer while he rolls in wealth." These were among the cries of the public, jealous of his wealth and power. He was even charged with trading military supplies, of lining his own pockets by discounting government paper, and (the old time-worn accusation) of cornering merchandise.

These accusations he could not permit to go unanswered. To Colonel Tilghman he wrote concerning these libels: "I am not much concerned about the opinions of such men while I have in my favor the voice of the wise and the good, added to the testimony of an approving conscience. I am not ignorant that many people employ themselves in defaming men whom they do not know and measures which they do not understand. To such illiberal characters and to all which they can write or speak, the best answer is to act well."

Some of the calumnies, however, he felt obliged to refute since he feared their effect upon the public and consequently upon national credit. He stated that on May 1, 1782, he had "totally quitted commerce." "Instead of being enriched," he added, "I am poorer this day than I was a year ago." As always he insisted upon having his accounts inspected. To the accusation of buying notes he replied in his *Official Diary:* "If I ever did buy one single note either for public or private account, either directly or indirectly, by myself or by means of others, I will agree to sacrifice everything that is dear and valuable to man. Never was a more malignant and false slander invented."

By "Centinel," a pseudonym used by some calumniator in the public press, he was called "Bobby the Cofferer," "a public defaulter," and was asked to "disgorge the public treasure." To this he replied that he had not touched one shilling of the public money; that the receipts of the government were published in the papers and his accounts were open to inspection. He wrote George Olney, one of the state Tax Receivers: "I know not what representations or misrepresentations are made with respect to my conduct, but I know that my greatest enemy having had an opportunity fully to investigate it, has not been able to show any color of impropriety. . . . It is extremely painful to think that the public service should be injured by personal malice."

One of the most malicious and vicious attacks was made in an anonymous letter addressed to Robert Morris, Esq., written presumably after he had publicly defended his conduct and mentioned his sacrifices for his country: "That submission to your absolute dictation should be the only rule of government are manifestly your sentiments," the letter ran, "so much has a sudden and enormous acquisition of wealth by speculating on the distresses of war, pampered your pride and inebriated your understanding. . . . You produce yourself as the Atlas on which the United States entirely rests. . . . Is it for you wallowing in wealth, rioting in voluptuousness, gorged with honors, profits, patronage and emoluments, is it for you in the bosom of your family, your friends and your affairs—is it for you to insult the public with your sacrifices of time, property and domestic bliss?" This venomous diatribe Morris naturally greeted with silence. All these slanders, however, hurt him, especially in view of his exhausting labors in behalf of the republic. He realized that the calumnies were due primarily to envy of wealth and position, to his economic measures which were naturally unpopular, and particularly to his inability to meet all demands upon the public exchequer. Nevertheless a number of these pin pricks wounded like sword thrusts.

Particular offense was taken because the necessities of the officers made prisoner at Charleston were not relieved. This seemed unavoidable since there was no money in the Treasury and all Morris's money and credit and that of his friends had been advanced to support the expedition against Yorktown. His political enemies, Paine and Arthur Lee, had tried to cause dissension between General Greene and Robert Morris; but Greene was too liberal to be alienated from a man he respected as much as he did the Financier. Of course, no doubt, the general often felt ill-used since the Financier could not meet his requests for money.

After the war in the South was ended, Greene was chatting one day with Morris in the latter's office. "Although I am not ordinarily superstitious," Greene remarked, "I believe that twice during the Southern campaign there was special intervention of Providence in my favor."

"The occasions?" Morris inquired with a twinkle in his eye as he leaned back in his chair to listen to the narrative.

"On one occasion," Greene related, "I was seated in my tent overwhelmed with gloomy apprehensions. My army, I felt, must be disbanded unless they could obtain food, clothing, and other supplies. At the battle of Eutaw Springs some of my men were as naked as the day they were born. They could not fight on against such odds. As I was thus lost in gloomy reflections, I was suddenly approached by a gentleman I had seen occasionally around camp, who placed at my command £30,000 on my personal note made payable to you as Minister of Finance."

Robert Morris smiled but remained silent as the General spoke of another similar occasion when the mysterious stranger had supplied him with funds required by the army, then vanished as mysteriously as he had come. Morris smiled more broadly.

"What do you know of the matter, sir?" Greene questioned.

"Only this," Morris replied. "Your camp visitor was no heavenly visitant, but merely Mr. George Abbott Hall, whom I employed to buy and sell produce in the South and to provide for your army when they most needed funds."

Greene, flushing at this, remarked drily, "Then, sir, you did not trust me."

"That indeed was not the case," Morris assured him earnestly, "but I realized that if I sent the money directly to you, you would spend it before the direst necessity arose and later would lack it when it was essential."

Greene nodded thoughtfully a minute. "Your precaution," he at last magnanimously admitted, "has been the means of saving my army. I commend your wisdom and foresight." Thus the misunderstanding between the two men ended.

Disheartened by the calumnies of his foes and even more by the total lack of cooperation of the states, the Financier felt the necessity for "quitting an office of incessant labor and anxiety." His position had grown insufferable. His health had become affected. His family, always devoted, had enjoyed only brief glimpses of him for two years. Since the war was virtually over, Morris felt justified in resigning. On January 24, 1783, he tendered his resignation to Congress:

"To the President of Congress

"Sir:

"As nothing but the public danger would have induced me to accept my office, so I was determined to hold it until danger was past, or else to meet my ruin in the common wreck. Under greater difficulties than were apprehended by the most timid, and with less support than was expected by the least sanguine, the generous confidence of the public has accomplished more than I presume to hope. . . .

"Many late circumstances have so far lessened our apprehensions from the enemy that my original motives have almost ceased to operate. But other circumstances have postponed the establishment of public credit in such a manner that I fear it will never be made. To increase our debts while the prospect of paying them diminishes does not consist with my ideas of integrity. I must therefore quit a situation which becomes insupportable. But lest the public measures might be deranged by any precipitation, I will continue to serve until the end of May. If effectual measures are not taken by that period to make permanent provision for the public debts of every kind, Congress will be pleased to appoint some other man to be the Superintendent of their Finances. I should be unworthy of the confidence reposed in me by my fellow citizens if I did not explicitly declare that I will never be the minister of injustice.

"I have the honor to be, etc.

"Robert Morris"

His resignation produced general consternation and dismay. It offended friends and foes. His enemies, especially, made the most of this letter, intimating that he was merely seeking more power and had no intention of resigning. To many it seemed an improper, ill-advised action, especially to those who side-stepped responsibility. Why should the patient bearer of their burdens seek to be relieved of the load? Why should this convenient scapegoat wish to escape their missiles? Congress enjoined secrecy upon him with regard to the resignation, but apparently it was generally known. The legislators feared the results of publishing abroad the tenor of the Financier's letter as it revealed the financial status of the country. It was a hush-hush affair, which like so many others of that sort was widely advertised.

Even close friends of Robert Morris did not seem to understand his actions or his motives. George Washington reproached him with deserting the cause. Only Alexander Hamilton, also a financier, appreciated his reasons for resigning. To Washington, Hamilton explained that the Financier "was reduced to making engagements which he could not fulfill." "Mr. Morris," he continued, "certainly deserves a great deal of his country. I believe no man in this country but himself could have kept the money machine a-going during the period he has been in office." This is praise indeed from another financial genius, Secretary of the Treasury under happier auspices.

Just after his resignation Morris, feeling the human need of sympathy and understanding, sent appeals to his friends to try to understand the motives for his action and to reserve their censure. In writing Greene, he said: "You and every other good man will I hope acquit me for leaving a post in which I am totally unsupported and where I must be daily a witness to scenes of poignant anguish and deep injustice without the possibility of administering either relief or palliation." This letter reveals his distress at not being able to relieve the sufferings of the army and civilians whose needs he could not meet. But the attacks upon him had embittered him, leaving scars even upon his sympathies. To the Paymaster General he explained: "It becomes impossible to serve a people who convert everything into a ground for calumny. . . . My desire to relieve the army has been greatly cooled from the information that many of them have joined in the reproaches I have incurred for their benefit." Morris felt, moreover, that owing to the disposition of many to traduce and vilify, "no prudent man would risk a fair reputation by holding an office so important."

The Financier could not refrain from laying the responsibility for his resignation squarely upon the shoulders of the recalcitrant states and the Congress, with its irresponsible, vacillating attitude toward the public debt. He stated his position very clearly in a letter to the Governor of Virginia: "If I had met with that support which though unmerited by my abilities, was due to my zeal for the public service, I believe that I should have continued in office until all accounts being settled and all debts provided for, I could have left to my successor the pleasing prospect of future wealth unclouded by any dismal retrospect of past poverty."

Humbly and despondently he wrote Congress: "I hope that some abler mind will point out the means to save our country from ruin." Congress, aghast, not knowing where to turn, appointed a committee consisting in part of Richard Peters, James Madison, and Alexander Hamilton, to confer with Morris concerning his continuance in office. Two conferences were held, as a result of which the Financier agreed to remain in office only long enough to complete the payment to the army and to fulfill his "present engagements." He stipulated, moreover, that he would not remain unless effectual measures were taken to provide for the public debt. Congress glibly promised to support his measures. In reliance upon that promise (he remained trustful and sanguine despite his experiences), Robert Morris agreed to continue as Superintendent of Finance.

But promises were futile, as Morris might have known. Congress

still presented no plan for funding the national debt. Bills drawn by
that body pressed heavily upon the Financier and threw into confusion the affairs of his department. The states remained apathetic.
Vilification of Morris continued. In fact, nothing was changed. "My
prospects," he stated, "are extremely gloomy, and unless greater
exertions are made universally, the public credit which has been so
long declining must at length die." He began to fear that the army,
"unfed, unpaid and unclothed," would have "to subsist itself or disband itself."

Fortunately for the poor harassed Financier and the poor suffering country the Treaty of Peace with Britain was ratified on September 3, 1783. There had in fact been rumors of peace since 1782.
Astoundingly enough, these rumors were not joyfully received in
America. Evidently even in that early day, there were war profiteers
unwilling for hostilities to cease. Patriots also felt that peace at that
time would be premature. This situation is shown in a letter written by Robert Morris on October 6, 1782, to Matthew Ridley, financial agent for Maryland, sent abroad during this period.

"I thank you for the political information contained in your letters," Morris wrote. "Peace seemed for a while to be forcing herself suddenly upon us, and altho the prospect is not now so strong
and clear as it was, yet it seems to me impossible that the war can
continue much longer. The expense of the Belligerent Powers in
Europe must be immense, particularly to Great Britain, and the people seem already tired of their burthens; for my part I wish most
sincerely and ardently for Peace that I may get rid of a most troublesome office and spend the remainder of my days with more ease and
in less hurry than those that are past. But was I to confine myself
to the language of a patriot, I might speak in another manner and
tell you that a continuance of the War is necessary until our Confederation is more strongly knit, untill the obligations to support it
shall be more generally diffused amongst all ranks of American citizens, untill we shall have acquired the habit of paying taxes (the
means we possess already) and untill the several governments have
derived from experience and action the vigour and self-confidence
which is necessary to ensure the safety and promote the happiness

of the People. The expense of the War as now conducted is not very heavy to this country, and the payment of our Public Debt will hardly be felt by those that come after us, as the country has abundant resources as yet untouched.

"In the view of things, Peace may not be really so desirable as at first view one would think, and perhaps you may be surprised when I tell you that in this city the prospect of Peace has given more general discontent than anything that has happened for a long time, particularly amongst the mercantile part of the community. I have been much surprised at it, but so the fact, however again I repeat my wishes for a speedy and honorable Peace. It is idle for Great Britain to think of wheedling us into a separate and disgraceful Peace. No man in this country seriously thinks of such a thing, even the disaffected are convinced of the impracticability of it. For my part I will sooner sacrifice all my prospects of ease and enjoyment throughout the whole course of my life, than consent to close this contest by any act derogatory to the Integrity, Honor and Glory of a young and rising Nation."

Even the peace treaty, signed in Paris, September 3, 1783, brought Morris little relief. The unpaid army and the public debt still remained. He concentrated dynamic efforts on the settlement of accounts and the payment of the army. Seven hundred and fifty thousand dollars (three months' pay) was indispensable if the army were to be disbanded peacefully. This could be financed only by taxes and by the sale of public property. The Financier urged the immediate enactment of such laws. For unless the troops were dismissed at once with their arrearages of pay, an internal war of riot and crime, more serious than that with England, might result. The threat of mutiny rumbled through the land. The soldiers, having learned the use of firearms and having achieved their liberty, intended to use their weapons and privileges in securing their rights. Morris sympathized with them in their objectives and deplored his inability to meet their just demands. Fervently he prayed for guidance and for some response to his incessant pleas to Congress, to the states—to anyone who might assist him in his efforts.

To George Olney, Morris confided his discouragement and fears:

"If the engagements which I am taking for the relief of the army are not supported by liberal aids from the states, we must close our transactions with shame and disgrace, and this seems hard after having in about two years made a saving to the United States that will astonish every person who may be at the trouble to compare the expenditures previous to my administration to those which have accrued during its continuance." Shame and disgrace after his stupendous efforts—how the thought galled Morris, whose pride and patriotism were involved. He could balance the books of the nation, he felt, if only he had the cooperation of Congress and the states.

Taxes, however, did not amount to $750,000. Payments exceeded receipts by more than a million dollars. Morris continued his financial juggling. He obtained a loan from the bank on the issuance of his own notes—more "Long Bobs" and "Short Bobs"—to the sum of $100,000. At this time he turned again, too, to the "Good Samaritan of the Revolution," Haym Salomon, a patriotic Jewish broker from Poland. When the Bank of Pennsylvania was established, he had been among the most generous subscribers. Morris knew that he could count on him to contribute to any worthy cause. At one time Salomon had given $2,000 to relieve the distress of the poor in Philadelphia. Now Morris requested him for a large sum to save the country from financial disaster. Asking no interest from the government, this patriotic broker loaned the United States over $350,000. The government seemed to feel that if he eliminated the interest, it might eliminate the principal. At all events this loan was never returned to Salomon or his heirs.

Every day Morris felt more deeply that he could no longer remain in office. Although Congress had broken its pledged word to him, he was unwilling to break his promise to that body and to the nation. He came to believe despairingly that his successor could accomplish more than he. "At least," he remarked sadly, "that Voice of Party which has hitherto opposed the public service on private principles will be silenced." With fine sarcasm he observed: "The Peace having given our domestic and Coffee House politicians a little more leisure, they will have time not only to find fault but to find out where the fault lies, which is not always the less useful task."

To his *Diary* Morris confided his eagerness to be relieved of official cares: "I wish for nothing so much as to be relieved from this cursed scene of drudgery and vexation." "Neither the powers nor emoluments of the office," he told Thomas Jefferson, "have sufficient charms to keep me in it one hour after I can quit it with consistence."

Before finally leaving office, he wished to close all transactions in which he was concerned. He sent shiploads of tobacco to help cover overdrafts. There must be no blot upon his own escutcheon or that of the United States if he could prevent it. To the French Ambassador he sent this message: "It has always been my intention, Sir, to do equal justice to all, and if my conduct has in any instance been variant from that disposition, it has been from the situation I have found myself by the defect of ability."

His chief confidants in those busy, anxious days seem to have been the (so-called) Tax Receivers, especially George Olney. The verbal assaults of his enemies still wounded him, as he shows in one letter to Olney: "I wish to quit the painful, envied station which has given *some men so much trouble.*"

Before Morris finally surrendered his certificate of office, he observed: "I confess that I did wish to have been an instrument toward establishing our affairs upon a solid basis, and I thank God that be the event what it may, I have not to reproach myself with any want of the proper efforts for that purpose." He did succeed, thanks to Salomon's generosity and his own credit, in paying the soldiers a part of their arrearages and seeing them dismissed on furlough. They were not disbanded.

Still constructive, despite the blows of misfortune and the destructive criticism leveled at him, he made arrangements for an encyclopedic compilation of the principal facts about America—its geographical, political, commercial, and moral aspects. To the State Receivers, the representatives of the government in each state, he gave specific directions for gathering these statistics. Since they had been engaged in industry in the states, as taxes were paid—if paid at all—in "specifics" (usually agricultural products), they were acquainted with the resources of the states. Moreover since the receivers could not collect money, they might as well collect facts, and thus serve some worthy purpose. Morris, with inspired foresight, asked them to discover all the resources of each state in peace and war, especially the *number of fighting men available in case of war*. Although the peace treaty had just been signed, he foresaw the strong possibility of another conflict. Next time the government should be prepared.

To his last day in office Robert Morris sedulously attended to the minute details of his department. Having received a visit from Thomas Kilbuck, one of the sullen, disgruntled Indian youths maintained and educated at the public expense, the Financier advised returning the young men to their people "with some degree of splendor" since they were dissatisfied and might otherwise become troublesome. Here Morris's diplomacy and adroitness are evident.

Robert Morris continued in office until November 1, 1784, having served his country three years and five months with intense, self-sacrificing effort as Superintendent of Finance. To him the United States owes its establishment on a firm financial foundation. The Bank of North America, the restoration of credit, the feeding, clothing, payment, and finally the dismissal of the army—all these are monuments to Robert Morris, the Financier. Still solicitous for his own honor and the credit of the United States, he inserted an advertisement in the newspaper stating that Robert Morris's notes would be paid although he had left public office.

On retiring from the superintendency he made a complete report of the transactions of his office for the full term. Not content with this statement to Congress, however, he felt that he owed a similar account to the public. Consequently he had five hundred copies of his *Statement of Accounts* struck off for distribution at his own expense. He thereby hoped, he said, to give satisfaction to Congress and the young nation. In his *Farewell to the Inhabitants of the United States of America*, which prefaces his *Statement of Accounts*, he made a report to the nation he had served. In this truly remarkable document he said: "That every servant should render an account of his stewardship is the evident dictate of common sense.

When the truth is important, the necessity is increased; and where it is confidential, the duty is enhanced. The Master should know what the servant has done."

He stated in his own defense that want of funds made accounts intricate and complex; that although quarterly reports from the State Receivers had been requested, they had not been sent. He mentioned his efforts to "appreciate" money—to restore it to its expressed value. Although he had been forced to conduct mercantile operations for the government, he said, he believed that as a general rule a government should not carry on such operations. To the bank he paid enthusiastic tribute: "Without the establishment of the national bank, the business of the Department of Finance could not have been performed." Although the Superintendent of Finance had expressly stipulated before taking office that he would not be held responsible for debts contracted previous to his administration, yet he made considerable payments of such debts and retired the Continental bills without causing a financial panic. According to his *Statement* the only foreign debts remaining (except those on particular loans bearing interest and payable at a future date) were 846,770 livres due to the Farmers General in France. He urged a final adjustment with Beaumarchais and Deane, both of whom had suffered financial reverses through their mercantile operations for the United States (and with whom accounts were not to be settled until long after their deaths and that of the Financier). "The payment of debts may be expensive," Morris philosophized, "but it is infinitely more expensive to withhold payment."

The war he considered much more expensive than it should have been because "the needy can never economize." The expenses continued, moreover, even after the war had ended. He made a plea for a strong central government. "If there be not one government which can draw forth and direct the combined efforts of united America," he declared, "our independence is but a name, our freedom a shadow, and our dignity a dream." He desired "a firm, wise, manly system of government." America, like the army, he considered "crowned with laurels but distressed by want."

In that *Farewell Address* he could not resist a brief thrust at the enemies who had harassed him and hampered his conduct of affairs. Speaking of himself impersonally as Superintendent, he wrote: "In descending from that eminence on which your representatives had placed him, he avoids the shafts which calumny had aimed. He has no longer therefore any personal interest in those jealousies and distrusts which have embarrassed his administration and may prove your ruin."

That final *Statement of Accounts* must have brought Morris a glow of satisfaction—the satisfaction of having completed his task and saved his country financially. There remained the further blessed satisfaction of retiring to private life.

PART THREE

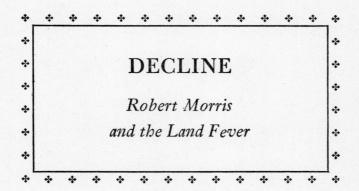

DECLINE

Robert Morris
and the Land Fever

CHAPTER XII

"THOSE CURSED BILLS"

❖   ❖   ❖

AFTER so many years of earnest, laborious effort for his adopted country, Robert Morris was entitled to an interlude in which to attend to his own business and to enjoy domestic life. While he was Superintendent of Finance he was still a member of the firm of Willing & Morris, but he had appointed someone, probably John Swanwick, to take charge of his affairs for him. Now he felt eager to place his own hand upon the helm of his private business. Although he was still considered a wealthy man, he had sacrificed at least some of his fortune to the needs of his country: over one million dollars (according to report) for the Yorktown campaign, and credit to half a million dollars for mustering out the army. Consequently for his family's sake he wished to recoup his losses.

Little did the nation as a whole appreciate the advantages accruing from his wealth and business success. Tongues of the envious wagged. These acrimonious critics observed his lavish hospitality, but did not realize how much it contributed to the pleasure and profit of the country. "His home, his carriages, his sumptuous hospitality" bred confidence among the representatives of other nations. His salary of $6,000 a year, which he received as Superintendent of Finance, was absurdly inadequate to meet all the demands upon him. Thus it was necessary that he supplement it from his own fortune. In order to maintain that fortune, he had to conduct his business.

He began by enlarging the firm's commercial enterprises, sending ships to China. In 1784, the year he retired as Superintendent of Finance, he dispatched the first vessel that ever appeared in winter in the port of Canton. The *Alliance*, sent on an out-of-season passage around South America, appeared at Canton toward the end of December, creating great astonishment. Morris also sent ships to China equipped with guns. One, the *Empress of China*, perhaps the first ship to arrive with such a cargo, received from the Chinese mandarin this amusingly ironic passport: "Permit this barbarian ship to pass. She has (so many) guns and (so many) men; consequently can do the Emperor no harm." These vessels, with other cargoes, brought back from the Orient fine china for the Morrises' table and art treasures for their home.

In the meantime another ship, sailing to Europe, had carried other treasures, their sons, away from them. In the fall of 1781, just after his acceptance of the office of Financier, Morris sent his two eldest sons, Robert and Thomas, abroad to study. They were placed under the care of Matthew Ridley, who as financial agent for the State of Maryland had business to attend to in France.

In a letter to George Washington, Robert Morris stated his reasons for sending the boys abroad: "Should an opportunity offer, Mr. Ridley will present before you my two sons who have the ambition to pay their compliments to you before their departure for Europe, where they are now destined under the care and protection of that gentleman untill he can place them with their tutors. I consider the step I have taken as advantageous to them and also of some public consequence, because if the example is followed and it becomes the practice to educate American youths in France, habitual attachments will strengthen those ties of affection which in gratitude is due from this to that country. I have written to His Excellency Count deGrasse excusing myself for depending on a passage on one of His Majesty's ships. Should you have an opportunity of addressing a word on the subject, it will procure to Mr. Ridley and the boys the favourable attention of the Commander they go with. I flatter myself with the fond hope that these boys may hereafter become useful to their country and that they will add to the number of those who shall publicly make repeated grateful acknowledgments for the blessings of Liberty and Peace transmitted to them by means of those noble, those glorious exertions of which your whole conduct in the War affords one continued and unparalleled example."

At the time of their departure for France, Bob was almost twelve; Tom, ten. Their father left Philadelphia with them to bid them farewell at the Chesapeake port from which the French warship sailed. He advised Ridley to take the boys upon their arrival in Paris to call on Dr. Franklin, who would assist in determining the best schools for them and who would help in placing them there. Their expenses were to be paid through the Paris bankers, Le Couteulx et Cie.

Soon Robert and Mary Morris heard that the boys had been placed at a pension at Chaillot. This arrangement their father did not consider satisfactory as he thought it unsuitable for learning anything but the language. Consequently he wished "a proper seminary chosen without further loss of time"—a school that would supervise their manners, habits, morals, and religion, as well as their studies. Morris felt that his sons' progress was retarded by a change in tutors, that their writing especially had been neglected. He wished them to learn to write in the English manner. They were to be supplied with English books suitable to their age and abilities in order to retain their knowledge of their native language. They were to be taught French grammatically as well as practically; to learn other living languages, especially German; to be well grounded in mathematics and in the sciences; to be directed to authors that would give them information and help form their taste. He insisted, moreover, on their studying the laws of nations and of nature, and on their becoming acquainted with the Constitution of the "German Empire" and of the other states in Europe. "A liberal education," Morris wrote Ridley, "has its use in every station of life, and I am very anxious that my boys should learn everything that can possibly be useful to them." The older, Bob, his father inclined to establish as a merchant; the younger, Thomas, as a lawyer if his talents warranted. They were to be well grounded in every branch of learning. Nor were the polite accomplishments to be neglected: they must learn to dance, to fence, and to ride gracefully. But their father was most insistent that their behaviour and their morals should be well watched and regulated. He stressed "the advantages of honesty and the sweets of integrity, the gratifications resulting from a conduct inspired by a high sense of honour, and the internal peace and satisfaction that might result from a rigid adherence to the principles of justice." "I think it of infinitely more consequence," he added, "that they should be good men than learned or great men."

With regard to their daily regimen, he wished their food to be plain and simple, their clothes and manner of living like that of other boys at the same schools. Their allowance and pocket money were to be regulated in the same way, for he believed, "nothing hurts a generous spirit more than finding itself bounded within narrower limits than its associates, and nothing is more pernicious than to breed youth up in profuseness and extravagance." To M. de Basseville, the boys' tutor, Robert Morris wrote that he wished his sons "taught economy, not parsimony." He requested monthly or quarterly reports concerning his sons' progress and letters from them regularly. The same meticulous attention to detail that characterized Robert Morris in his business dealings is revealed here in his plans for his children's education. Even today his educational theories seem wise and essentially modern. Throughout, the stress is on character development rather than mere "book learning," on the balanced individual rather than the student, on service as a life principle rather than self-gratification.

From friends abroad, especially John and Sarah Jay, the Morrises had reports about their sons. A letter from Jay, after he had been transferred from Spain to France, spoke of Robert and Thomas as having dined with them in Paris a few nights before. He described them as "fine boys with their full share of natural talents." Mrs. Jay (the beautiful Sarah Livingston Jay) wrote Mrs. Morris even more fully about a certain visit Robert and Thomas paid them in November, 1782. "Yesterday, your little sons, by passing their holiday with me made me very happy," ran the letter. "Robert so exceedingly resembles Mr. Morris, that I feel for him a respect mingled with my love; tho', at the same time, I regret his distance from his father's example and counsel. When (as it sometimes happens) among our little Americans, that my decision is referred to respecting matters of right and wrong, I always request Robert's opinion, and when he hesitates, I ask him what he thinks would be his father's sentiments upon such occasions, to which he generally replys very justly; and I remark to him the certainty of his acting with propriety while he imitates so worthy an example. Tommy (who is likewise a fine boy) told me that his last letters mentioned Hetty's and Maria's illness. I hope they are now quite recovered, as well as my dear Kitty. You will embrace them for me?" The "Kitty" mentioned here was Mrs. Jay's sister, Katherine or Kitty Livingston, who made her home with the Morrises during the war while her father's home in New Jersey was considered unsafe.

For a while the two youths were at school in Geneva with Benjamin Franklin Bache, Franklin's devoted, serious-minded grandson, who enjoyed nothing more than visiting his grandfather. After five years in France and Switzerland, Robert and Thomas attended the University of Leipzig for two years' study. Just before their transfer to Germany, Morris learned that Robert had become very careless with regard to his person and had boasted that he need not take care of his clothes because his father was wealthy and could buy him more. Bob, unquestionably, was a genuine boy. Thereupon Morris sent him a long letter filled with fatherly advice, written on July 29, 1786.

"I am told that you are not so careful of your person and clothes as you ought to be, and that you are disposed to be expensive because people have told you that I am rich. Whether I am rich or poor can be no reason for your being extravagant or nasty." The letter continued to speak of the pains taken at home to teach him habits of neatness and cleanliness. "Everybody is obliged to be clean," his father added reproachfully, "or they will not be received in society, and they must take care of their cloaths or go naked. . . . If you think that I am to supply those with new who commit to destruction the necessary cloaths provided for them, you will be deceived. . . . *I am ambitious not of giving you a large fortune but of teaching you how to make one for yourself.* If you do that, you will know the value of it and you will feel truely independent. You will then be able to act like a man and fear nothing *but to be in the wrong*." In speaking of Tom, he said, "I think this same son Thomas, although a little wild and funny, yet a good sort of a fellow."

There is great wisdom stored in these letters of Robert Morris to his sons and their tutors. As a self-made merchant and statesman he knew the value of a neat appearance as well as a noble character. Independence, self-respect, integrity—these were the attributes he wished inculcated in his sons.

While the boys remained in Europe, their parents kept open house for visitors. Gouverneur Morris, cultured and witty, made this his home. Kitty Livingston, a guest in the Morris home for several years, was a lively young lady, not above placing a bet now and then. One evening when the Chevalier de la Luzerne was visiting the Morrises, a famous bet was made that echoed across the Atlantic.

"All the ladies in Europe wear the paint and patches. You do not do so?" queried the Chevalier banteringly.

"No indeed," responded Kitty blushing. "And I'm willing to bet, Chevalier, that my sister, Mrs. Jay, is not so frivolous as to wear paint and patches. Nor will she attend entertainments on Sunday while in Paris although you implied earlier this evening that most ladies do so."

The Chevalier smiled and shrugged. "Ah, but, mademoiselle, such action is inevitable under the magic spell of the Parisian gaiety."

"What do you bet?" challenged Kitty as Gouverneur Morris grinned and Robert Morris chuckled.

"A beautiful dress cap for mademoiselle or whatever you wish, but you must furnish the proof," the Chevalier replied with typical French chivalry—and reservations.

William Carmichael, then in Paris, was named referee. Several months after this conversation, Morris received a letter from Carmichael giving the sequel in part. "Mrs. Jay informs me," said the letter, "that the Chevalier de la Luzerne hath deferred the determination of his betts with Miss Kitty Livingston to my decision. I thank him for the good opinion he entertains of my impartiality altho' even a Lady was in the case. But in the present instance I think I can justify his confidence in me, for without being biased by my partiality for Miss Kitty, I can assure him that Mrs. Jay hath neither worn Paint or Patches or been at one Public Spectacle on the Lord's day in Europe or the West Indies."

Mrs. Jay in a letter to Mrs. Morris corroborated Carmichael's statement: "Shall I request of you—that you will tell the Chevalier that Kitty is not mistaken in her sister; she has really won the bett."

To her sister Sarah Jay wrote almost as formally: "The bets depending between you and the Chevalier, I hope, are considerable since you are entitled to the stake, for I have not used any false coloring, nor have I amused myself with plays or any other diversions on Sunday."

The conclusion of the matter was recorded by Mary Morris in a letter to Sarah Jay, written July 12, 1871: "The Chevalier acquiesces in the loss of his bet, presented Kitty with a handsome dress cap, accompanied with a note acknowledging your firmness."

Much of the life of the period is reflected in the correspondence of Mrs. Jay and Mrs. Morris, especially the friendships, the manners, and the fashions of the day. A letter from Madrid to Mary Morris, dated April 22, 1781, shows the friendly esteem in which the Morrises were held.

"My Dear Mrs. Morris:

"As Mr. Jay and myself are interested in Mr. Morris' and your happiness, we were very anxious last fall about both your healths, for we had heard that they were impaired, and a letter from Kitty some time after, was doubly welcome by giving us the pleasing information of the recovery of persons we so much esteemed. How amply, my dear madam! does your affection compensate Kitty for the absence of her sister—but where can I hope to find such friends as I parted from in quitting America—not I am sure in the acquaintances of a few months or in the formal birthday visitors—preserve, therefore, I charge you the regard you honor me with, that in your company when I return, I may forget how long we have been separated. I dare say you were pleased with the marriage of Mr.

Bingham and Miss Willing [Thomas Willing's daughter Anne], as it promises happiness to the parties interested. Shall I request you to present to them our congratulations?

"Tell Miss Hetty if you please that if she thinks she can smile upon a Don, I'll use my influence to engage a few to accompany us, for we hope to return before she seriously thinks of paying her devoirs to Hymen. Kitty's accounts of Maria increase my inclination to see her; and I am quite happy that your little sons are likely to answer the expectations formed of them.

"You and Mr. Morris will do us justice in believing that you have not more sincere friends in the numerous circle of those who love and esteem you, than in Mr. Jay and

"Your humble serv't,

"SA. Jay."

It seems hard to believe that this formal letter was written by a young woman of twenty-four to a friend not ten years older. At this time Hetty Morris, mentioned as smiling at Dons, was only a little girl, and Maria a baby.

The next year from Paris [14 November, 1782] Sarah Jay for her friend's pleasure recorded certain fashion notes and gave her impressions of the French Court.

"At present," she told Mrs. Morris, "the prevailing fashions are very decent and very plain; the gowns most worn are the robes *a l'anglaise*, which are exactly like the Italian habits that were in fashion in America at the time I left it. The sultana, resembling the long polinese, is also *a la mode*, but as it is not expected that it will long remain so, everybody makes them of light silk. There is so great a variety of hats, caps, cuffs, &c., that it is impossible to describe them. . . .

"At the Marquis de LaFayette's table, I had the pleasure of hearing you, my dear Mrs. Morris, mentioned the other day, as well as Mr. Morris, in terms to me the most grateful imaginable. . . .

"The Queen has lately returned to Versailles, after a residence of eight or ten weeks at Passey. . . . She is so handsome, and her manners are so engaging, that almost forgetful of republican principles,

I was ever ready while in her presence, to declare her born to be a Queen. There are, however, many traits in her character worthy of imitation even by republicans, and I cannot but admire her resolution to superintend the education of Madame Royale, her daughter, to whom she has allotted chambers adjoining her own, and persists in refusing to name a Governatete for her."

This view of the much maligned Marie Antoinette, as seen through the kindly eyes of Sarah Jay, is novel and refreshing.

Other letters from the friendly, chatty Mrs. Jay to Mrs. Morris contain purely personal fashion news. One such letter starts:

"My Dear Madam:

"It was not without regret that I heard of Captain Barney's leaving Paris without having those things in charge, which you had requested might be sent by him. But I hope my dear friend will acquit me of indolence when I assure her that I never received the commission with which I was honored, till two days before the Captain's departure, and one of those was Sunday, on which you know business could not be transacted. Mr. Le Couteulx still flatters me that the box may arrive at the port in time to be taken on board.

"The measure for your gown cannot, it seems, be found, but it is of less consequence, as Mr. Ridley has sent out for Mrs. Powell two habits, which you can see before you have yours made. The Pistache and rose colour were most fashionable last autumn, but what will succeed them in the spring is difficult yet to divine; the trimming is made by the first milliner, and will either suit a sultana or habit, with both of which dresses they wear the petticoats of a different colour. You'll pardon the liberty I've taken in adding an handkerchief—it's to be ty'd on before the gown and then pinned down to the stays. . . . I can't imagine why it's called a Chemise, for I cannot discover any resemblance that it bears to that part of dress. . . . Your stays, tho' made according to your direction, is perfectly the mode, stiff ones having long since been laid aside—but you forget that your waist has length as well as breadth, and, therefore, you'll be obliging as to pardon your Taylor if he has not guessed right. . . .

"As black and white riding hats are equally worn, I've sent both, the one trimmed in the present taste, the other without ribbon, that your own may be consulted; they are likewise very much worn of a morning, with the hair dressed without a cushion, as for riding. Should I have been so fortunate as to give satisfaction in the choice of the things, I shall think myself vastly happy, and always proud in being honoured with your commands.—With my best wishes for Mr. Morris and my dear Kitty, I remain

> "My Dear Madam,
> "Your very sincere and Affectionate Friend
> "Sa. Jay"

During the course of this correspondence a romance was flourishing in the Morris home. Kitty Livingston received other letters from Europe besides those from her sister. Evidently she and Matthew Ridley were engaged at this time, for soon after his return from France they were married.

The elegant home of the Morrises became to an even greater degree the center of social life in Philadelphia and in the United States, since Philadelphia was then the country's most important metropolis. Distinguished foreigners, particularly French diplomats and officers, enjoyed the gracious hospitality of the "host" and "hostess" of America. The Marquis de Chastellux gave a revealing glimpse of the home and its occupants: "Mr. Morris is a large man, very simple in his manners, but his mind is subtle and acute, his head perfectly well organized and he is as well versed in public affairs as in his own. . . . His house is handsome, resembling perfectly the houses in London. He lives without ostentation, but not without expense, for he spares nothing which can contribute to his happiness and that of Mrs. Morris, to whom he is much attached."

In this home, located near the river, at Front and Dock streets, the Chevalier de la Luzerne often dropped in for tea. One day he presented Mary Morris with a silver waffle iron. On another occasion he was accompanied by the Prince de Broglie, who described that visit with evident enjoyment: "M. de la Luzerne conducted me to Mrs. Morris to take tea. She is the wife of the Comptroller General of the United States. The house is simple but well furnished and very neat.

The doors and tables are of a superb mahogany, and beautifully polished. The locks and hinges in brass were curiously bright. The porcelain cups were arranged with great precision. The mistress of the house had an agreeable expression, and was dressed in white; in fact everything appeared charming to me. I partook of most excellent tea, and I should be even now drinking it, I believe, if the Ambassador had not charitably notified me at the twelfth cup that I must put my spoon across it when I wished to finish with this sort of warm water. He said to me: 'It is almost as ill bred to refuse a cup of tea when it is offered to you, as it would be for the mistress of the house to propose a fresh one when the ceremony of the spoon has notified her that we no longer wish to partake of it.' "

Such hospitality as this was of inestimable value to the United States. Diplomats are often influenced more profoundly by social amenities than by political considerations. An early writer, Mease, gives an illuminating picture of the social life of Robert Morris. "His house was the seat of elegant but unostentatious hospitality, and his domestic affairs were managed with the same admirable order which had so long and so proverbially distinguished his counting house, the office of the Secret Committee of Congress and that of Finance. An introduction to Mr. Morris was a matter of course with all the strangers in good society who for half a century visited Philadelphia, either on commercial, public or private business; and it is not saying too much to assert that during a certain period it greatly depended upon him to do the honors of the city, and certainly no one was more qualified or more willing to support them." He was the Grover Whalen of his day, admirably suited to the role because of his geniality, sincerity, and wholehearted interest in his fellows. His naturally fine taste and that of Mary Morris added to the pleasure of his numerous guests.

As Samuel Breck records in his *Recollections:* "There was a luxury in the kitchen, table, parlor and street equipage of Mr. and Mrs. Morris that was to be found nowhere else in America. Bingham's was more gaudy, but less comfortable. It was the pure and unalloyed which the Morrises sought to place before their friends without the abatements that so frequently accompany the displays of fashionable life. No badly cooked or cold dinners at their table; no pinched fires upon the hearth; no paucity of waiters; no awkward loons in their drawing rooms."

The exquisite taste of Robert and Mary Morris revealed itself especially in the fine artistic furniture which may still be enjoyed in the Philadelphia Art Museum and in Congress Hall, as well as in the homes of his descendants. Had he retained his fortune, there might be entire rooms illustrating the elegance of the Morrises' home, instead of a few pieces of furniture and silver, repurchased from friends just before his death. There are three handsome sideboards, mentioned by Mrs. George L. Harrison in her privately published *Annals of the Ancestry of Charles Custis Harrison and Ellen Waln Harrison;* the largest, of mahogany inlaid with satinwood, with satinwood sunburst medallions on the cupboard doors. A pair of mahogany inlaid knife boxes with small silver feet and silver handles and escutcheons, recently on display in the Philadelphia Art Museum, usually rested on the satinwood sideboard. Mrs. Harrison also mentions a large mahogany desk, which Robert Morris left his daughter Maria, eight side chairs of dark maple artistically designed in the French style, and a large mahogany book-case or china closet with three sliding doors and three cupboards. There is still in the family a tiny mahogany four-post single bed with tester, that belonged to Mary Morris. One of the most interesting articles, certainly the most unique, belonging to Robert Morris was a mahogany "beau brummel" with compartments in the top for brushes, shaving apparatus, and other masculine toilet articles, and a large drawer below containing a wash basin. In Congress Hall in Philadelphia is a very spacious yellow satin divan (or sofa), owned by George Washington and bought by Morris when Washington retired to Mount Vernon at the end of his second term as President. It is unfortunate that the Gobelin tapestry and French marquetry work, considered the finest ever brought to this country, have been scattered and are no longer associated with the name of Robert Morris. More than anything else the beautiful pieces of Sheffield silver reflect the Morrises' elegance and fastidiousness. A handsome silver coffee urn, carved with the interwoven initials of Robert and Mary Morris, served many a distinguished guest. A delicately lovely silver cake basket, with a grape and wheat motif, decorated the table at many a banquet. These are but tantalizing souvenirs of the luxury and elegance that characterized the domestic life of the Morrises.

During the period after Morris's release from office, he moved to a brick mansion on High Street (now Market), between Sixth and Seventh. This was a most historic house. At one time owned by Richard Penn (1771–1775), it was later occupied by General Howe while the British were in control of Philadelphia. After the British evacuation of the city, Benedict Arnold, the military governor, resided there. This mansion was, in fact, the scene of many of the brilliant festivities that characterized his regime. Still later it was occupied by Sieur John Holker, the Consul General of France, who was living there when it was practically destroyed by fire. In 1785 Robert Morris bought the property and rebuilt the house. It was a three-story red brick mansion, connected by a long passageway with the kitchen, the smokehouse, and the washhouse. At the back of the property were the coachhouse and stables with accommodations for twelve horses. To the east stretched a spacious tree-shaded lawn enclosed by a brick wall. In that comfortable, elegant home Mary Morris, lovely, gracious hostess, gave her "petit suppers," her Wednesday night parties, and entertained more formally at dinners and receptions.

One morning in 1785, the same year the new home was built, Robert Morris was measuring wall space in his drawing room and in his attic—not an unusual activity in those days of construction, but this measurement was for a very special purpose. Morris had heard indirectly through John Jay that the French Ambassador, M. De Marbois, was leaving his house and that portraits of Louis XVI and Marie Antoinette, which he was keeping for the United States, would need to be stored elsewhere. These portraits had been sent the government by the King and Queen, but were housed by the Ambassador temporarily until the nation had a suitable gallery in which to hang them. Morris, always cooperative, wrote De Marbois offering his home for storage purposes. M. De Marbois replied that he had no intention of surrendering the portraits and intimated that Morris was entirely too officious in the matter. Robert Morris answered coolly but courteously that his offer was due to a misunderstanding and that he was most grateful to be relieved of the responsibility. His warm-hearted generosity led often, unfortunately, to a misinterpretation of his motives.

At this time Morris began his land speculations, which laid the foundations of his misfortunes. This period marked the beginning of the first great epidemic of land fever sweeping the United States, the forerunner of California and Florida real estate booms. Morris, al-ways adventurous, optimistic, with unbounded faith in the value of land in this new nation, eventually surpassed all competitors in his purchases, but even he bought slowly at first. He usually investigated carefully before purchasing, making extended trips through the South or through Pennsylvania, where hundreds of miles of fields or virgin forests fired his imagination. During this interval in his political ac-tivities, he traveled through Virginia, West Virginia, and Georgia, buying land and forming partnerships. One such partnership had been formed previously, in February, 1780, with Samuel Beall and John May of Williamsburg, to procure waste or unappropriated lands in Virginia. Robert Morris advanced £24,000 ($120,000). John May was to pay in tobacco for the money advanced and to act as manager of the business.

In 1787 Morris, with his friend and assistant, Gouverneur Morris, journeyed through Maryland and Virginia, remaining away from Philadelphia for many months. On his way to Virginia he visited the Halls' home at Sophia's Dairy, near Bushtown, Maryland, to which his family had fled during the Revolution. He spoke of being received by three charming young ladies, Molly, Polly, and Sophie Hall (Mrs. Morris's nieces), who gave him a hearty welcome and a good break-fast. He invited Molly, Mary Morris's namesake, and one of her sisters to spend the winter in Philadelphia with their aunt. In a letter to his wife from Baltimore he suggested that she arrange for Molly to re-ceive instructions on the harp at his expense, and that this matter be conducted tactfully as his Molly knew how to do it, without letting the niece feel herself the object of charity.

Early in December while her husband remained in Virginia, Mrs. Morris wrote him that the Federal government had been agreed to by the Convention. The joy of the populace knew no bounds. To her delight they gave three cheers for Robert Morris. Something of Mary Morris's feminine charm appears in all her gossipy, affectionate letters, especially in a naive remark like this: "You know that I am something of a politician."

She was a real comrade to her husband, dearly beloved through the years. Her sweetness, her dignity, her humor, her domestic efficiency were an unmixed blessing to Robert Morris, one of the few he was privileged to enjoy throughout his life. In every letter he showed his affection for her. He addressed her as "my dearest friend," "the partner of my happy moments and the sharer in my sorrowful hours," "the constant companion of my thoughts." "Your life is to me," he exclaimed, "the dearest object in this world." Here was a real marriage—of body, mind, and spirit.

Occasionally, of course, misunderstandings arose between husband and wife, usually as the result of impatience at the absence of the other or a failure to write. This letter to Mary Morris from her husband in Richmond, written just after Christmas in 1787, reveals such a situation: "If my having expressed some degree of impatience at not receiving a letter from you for some time after my arrival at this place, hurt your feelings in the least degree, I am sorry for it, my dear Molly, and you must attribute it to the true cause, an anxious solicitude to hear of the welfare of that family whose happiness lies nearer my heart than any other consideration in this world."

In a very newsy letter he told his wife of a visit to Williamsburg— of a fine journey and a sound sleep. He and Gouverneur Morris shared a room (but occupied different beds) at Benjamin Harrison's. Old Governor Harrison, he said, was staying with his son. They all lived well. One day, he reported, they dined with a Mr. Harvie. The conversation at the table between the ladies and gentlemen was well supported; the ladies, however, retired from the table, he noted, earlier than in Philadelphia. He went on many trips—one to see the Canal at the Falls of the James River. They got out of the carriage and walked three miles to view the falls and canal. There they enjoyed a barbecued shoat and a brandy toddy, the tables being set out-of-doors under the trees. In Richmond, as he needed considerable space for himself, his servants, and his horses, the Governor lent him a House of Stables and a room to write in, another for the servants, as well as accommodations for his horses and their hay and oats. During his stay in Virginia he felt rather unsafe in the wooden houses for fear of fire, and wished himself back in his brick mansion in Philadelphia. He and his companion had many invitations—one for Sunday dinner from the Governor of Virginia (the elder Benjamin Harrison). On another occasion he and Gouverneur Morris went in a phaeton to dine at Wilton. The iron axle of the carriage broke and the phaeton turned on its side. Morris leapt out and fortunately lighted on his feet, then proceeded to lift the carriage off Gouverneur's hand. By that time a hundred spectators had gathered. The younger Morris must have felt that there was a strange fatality about his riding in phaetons since in just such an accident he had injured and eventually lost his leg seven years before.

Through Morris's correspondence of this period is found the beginning of the refrain that rings through all his later years, concerning those "cursed bills," later changed to "creditors" and "debts." The return of his bills rankled. "My fortitude will be deeply probed," he told his wife, "but I shall stand the test and ultimately extricate myself with honor. Illiberal reflections of abuse will be my portion in the meantime." He advised Molly that the less she said or heard on the subject of the ill-fated bills, the better. "My greatest consolation," he told her, "is the certainty of being able to pay every farthing and of having sufficient left for my family. . . . You must compose yourself, leaving to me the vexations, mortifications and struggles which it is my part to sustain." Evidently he was again the victim of criticism in the papers. "If I was to fight," he confided to his wife, "it should be with the authors of that abuse so freely lavished on me in the prints." Despondently he reflected, "I sometimes determine to quit business and make myself easy for the remainder of my life." The fates decreed that he could not enjoy such ease. Had he, however, resisted the land lure, had he seen in time the handwriting on the wall, he might have led a comfortable, even prosperous, old age; at least, tragedy might have been averted.

In December Robert and Mary Morris began to write expectantly of the boys' return from Europe early in May. "There is an absent one," Molly admitted, "whose return is still more necessary to my happiness than even that of my dear children." Two months of his absence seemed twice as long to the entire family. A strong bond united Morris, his wife, and children. Molly sent him frequent bulletins concerning the family: "the little captain," Henry, playing in the back yard, wheeling dirt in a wheelbarrow for his brother William to make a garden, or playing with their servant, black Rachel. Hetty, as young as she was, was depicted as having affairs of the heart —one most unfortunate, in which "she was supplanted by a younger damsel." Her father philosophized that this was hard for her to bear but might teach her a lesson concerning "the vanity and uncertainty of human affections and pursuits." Maria was now spoken of as the "darling little daughter." In one letter Mary Morris mentioned a dream Maria had had about her father and "a certain chit-chat" with him after his return. This delighted him. "Dreaming is not in my power," he confessed, "unless it is waking dreams." His father spoke of Bill (William White Morris, the third son) as an agreeable correspondent, but advised that he take time to think before acting; otherwise he would have "a plentiful harvest of disappointments, mortifications and miseries."

When May came and still Robert Morris had not returned home, his wife wrote him a most reproachful letter. "It is indeed too long now that you have been absent from us. I find my patience indeed 'most exhausted," Mary Morris said. The boys had already arrived from Europe, speaking English with a French accent. She mentioned also the arrival of the new French Minister, Count Montier, his sister, the Marchioness, and her son, Count Breon. The boys waited on the Minister and Mrs. Morris on the Marchioness, who was in bed fatigued by the journey. That very same afternoon the Minister returned Mrs. Morris's call. The Marchioness she described as "small, plain in dress and of agreeable manner." Her English was "tolerable." Count Montier she depicted as "comely, plain in dress and manners." Robert and Thomas accompanied them on a sight-seeing tour, to show them the country and the "situations best worth seeing." She told her husband of the death of Charles Willing and of her going with the children on the wagon to Germantown—presumably to his funeral. Their new chariot she reported as being finished and admired by all the town. She put off getting it from the manufacturer, however, until she heard from her husband.

The latter suggested that she come down to Mount Vernon in the new chariot to meet him there. On the return trip he and she might ride in the chariot, accompanied by Bob and Tom on horseback, and Hetty with Gouverneur Morris in the phaeton. But this was a mere pipe dream, born of his desire to see the family as soon as possible. For there was an insuperable objection, Robert Morris realized—"the show of parade which agrees ill with my present situation. I cannot bear the idea of insulting my creditors," he continued, "by making a show in any way whilst I am in debt and not able to pay as fast as I ought." Debts began to weigh even more heavily upon him. "I mean on my return to make a great reform in our expenses," he wrote his wife that spring. It would be necessary, he said, for the boys to qualify themselves to make their own way in the world. He advised their being sent down to him so that he might help them select suitable professions. To Thomas he wrote telling him the requisites for becoming a lawyer and asking his desires in the matter.

Robert Morris was unwilling to force his own ideas upon his family. He wished to be a companion to his children. To him they were personalities, not chattels. Indeed there always remained in him much of the boy—boyish enthusiasms, youthful optimism, ardent, flamelike love of adventure. The flame burned brightly despite financial stringency, more severe than he had ever felt before personally, and destined to become more acute with the years of rapidly developing land fever.

CHAPTER XIII

CONGRESSIONAL WIREPULLING

❖ ❖ ❖

EVEN during the years of comparative rest from political activity, Robert Morris had not wholly retired from public life. When the charter of the Bank of North America was annulled by the Pennsylvania legislature in 1785, Morris sought election to the legislature to obtain a renewal of the charter. On the second day of debate on the subject in March, 1786, he made a long, logical and persuasive speech, in which he defended the management of the bank from charges of favoritism and demonstrated the value of this institution to the community and the state as well as to the Federal government. In his peroration he asserted: "It [the bank] promotes the grandeur of the state, increases its wealth and adds to its dignity." Partly through Morris's eloquence and powers of persuasion, the bank, his pet project, was restored to confidence and its charter renewed. He exerted a powerful influence in Pennsylvania politics over a term of years because of his wisdom, business acumen, force, and determination.

Morris was also one of those who most earnestly desired a convention to draw up a constitution for the United States. Pennsylvania at first selected six men to represent the state in this convention: Robert Morris, George Clymer, Thomas Fitzsimons, Jared Ingersoll, James Wilson, and Gouverneur Morris. On his return from France, Benjamin Franklin was added to the number. On May 25, 1787, a quorum attended for the first time. On this historic occasion only four of the Pennsylvania delegates were present. Robert Morris usually kept his appointments punctually. It was he who made the nominating speech and conducted George Washington to his chair as president of the Convention.

At this time Washington visited the Morrises as he usually did when in Philadelphia. Upon his arrival in the city on September 13, 1787, he had first gone to a boarding-house kept by Mrs. Mary House at Fifth and Market streets, but he was not permitted to remain there more than a few minutes. Robert and Mary Morris called upon him at once and insisted that he go to their home. During this visit Washington with Robert and Gouverneur Morris went on many short excursions on horseback. Sometimes the ladies accompanied them in carriages after Lady Washington arrived to join her husband. On one occasion the three men went to Trenton on a fishing trip, where the General had made a large "catch" during the Revolution. At another time they rode to Valley Forge for a picnic, Gouverneur Morris fishing while George Washington and Robert Morris looked around the camp. In Philadelphia dinners and receptions were given in the General's honor—public banquets for notables, the table lavishly spread with choice viands and rare wines. The evenings were spent "in great festivity and mirth."

At last the Constitution was completed and adopted by ten states of the Union, Robert Morris among others signing for Pennsylvania. This event was celebrated on July 4, 1788. At dawn of day Christ Church bells pealed and cannon boomed from the ship *Rising Sun*, anchored off Market Street. In the harbor ten vessels, honoring the ten states that had signed the Constitution, were decorated, each ship flying a white flag with the name of a state emblazoned upon it. That day there was a great procession of eighty-eight floats. The Constitution was represented by Chief Justice McKean and the Associated Justices in a car shaped like an eagle, drawn by six horses. A citizen of Philadelphia and an Indian chief sat in a car (chariot or float) together and smoked a pipe of peace. A float drawn by ten white horses and supported by thirteen Corinthian columns represented the structure of Federal government. Another float symbolized the ship of state sailing on a canvas sea, manned by four small boys dressed as midshipmen. Of especial interest was the Federal ship *Union*, mounting twenty guns, which was built from a barge formerly belonging

CORNER OF INTERIOR OF CHRIST CHURCH IN PHILADELPHIA

Showing the Morris Pew (54) and the Penn Pew, which Morris may have rented later, and from which the pulpit now rises

to the *Serapis*. Trades and industries were also represented. Richard Willing, as a farmer, guided a plough drawn by four oxen, while his brother as a ploughboy walked beside the oxen. An ode written by Francis Hopkinson and read during the day celebrated the event. In the evening there was a supper at Bush Hill.

When the celebrations were over and it was time for Pennsylvania to elect its senators, the state chose Robert Morris and William Maclay of Maclayville (later Harrisburg) to represent it in Congress. Morris drew the long term, six years; Maclay, the two-year term. That fact rankled in the latter's mind, arousing jealousy of his colleague.

On his way to his inauguration in New York, George Washington stayed in Morris's home. All along the route from Mount Vernon he rode beneath triumphal arches. At Gray's Ferry, near Philadelphia, as he passed under an arch—one of many around the city—a crown of laurel was lowered upon his brow. On his arrival and at his departure, whenever the President appeared publicly, he was greeted by the ringing of bells, the booming of cannon, the playing of bands, and the dipping of colors. When he left, Robert Morris accompanied him to New York, their progress by coach and ferry a royal triumph. The journey from Princeton to Paulus Hook Ferry, however, was most uncomfortable, Morris wrote his wife. At Princeton he met his colleague, William Maclay, and took him with him in his carriage. They arrived at Paulus Hook at seven o'clock in the evening, in a thick fog, with a strong nor'easter blowing.

The next morning, March 4, 1789, the four Pennsylvania delegates crossed the river together and reached New York "before a Constable was up." That day the members of Congress met and adjourned as there was not a quorum and consequently no business could be transacted. Only eight senators and thirteen assemblymen attended those first sessions. As a matter of fact, Senator Morris and the other early arrivals had to wait five weeks to transact business since New York, the temporary capital, was too far away to be reached easily by the southern senators. Morris reported that the Federal Edifice was still unfinished.

He described graphically for Molly's entertainment and information the pageantry accompanying the beginning of the new era. On the night of March third, thirteen cannon were fired from the Battery for the funeral of the Confederation. The new government was saluted next day with eleven guns, one for each state that had so far adopted the Constitution. The flag was hoisted, the Federal colors displayed on top of the new building, while the bells rang and people thronged the streets. It was "like a grand festival," Morris thought. The fourth of March, 1789, "no doubt will hereafter be celebrated as a new era in the annals of the world," he prophesied.

Soon after his arrival Morris sent an express rider to Philadelphia with the news that Lady Washington and her grandchildren, Eleanor and George Washington Parke Custis, would breakfast at Chester on their way to New York. On May 21, Mrs. Morris accompanied a cavalcade consisting of two troops of light horse, the governor, and a number of prominent ladies and gentlemen, to meet the distinguished visitors at Gray's Ferry. There, at Gray's Gardens, the entire party of seventy-nine guests enjoyed an "elegant cold luncheon," at which the guests drank ten bottles of Madeira and forty-five bowls of punch as well as bottles of porter, claret, ale and champagne. They were hearty drinkers in those days. Amid shouts and cheers, the ringing of bells and thirteen peals of artillery, the guests entered the city. The ovation became even more vociferous as the procession approached the Morrises' residence on High Street, where Martha Washington was to be entertained during her stay in the city. From Thursday to Monday the President's lady remained in Philadelphia as the guest of Mary Morris. On Monday morning, Mrs. Washington, taking Mrs. Morris and Maria with her in her carriage, set out for New York. At Elizabethtown they were met by Washington and Morris and crossed the river in the presidential barge, rowed by thirteen pilots in white uniforms.

On May 29 the First Lady (literally the first) held her initial levee, at which Mrs. Morris, resplendent in diamonds, occupied the place of honor at her hostess's right. This position was always accorded her when she attended all subsequent levees. Soon after her arrival the Pennsylvania delegation in Congress called upon Mrs. Morris, who was not at home to receive them. On the fifth of July, just after the usual celebration on the Fourth, Mary Morris returned to Philadelphia. Not long afterward she received a letter from her husband requesting her to entertain and otherwise pay marked attention to certain strangers to the city, the Macombs, who had shown him great hospitality, and to friends of theirs from London. He suggested that they be taken to "The Hills." Mary Morris, gracious hostess and charming woman, contributed to a large degree to Morris's social and political success.

Unfortunately the only picture obtainable of Senator Morris is in the *Journal* of William Maclay, his colleague in the Senate and bitter opponent on most measures. Senator Maclay was evidently a provincial-minded, strait-laced, utterly unyielding individual, to whom the interests of the country were secondary to those of his section of Pennsylvania. He was a more intense, certainly more stubborn Democrat than Thomas Jefferson. According to his view of the political arena, moreover, he was the only thoroughly upright member of Congress. His photographic, acidulous comments on persons and events are worthy of a Sinclair Lewis. "The President," he remarked bitingly, "has become in the hands of Hamilton the dish-clout of every dirty speculation, as his name goes to wipe away blame and silence all murmuring. . . . Would to God this same General Washington were in heaven!" In reference to a speech made by a fellow senator, he objected to "the belchings of this bag of blubber." John Adams, he ridiculed on all occasions. Maclay spoke of Gouverneur Morris as "half pimp, half envoy" (for Robert Morris), "or more properly a kind of political eavesdropper about the British Court." The Yorkers he depicted as the "vilest of people." No one escaped his jaundiced eye and envenomed tongue.

At first he seemed surprisingly respectful toward Robert Morris, but when their policies clashed, as happened most frequently, Morris came in for his share of abuse. Before he had "lost confidence" in Morris, he spoke even flatteringly of a speech Senator Morris made on the tariff in opposition to the New Englanders. "Charmingly did he unravel all their windings," recorded the *Journal*. "He was clear and conclusive." "His weight in our Senate is great on commercial subjects," Maclay admitted. Later when he found that he and Morris did not view matters eye to eye, he depicted him as raging "in a violent chaff" and spoke of his (Maclay's) answering him "in a way that gave him a bone to chaw." On several occasions he called him a "blackguard"—his favorite epithet, or accused him of "perfidy." He considered that his colleague did not like close thinking, but said he had "a strong and vigorous mind" when it did act. According to the observant Maclay, Morris was invariably absent when questions presented themselves for debate. In fact, Senator Morris was depicted as a restless, peevish schoolboy, who on one occasion, becoming angry or disgusted, left his hat and stick in the Senate Chamber while he went into an adjoining room to write letters until the Senate adjourned. At other times he was pictured as being so angry that "his collar fairly choked him," or as "running backward and forward like a boy, taking out one Senator after another," or as "laughing heartily every time he got up" to present a motion. "There is too much levity in his conduct," this Mirror of Propriety objected.

Those were busy days for Robert Morris. He was offered the Cabinet post of Secretary of the Treasury, but refused it, suggesting the name of Alexander Hamilton. In view of the events immediately preceding the war, notably the Boston Tea Party and the treatment of the Tea Ship *Polly*, it is interesting to note that Morris favored raising the duties on tea. He also presented his opinions on the importation of sugar and moved that cotton be exempted from duty. Among other questions, he debated upon the Judiciary Bill, the Tonnage Act, senators' and judges' salaries, Constitutional Amendments, the Bank Bill, the Excise Bill, and the Foreign Affairs Bill. Like a good Philadelphian he defended the Quakers when they were attacked in a religious controversy. This seems a fair record for one who was "invariably absent when questions came up for debate" (according to his worthy colleague).

But Senator Morris's chief efforts those busy days were concentrated on the question of a permanent residence for Congress or a temporary residence for the next few years. At first he advocated moving the capital to the Falls of the Delaware, at Trenton. Since Morris had property there, Maclay accused him of wishing to advance his own interests. A schism resulted between Robert Morris and the rest of the Pennsylvania delegation, both in the House and in the Senate. Morris began negotiations with Jay and Hamilton to make the Falls of the Delaware the Federal residence. Maclay in the meantime was pushing the Susquehanna as the seat of government because of its central location and the benefits it would bring commercially to that section of the state. He remarked on Morris's "perfidy" in trying to influence votes against the Susquehanna when he had promised to support that location. Robert Morris was in close connection with the despised Yorkers. Indeed the upright Senator Maclay accused him of being the tool of Alexander Hamilton. Early one morning Morris and Hamilton met by appointment at the Battery to try to reach an agreement. Alexander Hamilton agreed to vote in favor of placing the permanent residence at the Falls of the Delaware or at Germantown in exchange for certain votes for a bill he was sponsoring. "Never had a man a greater propensity for bargaining than Mr. Morris," reported the *Journal*.

Morris proved himself a diplomat in all the intrigues that characterized the Senate. It was apparently an activity that he vastly enjoyed, a type of service to his country that utilized many of his talents —his mercantile ability, his sociability, his powers of persuasion. No longer in a position of isolated responsibility, he derived intense pleasure from sharing problems with his colleagues—from manipulating men as well as measures. For some reason he abandoned the Falls of the Delaware as the seat of Government and urged the removal of Congress to Germantown. On behalf of Pennsylvania he offered $100,000 toward establishing Congress in the latter city. His colleague wished to know on whose responsibility he made the offer. He replied that if the state would not supply the money, he himself would. (Thereupon the *Journal*'s author, horrified, raised his eyebrows.) When that scheme appeared impracticable, he began bickering for the temporary capital at Philadelphia, since the Southerners insisted upon establishing the permanent residence on the banks of the Potomac. Robert Morris confided to his wife that he intended to move, when there was a full Senate, that the next session of Congress be held in Philadelphia. After a series of compromises it was agreed that Congress should meet in that city for a period of ten years before taking up its permanent abode on the Potomac.

As a result of these negotiations he was abused by the New Yorkers in "the public prints, private conversation and in the streets." "Yesterday," he told his wife, "I nearly engaged in a serious quarrel with one of them." The New Yorkers were really angry with him for his efforts to move the capital. A caricature of Morris appeared in a New York paper, representing him as carrying off Federal Hall on his shoulders, with the faces of the members of Congress appearing at the windows. In the foreground the Devil beckoned him on crying, "This way, Bobby!"

Although Morris could accept criticism patiently or even laughingly, he had a red-headed temper which displayed itself frequently during this period. He often blazed away and once came into the Senate "raging angry and swore he would vote against everything." After the battle was won for his beloved city, however, he regained his poise and amiability.

While he remained in New York, the sociable Senator spent a great deal of time in social activities. He attended levees, ate dinners at various places of interest, and visited Morrisania, Gouverneur Morris's home, from which the latter was absent at the time. His son Tom spent much time with him there and in the city. Once during such a visit the weather was "terrible" and he was "forced to read [on account of the rain] when he meant to rove." From Morrisania he wrote Molly a long, newsy letter, telling her of a visit he had paid the President and Mrs. Washington the preceding Friday night and of their inquiries for Mrs. Morris and Maria. Mr. Constable, he said, was so charmed with Maria's playful disposition that he had named a ship for her. Evidently Robert Morris had kept his own phaeton in New York, for he spoke of expecting a black horse from "The Hills" to be put with one he had purchased from Alexander Hamilton, the pair to be attached to the phaeton.

Two matters distressed him at this time. He had begun to feel the pinch of financial stringency. A new note was struck in his letters when in sending his wife $100, he said that he knew her "prudence would make it go as far as possible," as he was having difficulty in collecting money. Another cause of anxiety was his failure to hear from Gouverneur Morris, who was then attending to Robert Morris's interests in Virginia. He feared his letters were being "intercepted for some villainous purpose or other." He had, however, received a barrel of hams from him.

Like young lovers, Robert and Mary Morris—these two who had been married for twenty years—rose early on the very same morning to write each other. He related to her, his confidante of a lifetime, bits of political gossip; she in turn told him of his gardens and of the first pineapple from their hot-houses. Eager for him to share the pleasures of the season with her, she sent him some fruit from "The Hills." Only once did Morris write his wife sarcastically: that was in reference to a bundle of clothing he had received from her, some articles of which needed repairing. He had been forced to request Mrs. Constable to sew some buttons on the shirt collar as it came "without any conveniences for fastening round the neck, which is not the way used in these our days."

Soon after this, Robert Morris was at home again. The next year Congress convened in Philadelphia, to remain there for ten years. This was owing largely to Morris's influence. Since his new home on Market Street was the most commodious in the city, Morris insisted that President Washington occupy it as long as he remained in office. Washington gratefully accepted. The Morrises, therefore, moved next door to a smaller brick mansion on the corner of Sixth Street, formerly owned by the Tory, Joseph Galloway, and now the property of Robert Morris. While the President's secretary, Tobias Lear, was attending to the details of settling in Philadelphia, Washington wrote him the following letter concerning the Morrises and certain domestic complications:

"Mr. and Mrs. Morris have insisted upon leaving the two large looking-glasses which are in their best rooms, because they have no place, they say, proper to remove them to, and because they are unwilling to hazard them down. You will therefore let them have, instead, the choice of mine—Mrs. Morris has a mangle (I think it is called) for ironing clothes, which, as it is fixed in the place where it is commonly used, she proposes to leave and take mine. To this I have no objection provided mine is *equally good and convenient;* but if I should obtain any advantage besides that of its being up and ready for use, I am not inclined to receive it. . . . Mrs. Morris, who is a notable lady in family arrangement, can give you much information on all the conveniences about the house and buildings, and I daresay would rather consider it as a compliment to be consulted in those matters, as she is near, than a trouble to give her opinion of them."

This is one of Washington's most unconventional letters, filled as it is with domestic details and considerations of friendship. Indeed throughout their association, Robert Morris by his own simple friendliness seemed to draw forth the President's most human traits.

On Christmas night in 1790, George Washington held his first levee in Philadelphia. It was a brilliant occasion, lights from a thousand candles glistening in the crystal chandeliers and gleaming upon the polished mahogany and shining brass and silver. The President stood in front of the fireplace facing the door, the light glinting on his knee and shoe buckles and on the long sword at his side. As guests approached him, he bowed in the formal fashion of the day, without shaking hands, but when Morris entered, he grasped him cordially by the hand. Every second Tuesday afternoon Washington held formal levees, wearing yellow gloves and holding a cocked hat with a black cockade, the edges adorned with a black feather. On these occasions Robert Morris was often beside him in the place of honor. In fact, Morris was the friend and adviser closest to Washington during his two terms as president. He was, moreover, a social and political power, adroit in handling situations in the drawing room, the counting house, or the Congressional arena.

The social life of the two families intermingled throughout those years. At Mrs. Washington's levees on Friday evenings, Mrs. Morris continued to occupy the first place at her hostess's right. Trained in social usages, naturally witty, charming, and gracious, Mary Morris was considered the "second lady in the land"; in elegance and taste, the first. She had a store of anecdotes and other narratives, some reserved merely for the ears of her family and closest friends. One that she recounted privately concerned a dish of rancid cream (probably clabber) served at the President's table, when Mrs. Washington "ate whole heaps of it," but the President "changed his plate." Dinner parties in the presidential mansion occurred at four in the afternoon. The President sat half-way down the table between the head and the foot, and invariably asked the blessing. The dishes were without covers. Silver trays and alabaster mythological figures about two feet high decorated the table. At each gentleman's place there was usually one cup or mug of beer and one glass of wine. After the ladies had withdrawn from the table, while he chatted with the men, the President often drank another glass. These dinners Robert Morris enjoyed because of his natural sociability and his admiration for George Washington.

The President's second inauguration was a gala occasion in Philadelphia. In front of the President's mansion appeared the cream-colored coach, ornamented with cupids, festoons, and wreaths of flowers, and drawn by six white horses. On the box sat the German coachman Fritz, tall, muscular, erect, obviously impressed with his position. The postilions and outriders were also clad in the Washington livery, white trimmed with scarlet or orange. Upon the steps of his home Washington appeared in a suit of black velvet with black silk hose and diamond knee buckles. His powdered hair, gathered in a black silk bag, was tied with a bow of black ribbon. He carried a cocked hat with the American cockade and wore a light dress sword with richly ornamented hilt, in a green scabbard. Over his left shoulder was draped a rich blue Spanish cloak, faced with red silk velvet. On the sidewalk outside the gate the spectators gathered in throngs to watch the President's departure. From the windows of their home the Morrises could view the entire spectacle—the cheering crowds and the elegance and dignity of President and Mrs. Washington. At Congress Hall another throng was waiting to greet the President with vociferous enthusiasm upon his arrival and at the conclusion of the inaugural ceremonies.

In the Senate in Philadelphia Robert Morris was especially interested in the Funding Bill to provide for the domestic debt of the United States and the Assumption Bill whereby the Federal government would assume the state war debts to the amount of $21,000,000. Here, too, a compromise was agreed upon by the proponents and the opponents of the bills. At first Morris "showed an ireful disposition" but at last yielded, remarking: "Half a loaf is better than no bread. I will consent to the bill on behalf of the public creditors for whom I am interested—as well as for the rest of the Union." Despite their political differences, Morris invited his peppery colleague, Senator Maclay, to dine with him on several occasions, and once at least to eat Philadelphia "pepper pot" with him. When he was with Morris, Maclay could not believe that the Philadelphia senator would fight his reelection; but later he would become convinced that such was the case. "The city hates me," he commented in the *Journal*, "and I have offended Morris, and my place must go." Unfortunately after William Maclay left, no detailed record was kept of the activities of Robert Morris, Senator. He is known to have assisted Alexander Hamilton in framing a tariff bill and no doubt advised him on many financial matters.

At the end of his six years of distinguished service in the United States Senate, Morris determined to withdraw from public life. Members of the Pennsylvania Legislature assured him of his unanimous reelection, but his private affairs had become so involved that he felt his retirement imperative. The cloud of debt and financial difficulties was beginning to lower. Even as early as May, 1790, he wrote his wife: "The bitterest moments of my present life are those in which I contemplate you as the partner of misfortunes of which I am not only the victim, but in some degree perhaps culpable in not having guarded better against them." Robert Morris was always honest with himself as with others.

In addition to serving in the Senate, he was interested in state enterprises. In 1791 he was president of the Schuylkill, Susquehanna and Delaware Navigation [or Canal] Company, one of the first organizations to foster improvements in Pennsylvania. Always public-spirited and energetic, he gave freely of his time to all worthy objects, intent on ameliorating conditions in the state and the nation.

During this period his home was the center of informal social life in Philadelphia. Both at the Market Street residence, next door to the

President's mansion, and at "The Hills," guests enjoyed the elegance and comfort of the Morrises' hospitable menage—the imported china, the magnificent French tapestries, the fine linens, and art objects from all over the world. Their library was filled with valuable books, their larder stocked with the rarest wines and the choicest viands. On the Chippendale chairs in the Morrises' drawing room sat the great men of the day—Alexander Hamilton, John Jay, Thomas Jefferson, Nathaniel Greene, and George Washington. Here came also the distinguished French emigrés—Talleyrand, La Rochefoucauld, Rochambeau, and De Noailles. Perhaps in the midst of the refined luxury of the Morris home, they felt themselves back in their native France. At least their tactful host and hostess had the art of making them feel at home.

In Philadelphia at that period there was strong partisan feeling. The entire population seemed divided into pro-English and pro-French groups. Riots occurred among the street mobs and heated discussions in the taverns. With the arrival of Citizen Genêt an attempt was made to force the Republic into an alliance with France. Revolutionary societies were founded, the Marseillaise was sung, and the Carmagnole danced with true French *abandon* upon the streets. Minister Genêt demanded in the name of the new Republic of France the two million dollars the United States owed his country. Ten thousand sympathizers thronged the streets of Philadelphia threatening to drag Washington out of his house and to force the Government to declare itself in favor of France and against England. Around a liberty pole erected in Girard Street danced young and old, singing and shrieking. The crowd broke the windows of Mr. Bingham, wealthy Englishman and Willing's son-in-law, as well as those of the English consul. After these demonstrations Citizen Genêt became insufferably insolent and was finally succeeded by Citizen Fouchet. The French, moreover, were divided into two parties: the ultra-reds, those who favored the Republic, and the royalists or loyalists, who wished the restoration of the monarchy. In Morris's parlors, seated on the satin divans and Chippendale chairs, a brilliant assemblage of these royalists conversed many an evening. The clever, scheming Talleyrand limped in, a satiric smile upon his lips. Excommunicated bishop, ex-Revolutionary

emigré, Charles Maurice Talleyrand de Perigord continued his machinations even in America. Here came, too, the graceful, talented
Vicomte de Noailles, who had served under Lafayette during the
American Revolution and had at first sympathized with the French
Revolutionists. They and other emigrés enjoyed Robert Morris's
famous hospitality. Intrigues flourished among the Gobelins tapestries
which recalled to these exiled Frenchmen their native land. In great
secrecy, almost in whispers, a company was formed—the Asylum
Company—to form a refuge for the emigrés themselves and (here
their voices dropped) for their Majesties, Louis XVI and Marie Antoinette. The royal couple were to be spirited away from France and
kept in this country until they might return in safety to their own
land and throne. Details had not been completed for the escape from
France. In the meantime, however, these *intriguants* were preparing
a haven for their Majesties.

Since much of the land in the northeastern part of Pennsylvania,
purchased by this company, was owned by Robert Morris, he held
a large number of shares, probably a controlling interest. "No better
refuge could be found, gentlemen, than the site you have chosen,"
Morris remarked. "The acres are fertile; the valley beautiful, embraced as it is in the folds of the Susquehanna." Morris was a successful real estate salesman.

"Their Majesties should be delighted," Talleyrand spoke drily.
"The location should prove safe enough, so far inland. There the
King may play farmer and the Queen again rehearse her role as dairy-
maid. Let us hope, however, that they will eventually escape from
the Asylum," he concluded with a sardonic smile.

"A town is already being settled, is it not?" asked De Noailles.

Morris nodded, his eyes lighting with pleasure. "It looks like a
picture village with its homes and stores, snuggled among the trees on
the banks of the river. You must see for yourselves, gentlemen. Shall
we plan a trip on horseback?"

Not long after such a meeting in Morris's home, flaming, searing
news reached the emigrés of the trial and execution of Louis XVI.
There was less reason now for the establishment of the town of
Asylum. The emigrés preferred to remain in Philadelphia or other

cities near the coast. Building languished. Only a few hardy pioneers remained to face the lonely winters in the picturesque valley.

In 1797 Louis Philippe, son of that Philippe Egalité, Duke of Orleans, who had helped usher in the French Revolution, came to America as an exile from France. While in Philadelphia he was often the guest of Robert Morris. One day on noticing the bronze bust of John Paul Jones in his host's drawing room, Louis Philippe exclaimed: "One of my proudest memories is that, when a little boy, I enjoyed the society of that wonderful man. And next I cherish in memory that my mother, more than anyone else in France, helped him at the most critical moment of his fortunes to obtain the instruments of victory. . . . During the three years, 1778 to 1781, while Paul Jones made France the base of operations, while your Congress was too poor to even give him the pay and allowances of his rank, my mother with her own hand gave him personally over ten thousand louis d'or [the louis d'or was worth approximately $4.70], besides contributing large sums toward the outfit and supply of his ships and crews. If he hesitated to accept her benefices, she would say, 'Commodore, I command you! This is not charity; it is not even gratuity. It is my offering to the great cause of which you are by far the ablest and bravest champion on the sea.'"

Led on by Morris's tactful questions, the prince continued talking, telling how his mother, wild with enthusiasm over Paul Jones's victory in the *Bonhomme Richard*, gave a ball in his honor after she had received this characteristic message from him: "The enemy surrendered at 35 minutes past 10 o'clock in the evening, by your watch, which I consult only to fix the moment of victory."

Undoubtedly, too, Citizen Louis Philippe delighted his host with another anecdote belonging to the same period. One day at a banquet, a few months later, Commodore Jones asked the Duchess if she remembered his promise that if fortune favored him, he would "lay an English frigate at her feet." She bowed assent, smiling. The Commodore thereupon requested an attendant to bring him a leather case from his apartment in the palace. (Both the Duke and Duchess of Orleans insisted that he make his home at their palatial residence, the Palais Royal.) When the attendant returned, Jones took a sword from the case and presented it to the Duchess with these words: "Your Royal Highness perceives the impossibility of keeping my promise in kind. The English ship captured was a 44, with two decks. The best I can do is to place in your dainty hands the sword of the brave officer who commanded the 44. I have the honor to surrender to the loveliest of women the sword surrendered to me by one of the bravest of men—the sword of Captain the Honorable Richard Pearson, of His Britannic Majesty's late ship, the *Serapis*." "This sword," concluded Louis Philippe, "is among the most valued relics of the House of Bourbon-Orleans."

In return for these confidences, Robert Morris, testamentary executor of Jones's will, told the story of another sword, a jewelled sword given Paul Jones by King Louis XVI. Shortly before the Commodore's death in Paris on July 18, 1792, Gouverneur Morris, Ambassador to France, called on the sick hero. In the course of their conversation Jones bequeathed this gift to Richard Dale, first lieutenant on the *Bonhomme Richard*. "My good old Dick," Paul Jones told Gouverneur Morris, "is better entitled to it than anyone else because he did more than any other to help me win it." Jones remembered that moonlight battle when Richard Dale and his men, armed with pikes, had stabbed the British gunners as they leaned out the ports to fire. His "good old Dick" had also been the first to board the *Serapis*, just as Captain Pearson lowered the British flag.

"Of course I considered this oral bequest a sacred duty," said Morris, "but my action aroused a storm of protest."

This conversation between the young French guest and his host may have continued to that last dramatic scene in the life of John Paul Jones—his death, when upon entering his room from the garden, he fell lifeless across the bed. In his clenched hand rested the watch given him by Marie Adelaide of Orleans, with her miniature on the dial—the watch he consulted only in moments of victory.

While Louis Philippe was in Philadelphia, he occupied a room over a barber shop. When he gave a dinner to distinguished guests one day, he was forced to seat half the visitors on his bed. Of course he was entertained at the homes of most of the leading citizens; among others he visited Thomas Willing, who had a large family of attractive daughters. There or perhaps at the home of her sister, the beautiful and charming Mrs. Bingham, Louis Philippe, later the Citizen King, met and fell in love with Abigail Willing. When he asked Thomas Willing for her hand, the father said: "If you have no claim to the throne of France, you are no match for my daughter, and if you ever become King, she will be no match for you." Thus Miss Abigail lost her chance of becoming a queen; instead she married Richard Peters.

Another visitor at the Morrises' home during this period was Gilbert Stuart, the distinguished portrait painter, who arrived in Philadelphia in 1794 while Congress was in session there. In the Republican Court, as it was called, in this city, were congregated all the most noted men and the loveliest women of that time. Aside from painting their portraits, the artist attended their gay assemblages, the musical parties, the informal dinners, and more ceremonious entertainments so characteristic of a national capital. Stuart was an addition to any gathering. He was a musician as well as an artist, playing on the harpsichord and other instruments. Since there were few paid performers in those days, the guests themselves provided the entertainment at these musicales. His sparkling wit and talent for mimicry made him also a capital storyteller. At the Morrises' table he probably repeated his favorite story about himself.

"Once when I was visiting in a town for the first time, some of the citizens seemed curious about my occupation, so I decided to lead the questioners a merry chase. After considering me in turn doctor, lawyer, business man—everything but a burglar—they shook their heads in despair. Whereupon with mock seriousness, I said, 'I will tell you the truth. I get my bread by making faces.'" To illustrate, he screwed up his features in a grotesque grimace to the amusement of the other guests. "Those who had been questioning me then nodded at each other," Stuart continued, "saying that they had known all the time that I was a comedian. Solemnly I replied that I had never been on the stage in my life. At that they were more puzzled than ever. At last I admitted the sad truth that I was a portrait painter." The guests, amused by Stuart's grimaces and inimitable gestures even more than by the tale itself, laughed merrily. Robert Morris's side-shaking laugh boomed above the others.

The best pictures of Robert Morris and his family were those painted by Gilbert Stuart about 1795. There is the speaking likeness of Morris himself, with his broad shoulders and rounded oval face, dominated by the large deep-blue eyes. It is a human, kindly face, the full lips half smiling, the rounded brow expressing philanthropy (according to phrenologists), the well-formed nose broad at the nostrils, the gray hair (his own) falling loosely to his coat collar. Something of his magnificent vitality vibrates from the portrait. "Here," we say as we look at it, "was a man who accomplished things and yet was bigger than any job he undertook." This portrait, inherited by Thomas Morris, is now in the possession of Lieutenant Colonel Robert Morris of Harrisburg. Stuart also painted other family portraits for Robert Morris: the lovely one of Mrs. Morris, now in the Lenox Collection in New York; one of William White, Morris's brother-in-law, Rector of Christ Church and Bishop of North America; and the portraits of Morris's two daughters.

An interesting story is told with regard to these portraits of Hetty and Maria Morris. The canvas is defaced by ridges; another obvious defect is the non-existence of Hetty's hands. A tale persists in the Morris family that when Gilbert Stuart asked Robert Morris for his criticism of the partly finished portrait, the latter made some slightly disparaging remark on the painting of Maria's hands. Thereupon the temperamental artist, who prided himself especially upon his technique in painting hands, became so infuriated that he seized his palette knife and slashed the picture. Other authorities maintain that the cuts are attributable to an effort to separate the portraits of the two sisters. At all events, the picture remained unfinished and has definite ridges showing where it was cut, by temperament or by design. After Stuart's death many years later, his daughter found the pieces in a garret. Piecing the canvas together, she sold the portrait to Hetty's husband, James Marshall, for thirty-six guineas, twice the price originally agreed upon by Gilbert Stuart and Robert Morris.

The most famous of all portraits of the period were Stuart's numerous studies of George Washington and other members of his family. Since the artist knew the President so well socially, he was able to study him under various conditions and thus present well-rounded, interpretative portraits of him.

Other portraits of Morris taken at this period or a little earlier were the one by Robert Edge Pine, for whom Morris had erected a house in which to exhibit his paintings, and those by Savage, Trumbull, and Peale. The last mentioned, now in Independence Hall, Mary Morris considered such a poor likeness of her husband that she would not permit it in her house or even in her sight. In this portrait Morris appears not merely corpulent but apathetic. Not a trace of his dynamic vitality is evident. But after all, Charles Wilson Peale was a political enemy of his.

After his retirement from the Senate, Morris enjoyed a greater degree of domestic tranquillity than he had known for many years —a lull before the storm. In 1795 Hetty married James Marshall, a younger brother of Chief Justice John Marshall, and himself a noted jurist. Robert managed his father's estate at Morrisville, opposite the Falls of the Delaware. Thomas in the meantime attended to his father's property in New York State. These older sons were, consequently, at home only on occasional visits. The two youngest children, Maria, the "darling daughter," and Henry, "the little captain," proved also a blessing to their father.

The two middle sons, William and Charles, were, however, wild, idle, and extravagant. The former, after studying law at the University of Pennsylvania, went abroad with Gouverneur Morris on business connected with his father's property. Like his father's half brother Thomas, William proved untrustworthy, at least in those salad years. He gave no report of his expenditures but made frequent drafts on his father while he remained in Paris. From London, however, he wrote home of his enjoyment of the theatre, especially *Macbeth* at the new Drury Lane. On his return from Europe William redeemed himself by trying to straighten out his father's accounts and by assisting him in every possible way. Charles, the black sheep of the family, also attended the University of Pennsylvania and later was apprenticed to a Philadelphia firm, Nicklin & Com-

pany, where he seemed an utter misfit. Thereupon his father placed
him in his own counting house, the position in which he himself
had started his mercantile career. There he gave him courses in
reading, writing, and bookkeeping, so that he might become a useful member of society. Charles, however, had no mercantile ability
or interest; he was a "throwback" to an earlier generation, that of
his great-grandfather, Andrew Morris, "saylor." The sea was in his
blood. Unhappy years passed, unfortunately, before that atavistic
tendency was discovered. In the meantime he caused his father and
mother many heartaches. Disliking routine, he left home, wander-
ing through New York and Pennsylvania, lodging now with Thomas
in the Genesee Country, now with Robert at Morrisville. His father,
usually patient and indulgent, threatened not to do anything more
for him until he made "submission and amendment." On the whole,
however, Morris lived contentedly with his family and his host of
friends.

At last the era of social brilliance in Philadelphia approached an
end with Washington's last levee and farewell dinner. On a gloomy
day in March, 1797, a few days before Adams's inauguration, President Washington stood between the windows in his back drawing
room to receive his guests. The company, entering a front room,
passed through a wide door and bowed in stately fashion to the President. The ceremony was somewhat like a royal presentation. Washington, as usual, was grave, courteous, reserved. He did not extend
his hand to the guests but merely bowed, according to the custom of
the times. But when the President saw Morris enter, he advanced to
meet him and shook hands with him most cordially. As Robert Morris grasped the hand of his Chief, he repeated the appropriate lines:

> "The day is overcast, the morning lowers,
> And heavily in clouds brings on the day—
> The great, the important day."

At the farewell dinner on March third, the guests with difficulty
controlled their feelings. Bishop White, who was present on that
occasion, wrote this account of the event:

"During the dinner much hilarity prevailed, but on the removal of the cloth it was put an end to by the President, certainly without design. Having filled his glass, he addressed the company with a smile on his countenance, saying, 'Ladies and gentlemen, this is the last time I shall drink your health as a public man; I do it with sincerity, wishing you all possible happiness.' There was an end to all pleasantry, and there was not a dry eye among the company." After the dinner Washington presented Robert and Mary Morris with a small profile portrait of himself with his compliments.

This banquet marked not only the termination of Washington's public career but that of Morris's as well. Here ended the glorious chapter of the Financier's services to his country, ushered in by the banquet on St. George's Day, when he had dedicated himself and all that he possessed to his country, and extending through years of the most arduous labor to keep the "money machine a-going" and thus help establish the United States of America. Here began the last sad chapter of financial ruin, when his country requited those services by ignominy and neglect.

CHAPTER XIV

MILLIONS OF ACRES

❖   ❖   ❖

WHILE he was Superintendent of Finance, Robert Morris seemed guided by a special Providence. Now, as in a Greek tragedy, an evil Fate appeared to direct his life. The first warning came from abroad with the news of bank failures in London and Dublin, in which he lost over $600,000. This loss, which might have been less serious at another period in his career, was tragic at this time when he had become involved in enormous land purchases. Wishing to recoup these losses and to provide handsomely for his family, he plunged into ever greater real estate ventures. Some critics have suggested that a degeneration or disintegration of character was responsible for the calamities that overtook Robert Morris—the ruin that was slowly engulfing him. There is no evidence to support this theory—no sign of a diametric change in his character or personality. His land speculations, the chief factor in the collapse of his fortune, resulted from a thoroughly natural group of reactions. In his office as Financier he had been accustomed to gigantic enterprises, stupendous financial operations. Every negotiation was on a grand scale. The Financier was ever the giant, never the pigmy, thinking in millions when other men thought in hundreds or in single units. He was forced to "play the market," to deal in "futures." Such methods were imperative to save the tottering finances of the United States, and because they succeeded, he was hailed as the "Great Financier of the Revolution." Now in applying these same tactics to his own affairs, he gambled and lost, owing to many unforeseen circumstances.

His sanguine nature, his sunny optimism which had cheered an entire nation through the darkest days of the war, misguided his own good judgment and led him into extravagant land speculations. His active, exuberant imagination directed his vision beyond the present to a distant future. He saw the United States as a "land of promise flowing with milk and honey." His unbounded faith in America, which had infected even the courts of Europe and opened their coffers, made him risk all that he possessed. Opportunities in the new nation loomed large before him—opportunities which would not exist in reality for many decades. He, the supersalesman who had sold the greatness of America to European nations, ended by selling the idea to himself. Here were hundreds of millions of fertile acres, countless virgin forests, for which there would naturally be a great demand. The inhabitants of European countries, cramped within narrow boundaries and bound down by harsh laws, would welcome the opportunity of purchasing fertile fields in a free new land. Moreover, the rapidly growing population in America would demand room for expansion. So Robert Morris reasoned. His faith made him willing to hazard his fortune. He ventured and lost, but had he won, the world would have acclaimed his foresight. His greatest error was his belief that this expansion would come quickly. His enthusiasm, leaping over obstacles of reconstruction and financial stringency after the war, pictured the tides of immigration and westward movement that would not eventuate for half a century. That is the penalty of enthusiasm: it is blind to the guarded actions of the cautious or the pessimistic.

Coupled with this ardent faith in the development of the United States was a powerful, courageous self-confidence—not a belief in his destiny or in his own ability or his wealth, but rather in the integrity of his character and the honesty of his motives, combined with a dogged determination that these qualities should win. He had always a naive faith in the doctrine that "right makes might." The Americans must win the Revolution because their cause was just. Land must sell because it offered golden opportunities to the oppressed. Thus it seems evident that Robert Morris's real estate speculations resulted from his imagination, his optimism, his faith in

America and in the victory of the right. Had he not become involved with others, however, his magnificent fortune might not have been wrecked even by his stupendous purchases.

His early real estate ventures were highly successful. There was every reason to anticipate greater profits. His imagination soared. "The country is rushing into wealth and importance faster than was ever expected by the most sanguine of the sanguinous," he exclaimed enthusiastically. He spoke of the land purchased for $50 per one hundred acres, which sold for $200 per acre. The first large purchase Morris had made even before the Revolution—three thousand acres in Louisiana, which he bought for the proverbial "song" and abandoned during the war. He foresaw rapid development of the country, especially the South, and expected values to double and treble quickly. When he visited George Washington at Mount Vernon on his way to inspect land in Virginia, the general tried to dissuade him from making large purchases. As a landowner Washington knew the dangers of becoming "land poor." When he remonstrated with Morris, the latter replied, "I must either be a man or a mouse." It is unfortunate that he did not heed his own precept: "All earthly things have some limits which it is imprudent to exceed, others which it is dangerous to exceed and some which can never be exceeded." Perhaps, to his subsequent regret, he thought real estate belonged in the last category.

By 1790 the era of unrestricted land speculation had begun for Robert Morris. In 1794 he severed his connection with the firm of Willing & Morris, selling his interest to his former clerk, John Swanwick. Thomas Willing, always cautious, had tried to curb his partner's exuberant real estate ventures and failing, suggested his withdrawing from the firm as Willing did not wish to become involved in such a precarious business. With the severing of these ties, all restraint was ended. Robert Morris soon became the largest private property owner in the United States of that period, or, perhaps, of any period in its history. He owned or held a controlling interest in six million acres in Pennsylvania, Virginia, North Carolina, South Carolina, Kentucky, and Georgia, and later acquired several million acres in New York State—all this in addition to his homes and private estates.

With John Nicholson, at one time Comptroller General of Pennsylvania, and James Greenleaf, former consul of the United States at Amsterdam, he organized the North American Land Company, with a capital stock of three million dollars, 30,000 shares to sell at $100 a share. The members were pledged not to sell for less. The land titles were vested in Thomas Willing, President of the Bank of the United States; John Nixon, President of the Bank of North America; and John Barclay, President of the Bank of Pennsylvania. Offices were opened for subscriptions in Philadelphia and New York. The leading men in the United States were invited to become stockholders. All the sales machinery was in smooth running order. But Morris's fortune was tottering. As early as 1787 his bills were protested. The trustees, realizing this fact, refused to serve, whereupon Morris visited them and persuaded all except Willing. (Partners and wives are proverbially obdurate.) The most unfortunate circumstance of all, however, was the formation of his partnership with Nicholson and Greenleaf. After calamities had befallen him, Robert Morris admitted that this association was a serious error of judgment on his part. To the firm of Wilhem and Jan Willink of Amsterdam he confided: "My difficulties have been brought on by an unfortunate connection by which I was led into speculations too deep and extensive." Greenleaf, it seems, had promised to interest capital in the Netherlands—had virtually sworn that he would sell a large number of shares. It was upon this promise that Robert Morris had counted.

In his *Private Letter Book* for the year 1795, hope seems to alternate with despair. "Lands are everywhere rising in value," he wrote; and again two months later, "Lands are daily rising in value throughout America, and immense fortunes are made by those who purchased early." On the other hand, he spoke of his vexations and repeated disappointments, but even in such complaints there was usually a note of optimism. Resourcefully he laid his plans for the effective relief of all his wants.

The North American Land Company was such a plan, designed to promote the public good as well as private profit. The lands were to be sold to actual settlers upon easy terms of annual payments with interest. Large tracts of uncultivated lands would thus be improved, and the natural strength and wealth of the country increased. The Board of Managers were men of "the first character and abilities," with a secretary "bred to the law." The lands were to sell first at half a dollar an acre, the price later to be increased to two or three dollars an acre. The plan for each community showed forethought and real interest in the settlers. A surveyor-manager was to build farmhouses and barns, and to lay out a town in the vicinity of each farm, in order to attract mechanics. This desirable property was to be advertised throughout the United States and Europe. Robert Morris confidentially expected an enthusiastic response since the population of the country was increasing so rapidly. Moreover, a plan similar to this, which Morris had chalked out for Captain Williamson in New York State, had proved a brilliant success.

Robert Morris, optimistic promoter of the project, believed that the North American Land Company should be even more successful. He felt assured that shareholders would receive not merely ordinary six per cent dividends but in the course of fifteen years, at least four times, probably ten times the original investment. The shares, one hundred dollars at first, should be doubled or trebled in two or three years, Morris thought. He had complete confidence in all his property. The southern lands he considered of more intrinsic worth than even the valuable Pennsylvania property, the acres in Georgia being mentioned as especially fertile.

In order to sell stock or land and raise money for his real estate projects, Robert Morris sent to Europe Gouverneur Morris, and his sons, Robert and William, and later his son-in-law, James Marshall, and Hetty, who sailed on the ship *Pennsylvania* in October, 1795. For weeks Morris made preparations for the Marshalls' favorable reception in London, Paris, and elsewhere on the continent. He was particularly concerned about Hetty's happiness and comfort since she was pregnant. He wrote Mr. Church in England recommending Hetty to his wife's care, saying that she expected to land at Falmouth. Another letter recommended the Marshalls to Richard Penn. Soon after their departure, Morris sent Marshall a letter expressing his desire to borrow $60,000 to $80,000 or $100,000 upon security of his estate "The Hills." He wished also to sell Morrisville for $300,-000 or to borrow $200,000, using that estate as security. Over six thousand shares in the North American Land Company had been committed to Marshall's care on his departure.

Despite all his efforts and his resourcefulness, financial troubles swarmed upon Robert Morris. On April 16, 1795, the Bank of North America threatened to bring suit against him unless "paper lying in the bank" was paid. Morris replied immediately: "Disappointments have put it out of my power to pay punctually." He could not refrain from suggesting that "in other countries banks generally give aid to those who have property instead of increasing their difficulties." At the same time he was disappointed with regard to money expected from Europe. A loan on the point of being consummated in Holland was stopped by the French invasion. Thus the fates seemed aligned against Robert Morris.

It became increasingly difficult to borrow money. He felt himself wrestling with endless embarrassments and perplexities. "I do assure you," he wrote William Constable, "my only desire now is to get out of debt, settle accounts with everybody and quit work. These are to be sure dreadful times for a man to be in want of money. I know too well what it is. . . . I am obliged to sustain the whole weight of the payments from which I was promised total relief." (This was no doubt a reference to the facile promises of James Greenleaf.) To William Temple Franklin, his agent in England, he made this statement: "When my existing engagements are satisfied, . . . I mean to retire from all dealings in future that require credit." Yet he still felt hopeful of fulfilling his engagements; he could not wholly despair, realizing the vast extent of his domain. "My property is so extensive," he said, "that it cannot fail to carry me through, and all I want is a little time. . . . I expect before long to come forth in triumph."

There was, however, he was well aware, an apparent scarcity of money. This he felt was not a real lack, the truth being that there was a great influx of wealth. Of course there existed the greatest source of wealth in the world—the land, wide-spreading, fertile acres. In the value of this property Robert Morris believed wholeheartedly. Of course he knew that commercial men, himself among them, had made commitments beyond their capital and that speculators had exceeded proper bounds, but the real worth of the land remained.

Again he was attacked, groundlessly, needlessly. Envious and malicious persons circulated lies concerning the North American Land Company, in England, France, and the United States. His reputation was assailed by the French Minister, Fouchet, who based his attack upon a letter from Jonas Faucher, a blackguard Frenchman, who kept a tippling-house in Georgia and was not even acquainted with Robert Morris. This cowardly literary assault appeared in a French gazette, *Feuille de la Republique.* Upon reading the letter, Robert Morris insisted that his answer be published in the same magazine in which the original had appeared. As "an American citizen publicly traduced," he wished "justice done." He always endeavored to meet his enemies face to face, and in a manly, stalwart fashion confronted his assailants, thus attempting to silence their "croakings and reproaches." In this instance, the French Minister finally apologized, but not before the Land Company had suffered infinite harm.

Although he could not borrow on his holdings, Morris continued to purchase land in all unsettled parts of the Union, sometimes buying it for as little as fifty or even twenty-five cents an acre. He felt utterly confident that the land was valuable and that consequently he would eventually recover his losses and make a handsome profit. He refused to read the handwriting on the wall.

The greatest purchase, one that Morris felt would have made his fortune had he confined his interest to that alone, was the purchase of several million acres in the Genessee country in the western half of New York State, a section to which Massachusetts laid claim. On November 15, 1790, he bought a million and a quarter acres from Gorham and Phelps. The next year he sold the largest part of this tract to an Englishman, Sir William Pulteney, who appointed Captain Charles Williamson as his general agent. Robert Morris assisted Williamson in his plans for reselling and settling this territory—plans which were most successfully carried out and netted the owner a handsome profit. During this time Morris also became interested in promoting the Erie Canal project.

Delighted with the success of his first real estate venture in this section, he purchased several thousand additional acres in the Genesee country. Morris needed little encouragement to stimulate his imagination and arouse his optimism. In four separate deeds he conveyed four tracts of almost a million acres each to certain New Yorkers to hold in trust for firms in Amsterdam, notably the firm of Willink & Company, with whom Morris had dealt during the Revolution. A million and a half acres of this land sold for £112,500 (approximately $562,000), of which he was to receive £75,000 down and the remainder within a few months. This sale was made by Morris, however, before the Indian title was extinguished and was contingent upon the purchasers' securing a clear title to the land.

In order to carry out a favorite project of his own, Morris retained 500,000 acres, the Holland Reserve. Here he planned to establish a farm and town development, a haven for the Continental soldiers who had little money and no homes. His real estate ventures, like his mercantile business, were not wholly selfish but rather a means toward an end—an altruistic goal of improved conditions for mankind. According to his plan, farms were to be sold and settled and towns established, each community as far as possible to prove self-supporting. The purchase price of the land Morris wished to reduce to a minimum, and the cost of the houses and other improvements to be carried like a mortgage and paid for over a term of years. Here was the prototype of Federal Housing developments. As a first step toward the achievement of his purpose, Batavia in this tract was founded and named. "The founding of Batavia," states J. M. Kennedy in *Robert Morris and the Holland Purchase*, "was the last act in the great private tragedy by which the Revolutionary War was saved."

In order to sell these homesteads and consummate the Holland Purchase, a treaty must be signed with the Seneca Indians so that a clear title might be obtained. While this territory was being explored and surveyed by James Ellicott, Adam Hoops, Augustus Porter, and a surveying party, the Indians who held certain rights to the land became displeased and came to present their grievances to Robert Morris. They relied as did so many others upon his sense of justice and his innate sympathy and kindliness. With the adroitness and tact born of a kind heart and a democratic spirit, Morris treated them like princes.

One day a majestic figure wrapped in a gayly colored blanket, and wearing a sheaf of eagle feathers, alighted from the Morris coach and strode up the steps of the Morris mansion. This was Cornplanter, a chieftain of the Senecas, more intelligent and cooperative than some of the others. Morris, who had requested this visit, welcomed him with due ceremony and entertained him handsomely with drives around the city and out to "The Hills" and at dinners more sumptuous than usual. After a number of days Morris began to discuss business with him, through the interpreter he had brought with him. Tactfully Morris urged him to use his influence, a gift of the Great Spirit, to persuade his brother chieftains to sell their lands for cash or for annuities kept in trust for them always by the Great White Father in Washington. Cornplanter at first, with typical Indian reserve, maintained a haughty silence, but gradually succumbed to Morris's graciousness and tact. When Robert Morris sent him back to New York, laden with gifts for his people, himself, and his family, Cornplanter had promised to try to persuade the other chiefs to sell the Indian lands.

Morris sent his son Thomas to the Genesee country to attend to his affairs there. With him Robert Morris carried on an extensive correspondence, placing in him more and more confidence and giving him an increasing degree of power. He explained to his son that his primary consideration was not merely his own purchases but the welfare and contentment of the Indians. "I would sooner relinquish the bargain," he told Thomas, "than create any disturbance with the Indians; nothing less than that should induce me to give it up." As soon as the British had delivered up their posts, which they were dilatory in abandoning, Morris planned to hold a council with the

Indian chiefs, Red Jacket, Little Billy, Cornplanter, Hotbread, and others. He made application to Congress for permission to hold the conference at Buffalo Creek, the place of meeting Thomas had suggested. Although he had expected opposition from some unknown source, none was forthcoming. As far as the United States was concerned, his plans progressed smoothly. Jeremiah Wadsworth was appointed Commissioner for the United States to hold the treaty with the Senecas and William Shepherd, agent for Massachusetts. But all the tact and ingenuity of Morris and his son were required to put and keep the Indians in the humor to sell. Thomas was adjured not to tell Red Jacket and Little Billy of his father's conversations with Cornplanter, nor must the latter learn of Thomas Morris's talks with the others.

In August, 1797, Morris sent his power of attorney to Thomas and Captain Williamson for the purchase of the tract bounded on the east by the Genesee River and the boundary line of Gorham and Phelps Purchase, at the south by the northern boundary line of Pennsylvania, on the west by Lake Erie, and on the north by Lake Ontario. Robert Morris sent most explicit directions concerning the arrangements for this treaty. Jones, Smith, and Johnson of Niagara were to act as interpreters. The entire meeting should be conducted on the principle of "liberal economy." Liquor, which often caused trouble with the Indians, was to be paraded before them but withheld until the treaty was signed. Annuities, if possible, were to be arranged for the chiefs, to be scaled down depending upon the amount of land delivered. The Indians should be advised, Morris thought, to choose an annuity consisting of bank stock for the use of the Seneca Nation, dividends to be paid their representatives annually. They were to remain free, however, to choose a cash payment if they preferred. The main point was to induce them to sell. As an extra inducement, the kind they understood best, Robert Morris sent $6,000 for provisions, liquor, and trinkets for the Treaty to be held the last of August, 1797.

Although he knew the Indians would demand his presence at the Great Council, Morris felt unable to go as he was not well and had many obligations and business complications to hold him in Philadelphia. He realized, moreover, that the matter rested in capable hands, for Thomas had shown exceptional tact, resourcefulness, and courage, traveling unarmed by foot without a guard from Canandaigua to Niagara, visiting all the chiefs of the Senecas. By the messenger who carried his power of attorney, Morris sent also a speech to be delivered to the Indians at the conference. "Brothers of the Seneca Nation," the speech began, "it was my wish and my intention to have come into your country and to have met you at this treaty, but the Great Spirit has ordained otherwise and I cannot go. I grow old, am corpulent and not very well—am fearful of travelling so far during the hot weather in the month of August." With diplomatic skill he assured them that, although he possessed the right to buy the property, they only had the right to sell. He had heard that they were willing to sell. This seemed a wise decision on their part since the whites were settling around them and thus the land would probably be of less value to them than an annuity, which would be theirs forever. "I bid you farewell," the speech concluded. "May the Great Spirit ever befriend and protect you." Circumstances prevented this message from being delivered at the Council.

In the meantime Thomas had made all the arrangements for the Treaty. Thirteen to fifteen hundred rations of beef were provided with mutton and pork enough for thirty days. Large stores of rum, whiskey, and tobacco were purchased and all kinds of baubles for the women and children. Tench Francis, so successful in conducting other financial operations, made the purchases. Two large wagons were sent from Philadelphia loaded with wines, porter, tobacco, pipes, gaudy cloths, trinkets, and showy gifts of various kinds. At Wilkes Barre the goods were carried by boat to Tioga Point, where they were reloaded on wagons and taken to the shores of Lake Geneva to the home of Thomas Morris.

On August 20 the Council was scheduled to begin, but all the Indians had not yet arrived. On August 22, however, twelve hundred Senecas had gathered at Genesee on the Genesee River. Daily more arrived and still others were expected. A council house had been erected according to Robert Morris's instructions—an enormous tent covered with green boughs, containing seats and a platform.

For many days the Indians, clad in their finest blankets and bedecked with their gayest feathers, rode in on their favorite horses. With them on horseback or on foot came the squaws with papooses on their backs. It was customary to have a revel and frolic for a week before a council, during which time the savages became dissipated and engaged in brawls. It was in an effort to avoid this, that Morris stipulated that the liquor should not be distributed until after the conference had been held and the deeds signed. All might have been well had there not arrived with the Indians the ubiquitous frontier traders, who carried on a thriving business during the two weeks of the council. Some of the Indians, among others Red Jacket, got hold of a barrel of whiskey sold by these traders and became drunk, disorderly, and boisterous. All treaty proceedings had to be postponed until they had time to sober up. Again Thomas Morris's patience, courage, tact, and resourcefulness were severely tested and not found wanting. He proved to be the son of his father carrying out a commission faithfully and efficiently.

Two weeks of fruitless debate were enough to tax the patience of any man. Cornplanter, Red Jacket, Little Billy, Little Beard, and other chiefs wrapped their blankets around them in stubborn silence. They wished to treat with Robert Morris in person. He was the only one they were willing to trust. With dissatisfied grunts they prepared to leave for the forest. All Thomas's diplomatic skill was needed to persuade them to return. By gentle words and the offer of food and drink, by proposing annuities to some, to others cash gifts, he finally brought them back and induced them to sell their lands for $100,000. The money for the purchase of these Indian rights was derived from a fund, £37,500, reserved to Robert Morris by the Holland Company and placed in the hands of a New York firm, Messrs. LeRoy and Bayard. Thus despite his financial difficulties, although he had not a dollar to meet his own needs or the demands of his creditors, Morris was able to transfer to the name of the President of the United States as Trustee of the Senecas, the sum of $100,000.

But his troubles with the Indians did not end there. The chiefs were not wholly satisfied. Rivalries and jealousies had sprung up among them. As late as November of that year, Hotbread, one of the chieftains who felt himself neglected, complained to Thomas that he was the first to propose the Treaty, yet he had received nothing for himself, whereas Red Jacket, although he had opposed the Treaty and had caused trouble, received $600. Other chiefs continued to plague Thomas, who tried to satisfy them with money, gifts, and soft words. Red Jacket, appropriately named, swaggered and boasted of his actions and his money, arousing envy and ill will.

Thus was consummated the purchases of lands in the Genesee country, Robert Morris's most successful real estate transaction of that troubled era of speculation. A century later, on October 13, 1894, the Holland Purchase Land Office was dedicated to his memory, the only official shrine to Robert Morris in the United States.

CHAPTER XV

ROOFLESS CASTLES IN SPAIN

❖   ❖   ❖

LIKE a man running with a smile on his face to meet his doom, Morris continued his purchase of land. Not content with his vast real estate holdings all over the country, he invested in lots in the Federal City (Washington), feeling assured that they would soon become much more valuable since the capital was located there. This might have proved a profitable venture had Morris confined his attention to these purchases and, above all, had he remained free from "entangling alliances." But unfortunately he had already formed the partnership with John Nicholson and James Greenleaf, who proved his nemesis. With them he bought at first six thousand building lots in Washington and later twelve hundred more, on some of which they began building operations, forty or fifty houses, according to some accounts. Most unhappily the early negotiations were left to James Greenleaf, who showed himself thoroughly unreliable, if not actually dishonest. Consequently for many years afterward the partners suffered embarrassments with regard to titles to the property and payments to the Commissioners; in fact, annoyances of every sort.

Morris did not make this investment blindly. He investigated property before making a purchase. Unlike gullible modern real estate speculators, he did not buy Florida lots under water or part of the California desert. On September 2, 1796, he left for a ten weeks' trip to Washington, where he made his headquarters at a hotel near the President's mansion. He praised Major L'Enfant's taste and judgment in planning the City of Washington, with its spacious avenues and extensive vistas. The Commissioners should not have parted with the Major's services, Morris thought, but should have paid due honor to his genius. It would undoubtedly have been better for Robert Morris had L'Enfant remained in Washington engaged upon Federal projects. Morris was full of enthusiasm. Property here was of more value than he dared contemplate. His letters sounded at times like real estate advertisements. Lots that had cost $160 were now selling for more than $1,000. He mentioned two Washington lots that had sold for more than $4,000 each. "Washington building lots," he prophesied, "will continue rising in price for one hundred years to come." He deplored restrictions placed upon building in the city, yet he admired the fine edifices resulting from those restrictions. The opening of canal navigation from the Great Falls of the Potomac to Georgetown, a project which should be completed in twelve to fifteen months, would, he felt sure, introduce to Georgetown and Washington an immense quantity of produce and convert them both into commercial centers.

Robert Morris was especially delighted with the "genteel families and easy polite manners" of the residents of the Capital City and felt that, if he were younger, he would prefer living in Washington to residing in Philadelphia. He told Molly of the crowds that had gathered to see the races—a social event that impeded his business. Of course he went to Mount Vernon to call on Washington and visited other friends in the capital. With regard to the public buildings being erected in the city, he feared that the President's house would lose by "the parsimonious conduct of Congress," but thought that the Capitol gave promise of becoming "a grand and beautiful edifice."

In swift succession came a series of misfortunes. Morris and his partners had trouble completing the titles to their lots. Greenleaf "applied to his own use" $7,000 which Morris had given him to pay the Commissioners of the Federal City. As soon as he discovered his partner's perfidy, Morris wrote him: "I must request that they [the Commissioners] be made acquainted that the delinquency does not arise on my part." Greenleaf's bills descended upon Morris, and to a slighter degree upon Nicholson, who wrestled with constant dis-appointments and annoyances. "The return of all Mr. Greenleaf's bills falls heavy on us," Robert Morris wrote his friend, Benjamin Harrison. " 'Twas he that encouraged the very extensive land pur-chases which we made under a promise that he would procure in Holland the money necessary to support the same without depend-ing on resales." Every day brought fresh discoveries of Greenleaf's dereliction and treachery. The latter had not settled financial matters with Alexander Hamilton, Secretary of the Treasury—negotiations which his partners had entrusted to him. In order to meet obliga-tions which he himself had not assumed, Morris, who had never ex-acted usury, was now forced to pay it. "The blood hounds want food," he exclaimed.

From the Union Tavern in Georgetown, at the beginning of his trip homeward in November, 1796, he wrote whimsically to John Nicholson: "Various and numerous are the tales against not only John but Robert—knowest thou these men? May truth prevail, and Robert and John obtain the voice that impartial justice ought to be-stow."

The entire journey back to Philadelphia was marked by unfor-tunate adventures, which he recounted in a letter to Nicholson on November 20, the day after his arrival. On the trip he reached Frederick, Maryland, at 5:30 P.M., just as it began to rain. After it had cleared, he continued to Baltimore. As he was "cantering pretty fast," his horse slipped and laid him sprawling. As Morris described the accident: "The horse's forefeet came on some tottering stones, which rolled from under them and brought him down on all fours. I flew over his head and hurt myself a good deal. The carriage was gone before I was obliged to mount again." The cork had come out of a phial in his pocket when he fell and spilt the liquor which might have revived him. He reached the Black Horse Inn at 7:30 P.M., passed the evening pleasantly with Colonel Bartley, and left the next morning at 5 o'clock with a cold wind blowing. "At the Ferry," his letter continued, "I had like to have met with trouble. The land-lord had lately taken his passage across the Styx, and the men he had left behind swore they would not cross the Susquehanna in such a high wind—lest the waters of the latter might bring them to seek also a passage across the other river; however a good breakfast, a good drink, and a hard dollar brought them to." Morris landed half starved in Columbia at noon. There he bought a Susquehanna salmon which he took to Mrs. Hough's "where it was soon made palatable." After dinner he "pushed off" and reached Mr. Pettit's on the hill, forty-three miles from Philadelphia, where he spent the night. Early next morning he breakfasted at Downing's Town. After traveling until noon and eating a solitary dinner at the Buck Tavern, he set off again and "made a triumphal entry into this city at between 5 and 6 o'clock to the great joy of some and the vexation of others," his letter announced, "for I really came in the nick of time to defeat malevolent designs that had been formed against you and me."

There were those in Philadelphia who had wagered that he would not return, that he had gone to Washington to escape his creditors. They were evidently the ones who were "vexed" at his return. Upon his arrival he found a sheriff at the door—a shadow that never lifted from that moment until prison walls enclosed him.

After sending Mrs. Nicholson letters which he had brought with him from Washington and the horse and carriage that he had evidently borrowed from Nicholson, he called on her to give her first-hand news of her husband. Such thoughtful courtesies as these made Robert Morris popular with both men and women.

One of the problems facing Morris upon his return to Philadelphia was that of the completion of his new dream palace. Somewhat earlier than this, in the momentous year 1795 when he had quit public life, he had purchased an entire block in Philadelphia, between Seventh and Eighth and Chestnut and Walnut streets. This lot was originally Norris's pasture field. There Robert Morris was building a magnificent mansion. He had planned merely a large, comfortable home in which to enjoy his old age. All might have gone well had he himself supervised the construction of the house, for his tastes were elegant but simple. Moreover his realization of financial stringency would presumably have prevented him from lavish expenditures. He had made the error, however, of engaging the services of Major L'Enfant, the architect, to plan and superintend the erection of the mansion. Unfortunately he gave him free rein. L'Enfant's imagination, always exuberant, rioted in marble walls, bas reliefs, luxurious chambers, and spacious lawns. He planned a princely palace of marble, the most magnificent house in America. This was not Morris's original intention, but since L'Enfant assured him that the total cost would not exceed $60,000, he did not demur. Perhaps his imagination also was captivated by the picture the architect so graphically presented. Morris was, moreover, too busy with other ventures to attend to details. These he left to the Major, trusting in his judgment and willing to indulge his genius.

In the meantime Robert Morris had ordered furniture from Europe: handsome chairs and sofas from Paris, mirrors valued at $25,000, classic statuary for drawing room, halls, and garden. The luxurious furnishings and art objects arrived, but the mansion was still unfinished. The construction was prolonged from year to year until at last Morris's patience was exhausted. Three stories were built under ground, with arches, vaults, and labyrinthine passages in which many persons were lost, and which were so strongly constructed that they could not be demolished with the rest of the house. More and more money was demanded for the marble palace, many times the sum originally named. Yet the house remained unroofed, with marble extending only half way up the walls. It resembled a ruin rather than a new, unfinished mansion. Snow, rain, and sun spotted and streaked the walls; soot blackened the marble. The crowds who came to gaze at this magnificent ruin laughingly called it "Morris's Folly." Robert Morris himself was the first to admit that it had been a foolish project at this phase of his life and that he had made an error in leaving the supervision to Major L'Enfant. Once more he had been misled by an opulent imagination and by his blind trust in human nature, especially in specious promises.

Some of the amused spectators did not even admire the architect's elaborate plan, but thought it all in bad taste. Another architect of that period, Benjamin Henry Latrobe, thus describes the house in his *Journal:* "I suppose the front must be at least 20 feet long, and I think the flank cannot be less than sixty. . . . The windows, at least some of them—are cased in with marble with moldings, entablatures, architraves, and sculpture mixed up in the oddest and most inelegant manner imaginable; all the proportions are bad, all the horizontal and perpendicular lines broken to pieces. . . . There is a recess, across which a colonnade of one story columns was intended, the two lateral ones being put up, with a piece of their architrave reaching to the wall; I cannot guess what was intended above them. . . . The angle porches are irresistibly laughable things, and violently ugly."

At each corner of the house were the portico doorways supported by two marble columns. Handsome bas reliefs by Jardella, the Italian sculptor who had recently moved to Philadelphia, decorated the windows and doorways with sculptured festoons of flowers. Semi-circular tablets represented Tragedy and Comedy, somewhat symbolic of this marble palace, "Morris's Folly," so tragic to the owner, so amusing to others.

Finally when two stories had been built, no more marble could be secured. In despair Morris wrote the architect to finish the house in brick and roof it over as best he could, at least one wing, as the interior was exposed to the elements and the walls were already marred. Major L'Enfant had promised him that the house would be roofed by the fall of 1795. In September of that year Morris had written him: "I do not wish you to sacrifice anything to or for me, but if I am to pay, I am entitled to every information I may think proper to ask, and I have an unquestionable right to expedite my building and lessen my expense if I choose so to do." For the artistic, temperamental Major had evidently resented his employer's questions and suggestions. The letter after stating that he, Morris, had had no intention of using so much marble, continued: "An inclination to indulge your genius induced me to permit so much of it before I knew the extent to which you meant to carry it. Had you executed my intentions instead of your own, my family would now have inhabited the house instead of being liable to be turned out of doors."

In the meantime Morris had sold his High Street homes in the expectation of moving into his new mansion. While the house was under construction, he rented a residence between those of Thomas Fitzsimons and John Dickinson, just across the street from his marble palace, at an annual rental of $1,000. From this vantage point he could look daily at "Morris's Folly" and vent imprecations on himself and the architect, who had proved truly *L'Enfant terrible*. "I am being chastised for my folly," Morris exclaimed. He had already expended several times as much as he had been told it would cost, yet not a single floor was laid or wall plastered. A roof of sheet iron finally covered one wing. The mansion, his dream castle, which should have been finished in 1795, was still in 1797 and 1798 merely a pile of walls, with all work at a standstill.

Now his funds were exhausted. When the building was started, he had expected to receive £75,000. The London bank failure had involved him for almost twice that amount. Caustically Morris wrote his architect about the tearing down of last fall's work to put on more marble, "of which there is already vastly too much." Frequently he sounded the same refrain: "The delay and accumulation of expense becomes intolerable"; and he pled for "economy and dispatch."

This ruined mansion was not the only roofless building that belonged to Robert Morris. In what came to be known as "Morris Village" in Washington, on South Capitol Street, between M and N, were ten brick houses, unfinished and exposed to the elements. The site of these houses, now an undesirable section of the city, must once have seemed the choicest location in Washington—on Capitol Hill, close to the river. This was another of Morris's dream projects. He had planned well for his tenants but less wisely for himself. The substantial brick houses, set back from the street, had long strips of lawn extending to the sidewalk—really spacious lawns for a city. Unfortunately funds were exhausted before the houses were completed, and for years the roofless buildings gaped grotesquely at the sky.

Some time before this, Robert Morris and John Nicholson, wishing to rid themselves of the incubus of an untrustworthy partner who had brought disgrace upon them, bought Greenleaf's share in the North American Land Company and in the Washington property. William Lovering and William Cranch, the architect, both of whom lived in Washington, were put in charge of their real estate in that city. Morris feared that since the Commissioners' terms had not been met, they might advertise and sell the property. This, he considered, would be a great calamity for Washington City as well as for Morris and Nicholson, for he believed that the interest of the city and theirs were the same; one could not be promoted without promoting the other. He concluded that he and Nicholson must be in perfect agreement in their policies. The Commissioners, holding Robert Morris responsible for all outstanding obligations of his partners as well as himself, applied to George Washington to urge Morris to pay his debts. The latter replied that he was mortified at being in arrears. The loan mentioned in the President's account, he stated, was James Greenleaf's obligation. He assured Washington that he would send remittances until his part of the arrears, $15,000, was discharged.

In desperate need of money, Morris disposed of most of his shares in the North American Land Company. He had sold his shares in the Asylum Company to John Nicholson in 1795, but he still retained valuable real estate in Pennsylvania, with which in 1787 he organized the Pennsylvania Property Company, with a capital of $1,000,000— ten thousand shares at $100 a share. On March 18, 1797, Robert and Mary Morris signed a deed conveying to this company several hundred thousand acres, valued at more than a million dollars. This sale comprised "The Hills," with its "large and elegant greenhouse" and hothouse, its stone and brick farmhouses, its gardens and orchards, as well as the mansion itself; the Trout Spring estate on the Schuylkill; and "Morrisville" or the "Delaware Works" at the Falls of the Delaware, opposite Trenton—a really vast estate, comprising fourteen farms, a large brick house with "a charming view of the River Delaware," a stone barn and other outhouses; on an island in the river a grist mill, a rolling mill, a saw mill and several houses, and in the town of Morrisville, thirty-nine houses. The Upper Ferry and the Trenton Ferry also formed part of this last large estate. There were, however, mortgages amounting to several hundred thousand dollars on the property. The shares in the Pennsylvania Property Company were to be offered as security to satisfy Morris's creditors. This organization proved his determination to put up a good, honest fight to protect himself and his creditors from loss.

He tried in vain to borrow money on any terms. Two hundred

dollars was harder to secure than two thousand dollars a few months before. Not merely was he unable to obtain a loan, but he was harassed by "furious Duns, ravenous to madness." He told Nicholson, "The hinges of my Counting House door can not last until Christmas unless I shut it up." Suits followed in swift succession. Creditors tormented him with importunities. The times were hostile. Everybody was financially distressed, almost to frenzy. Distrust was universal, almost no credit being extended except for exorbitant rates of interest. While usury flourished, legitimate business drooped and pined away. "Who in God's name has all the money," Morris queried, "for everybody seems to want?" No more land could be mortgaged or sold at any price. Consequently the North American Land Company could not raise any money on its millions of acres. Taxes could not be paid. Banks refused to discount notes of the former Financier. The Bank of Pennsylvania, the Bank of North America, the Bank of the United States, all institutions which he had helped to found, brought suit against him. The Bank of Philadelphia obtained judgment against him for $20,997.40. Messrs. Wilhem and Jan Willink of Amsterdam held a £7,000 mortgage on his property. Creditors by the thousands became clamorous. Robert Morris, harassed and molested wherever he went, stayed away from public places or amusements. For the first time in his life he had no wish to mingle in society, but only to pay his debts and retire.

The machinations of the handsome, unscrupulous James Greenleaf still distressed Morris and prevented him from transacting business. This arch-villain of the tragedy, among other villainies, prevented his former partner from securing a loan of $50,000. Greenleaf also caused a stoppage of proceedings when Morris and Nicholson had certificates for the Washington lots made out and ready for the signatures of the Commissioners. By delays, evasions, and deceptions, he tried to injure his former partners—their business transactions and their personal reputations. Early in 1797 Robert Morris wrote John Nicholson: "Master Jimmy has opened Pandora's box, and if I am not mistaken much of the mischief will attach to himself. In the meantime he has injured us exceedingly." Greenleaf, moreover, had previously opened credit with the Washington lots as security and Morris unfortunately had endorsed his notes. When Amsterdam did not honor them, the latter had to pay $150,000, which he secured through a loan at a high rate of interest. The arch-villain's suits and bills continued to plague his former partners. Morris summed up the situation in these words: "He [Greenleaf] is the principal cause of all my late embarrassment, and it was the most unfortunate act of my life that I ever had anything to do with him."

The association with John Nicholson was also unfortunate. Although Nicholson was not dishonest or treacherous, his delays, his debts, and other obligations constituted a source of annoyance to his partner. "Do for Heaven's sake finish your business and then, but not till then, come home," Morris implored the partner, who remained in Washington. He reproached Nicholson with not hastening business in the Capital City and with leaving him to face the creditors alone. Lawyers asserted, he told Nicholson, that the latter did not intend to return, and that he (Robert Morris) was tired of putting off creditors with the promise of his coming "next week." Only a few months before this, Morris had written: "Under the severest and most urgent duns I ever met with, I feel an uncommon degree of confidence"; now he expressed himself as "almost faint-hearted." "This world nor anything in it," he told Nicholson, "is worth the plague that you and I have exposed ourselves to."

Nicholson's creditors became even more importunate, their patience exhausted. So was the forbearance of Robert Morris since he had borne the brunt of their solicitations. He said humorously that his partner's counting house would "get the pip" if he did not return to "reanimate it." Still Nicholson tarried in Washington, apparently preferring to let Morris meet the demands and attacks and face the sheriff and the hordes of creditors alone. Morris sent frequent messages urging Nicholson's return. Attachments of the partner's household goods threatened. Thereupon Robert Morris became even more insistent. "If I get under lock and key," he warned Nicholson, "you must then expect a domestic attachment." In the meantime, however, Morris paid some of his partner's creditors to prevent Mrs. Nicholson from losing her furniture. This occurred at a time when his own creditors were hounding him.

Finally he insisted that Nicholson should return at least for a conference. As he did not wish his partner to enter Philadelphia until they had conferred on the situation and their policies, he suggested that Nicholson meet him at the "little villa," Sansom's place outside the city, and that he should order the Negro caretaker to start a fire and send Robert Morris word of his arrival. At this secret rendezvous they should decide on their policies, Morris continued. Still Nicholson lingered in Washington. Finally after Morris had tried to frighten him with domestic attachments and other personal difficulties, the dilatory partner came home in February but returned to the capital in March. Morris remained to be sacrificed.

Only his family brought him the slightest respite from financial perplexities. "A delectable thing" was a visit to Morrisville to visit Robert and his Anna (Ann Shoemaker), "a charming, amiable young woman." Shortly afterwards Robert and Anna came to Germantown, where their son was born on January 28. In June, William, now home from Europe and eager to begin the practice of law, and Maria, the lively, attractive younger daughter, went on a visit to see the baby and his parents. Hetty had given birth to a son on February 6, 1796. She and her husband continued to wander through Europe attempting to sell or mortgage their father's property and sell stock in the North American Land Company, but without results. Persistently for more than three years James Marshall continued his efforts, traveling through England and the continent by boat, by train and coach. Another child was born to them before they returned home. Into the domestic cares and pleasures of his family Robert Morris entered whole-heartedly. He found time also to help other unfortunates. He contributed to the relief of a poor woman's necessities although she had made certain accusations against him and he had no money to meet the constant demands upon him.

"Shades of the prison-house" were beginning to close upon Robert Morris. He felt the earth fluid beneath his feet. Previously he had considered the Genesee country an anchor in the midst of billows of misfortune, but he lost even that consoling confidence. "In the perils and storms of the present day," he wrote Wilhem and Jan Willink, "there is no knowing with certainty what will hold and what give way." To another acquaintance he confided, "I blame myself for having gone so deeply into those speculations, and so do my friends—, but neither their blame nor my own reproaches will take me out of the scrape. This must be done by patience, perseverance and exertion." Although an idealist and an optimist, Morris was also a pragmatist, willing to face his situation realistically and eager to use his ingenuity in extricating himself.

In order to try to save the Washington property, he and Nicholson placed it in the hands of Trustees of the Aggregate Fund, who represented the interests of the creditors. It was in their power by selling or mortgaging lots to arrange for effective security and to pay the debts for which the property had been attached. Of course he hoped that such a sale would not merely save the property itself but leave a surplus for the partners, who needed money so desperately. To the Trustees he sent the admonition: "Do not run the hazard of disappointing your constituents or us, but entitle yourselves to the credit that will result from a faithful and liberal conduct in the management of your trust."

If there was one thing Robert Morris desired above everything else on earth, it was the ability to discharge his obligations. "If I can once get square, I will never contract another debt," he vowed. He spoke of being plagued most cursedly for want of money, "but it was impossible to borrow cash and equally impossible to sell land or mortgage it." With property worth millions Morris could not raise a dollar. A new note of despair crept into his letters: "I hate to complain, but in the bitterness of accumulated trouble my soul must have vent. Which way to turn I do not know." Without succour, he was, as he expressed it, "hard up against wind and tide." Although most eager to pay his debts, he was unable to do so. He wrote one creditor who threatened to bring suit against him: "It will not be worthwhile to institute such action as I pay as fast as I can and am always willing to pay when I can." Creditors could not understand his inability to fulfill his obligations. Was he not the wealthy Robert Morris, reputed to be worth millions? Was he not building a marble palace, considered the finest house in America? Did he not entertain liberally, even extravagantly? Did not his family travel and entertain and live luxuriously? It was hard for these creditors to understand that conditions had changed: that his houses and his lands and the extravagance of some members of his family were an incubus rather than a symbol of wealth; that his house was heavily mortgaged—and his handsome new furniture attached.

Even in those dark days of anxiety and despondency, Morris remained enthusiastic about his property and the resources and opportunities in the United States. Trying to persuade Europeans to immigrate and settle his lands, he depicted in glowing terms the richness of his tracts in Georgia, so fertile that the poor might become rich and independent. There were, he recounted earnestly, countless forests of timber and rich soil where crops could be raised without too much exertion—crops of grain, vegetables, lemons, oranges, grapes, peaches, tobacco, rice, and cotton. He spoke of unoccupied lands capable of providing food and raiment for millions, where there was "such comfortable space that they will not be willing to engage in broils as they do in crowded Europe." But despite all his efforts as a promoter and supersalesman, he received little response. While he, the Financier who had economized in the affairs of the nation, now became extravagant in his own investments, all the rest of the world had become cautious and miserly.

Still the creditors pressed in upon him, presenting their overdue accounts by messenger and post and personal application. Notes, interest, taxes had to be paid. Suits, duns, executions, attachments faced him wherever he turned. Creditors expressed themselves as no longer willing to subsist on promises. To liquidate his debt to Willink and Company he offered them his unroofed marble palace, which they refused to accept. Since he was unable to obtain a loan or credit, his lands in Georgia, one hundred thousand acres, were sold for taxes. He feared that he would lose other property in the South. "Oh, Kentucky, Kentucky," he exclaimed, "is there any faith in thy goodly land?" To add to his distresses a yellow fever plague drove the wealthy citizens out of the city just as they had been driven out in 1793. There was no one to whom he could turn for financial relief. He, who had borrowed millions of dollars for the nation during the Revolution on his own personal credit, could not now borrow one hundred dollars for his own needs. At this time he was indebted to Alexander Hamilton, Benjamin Harrison (the younger of that name who had once acted as clerk in his counting-house), John Dickinson, and Thomas Fitzsimons, as well as to many others. Harrison especially had almost beggared himself to assist his old friend. Rumors buzzed that Morris was planning to run away from his creditors although he had shown his good faith by returning from Washington and remaining in Philadelphia, facing his creditors and Nicholson's daily. Nevertheless, these whispers persisted, with the result that the last shreds of credit were destroyed and the duns became more urgent. The storm was brewing, the clouds lowering, and Morris felt that he must seek shelter from the tempest.

CHAPTER XVI

CASTLE DEFIANCE

❖   ❖   ❖

"THE HILLS" had alway been a refuge to Robert Morris—a refuge from business and political cares and from the attacks of enemies. Now he sought an asylum there from the importunities of his creditors. This flight did not signify an attempt on his part to avoid responsibilities or to evade his obligations. He merely wished peace of mind and the opportunity to plan methods of meeting the demands upon him without constant harassing interruptions. This was a strategic withdrawal, not a rout. In this way he had more time to devise schemes for selling property and settling accounts.

But even there he was pursued by his own and John Nicholson's creditors. Had it not been for the latter, he might have extricated himself from his most serious complications. As it was, he remained virtually a prisoner at "The Hills" during the autumn and winter, 1797 to 1798. He did not dare appear publicly or even leave the premises. Occasionally he walked over the estate, strolling along the river banks or climbing the hills, but on many days he did not venture out of the house. Since his books and papers had been moved there from his counting house, he was able to read, to review his accounts (a dubious pleasure), and to philosophize. Despite his distressing situation, he at first remained optimistic. In a letter to Benjamin Harrison he expressed himself as still hopeful of an improvement in his affairs. "Hope, the last resource of the unfortunate, stands by me," he remarked almost cheerfully, "and so long as that goddess is my companion, I shall fight a stout battle."

For a while after his eventful return from Washington, Nicholson was with him at "The Hills." The "splendid bankrupts," as they called themselves, tried to console each other. Indeed his partner's friendship seemed Morris's only consolation at this time, except of course his family's loyalty and devotion. They stood shoulder to shoulder, uttering few reproaches. Whimsically Morris admitted to Nicholson that he had begged him to return to Philadelphia for purely selfish reasons, because he wished his companionship. It became increasingly dangerous and uncomfortable, however, for Nicholson to remain at "The Hills." One day two men came to the kitchen door requesting a drink of water. They finally admitted to the servants that they had come to take Nicholson into custody. At last when the sheriff threatened to arrest him, Nicholson was transferred to another house and later to his own home in Philadelphia.

Then began that daily correspondence between "Castle Defiance," where Robert Morris held at bay the army of creditors, sheriffs, and other officers, and "Castle Defence," where John Nicholson lay hidden. The messages flew back and forth, sometimes more than a dozen a day—a remarkable correspondence full of humor and pathos. In fact, there were so many letters daily, especially from Nicholson, that they were numbered. At one time Morris said that letters "by the most indefatigable hand on earth" were staring reproachfully at him from the table. "If writing notes would relieve me," he told his partner sarcastically, "you would do it sooner than any man in the world, but all you have said in these now before me, numbers 5 to 9 inclusive, amount when summed up to nothing." Again he wrote caustically: "Here is a morning that will cool you and your letters so quick that I think you will dispatch the business they impart, without farther delay. I hope — — may get to a hotter place than my warm house before he can make a successful attack on you. We are hard threatened but I hope that care and vigilance will disappoint all of them as to our persons." Morris advised his partner to write less and think more.

Increasingly he was "harassed with new troubles from Nicholson's creditors." "How comes it to pass," he asked his partner, "that I am in a more responsible situation in these cases than you are?" That remains as much of a mystery to us today as it must have appeared to Robert Morris. "Good heavens," he cried in desperation, "where and when will end the persecution I meet with from your creditors?" Again and again he requested Nicholson to come to see him, by carriage or on foot, to discuss plans for discharging their indebtedness. "I had taken measures," Morris wrote, "and was progressing to settle my own debts for which Eddy is special bail. The others I never will pay nor suffer my property to be sacrificed from my own creditors to satisfy such enormities; therefore if you do not settle them, I am the victim." These complaints against the partner who refused to help himself or the friend being sacrificed for him seemed wrung from Morris almost involuntarily. He was forced to mortgage his Trout Spring estate to satisfy Nicholson's notes; of this sum Morris never touched a cent. During Nicholson's absence in Washington, Robert Morris had been obliged to sign bail bonds and enter a special bail. At another time he informed John Nicholson that if he (Morris) had to go to prison, it would not be on account of his own debts.

Many of the messages that flew back and forth were in humorous vein, especially those from the occupant of "Castle Defiance." "A curse on all suits, say I," wrote the besieged. "If they were good comfortable winter suits, one might dispose of them, the more the better, but these damned suits wherein a Lawyer is the Taylor are neither good for man, woman, child or beast. Away with them, away with them." Again he punned with regard to the flood of notes from his garrulous partner: "I wish to God these notes would take up those which bear promise of payments."

Some of the letters were in prayerful mood. "God help us," he ejaculated, "for men will not. We are abandoned by all those who want to get from us all we yet hold." And again he entreated, "Pray Heaven send us better times."

Occasionally he wrote bitterly as in the following note: "Good Heavens, what vultures men are in regard to each other. I never in the days of prosperity took advantage of any man's distresses, and I suppose what I now experience is to serve as a lesson whereby to see the folly of humane and generous conduct." He was seldom so cynical as that, however, and seldom so revengeful as in this message: "I should have no objection if R. Mathers and I. B. Church were tied back to back and left to tug one another for life. They are unfeeling wretches." Messrs. Mathers and Church were among the "blood-hounds" pursuing him.

"Castle Defiance" became Morris's fortress. Early in November he swore that he would let nobody in his house and would not go out-side the walls; thus he hoped "to disappoint them all." One day soon after Nicholson had left him, while the Mayor of Philadelphia was with him in the Long Room at "The Hills," John Baker, the sheriff, came to the front door and, not being able to open it, rang the bell. Morris looked out the window and told him he was engaged with a peace officer, but if the sheriff would walk around the garden and eat some pears, Morris promised to let him see him again. "Ah," said Baker, "I see you are all fast," and away he went. The prisoner in "Castle Defiance" advised the prisoner in "Castle Defence" to "keep snug."

Occasionally Morris escaped from his fortress. On November 19, he was in Philadelphia, where he saw John Nicholson and hinted at a plan of relief for themselves and their families. Although he had at this time no money and no credit, he still had resources within him-self—ingenuity and courage. His partner was very much more timorous. On another Sunday in November he requested Nicholson to visit him and dine on cold beef. Perhaps the prospect was not sufficiently alluring, for the partner did not come.

Many details of ordinary life obtruded themselves upon his atten-tion to divert his mind somewhat from the graver problems con-fronting him. A smoky chimney caused him great discomfort as the smoke choked him. As he had grown more corpulent, his asthma had grown worse. Thus he was especially susceptible to smoke-filled air. The windows, too, needed repairing, yet he feared to admit any-one, even workmen. Finally one day a glazier came. Robert Morris, suspicious of everyone, went out on the porch and locked the door after him as soon as he had admitted the man. Whimsically Morris posed this pseudo-legal question: perhaps the glazier might justifiably have broken into every room in the house in search of him, but had

he a right to break down a door into the open air, the front door being open and ready for him to go out?

This voluntary imprisonment was made more tolerable by frequent
visits from his family. William came to give him legal advice. The
Marshalls, on their return from Europe, shared his castle with him for
a while. Their children, "as hearty as bucks and as playful as kittens
but more mischievous," served temporarily to distract his mind from
his troubles. On Sunday Molly and the younger children came out
to bring him supplies and to spend the day with him. Even Charles
proved helpful, acting as secretary for his father.

Sometimes friends called. One day Morris had a visit from George
Washington Parke Custis, Washington's step-grandson, who was a
friend and admirer of Robert Morris. On another occasion a young
Englishman, Daniel Lester, recommended to Morris by Richard Penn
and others, called on the former Financier, to secure a letter of introduction to General Washington. Mr. Lester could not return contented, he said, "without seeing the saviour of this country." How
startled he must have been to find another of its saviours, the great
Financier of the Revolution, a prisoner in his own home, hounded by
creditors!

There were no banquets as in the olden days at "The Hills." There
was scarcely food enough for Morris himself and James, his gardener,
as he was "moneyless almost to starvation." What "victuals" he had
were supplied by James and a Negro cook, who were not permitted
inside the house. Only his own family, the friends for whom he sent,
and very special visitors were allowed "within the sacred walls of the
sanctum sanctorum" that contained his person. Some of those he
really wished to see were afraid of the eight or ten dogs at the farm-
house, "as harmless dogs as ever barked." He suggested that one man,
who feared these animals, should come out "under convoy." Unfortunately the creditors were not scared away.

Robert Morris's chief occupation seemed to be escaping from the
army of creditors, lawyers, sheriffs, and deputy sheriffs that besieged
the place. James, the gardener, acted as a faithful watchdog, bringing
him news of the besiegers—where they were camped and sometimes

what they intended to do. To all those who reached the door, Morris was "not at home." Sometimes, however, he talked to them from the upstairs windows, or peered through the shutters to catch a glimpse of spies lurking behind trees. One evening two creditors with officers and writs made a bed of leaves in an old quarry (Blackbeard's Hole). There they built a fire and planned to remain until they could place Robert Morris under arrest. James warned him of their designs. Soon after this he rigged up a peephole from which to watch the enemy. In December he was kept especially busy with detective work. On December 4 he wrote: "I have been very busy this morning watching the man that is watching me. I rose early and lighted my fire, then went down to let in the boy, and casting my eyes toward *the Old Peephole*, there was my gentleman snug enough. However I sent James to disturb him and from his description it must be West."

At six o'clock one evening that eventful week, an officer arrived, piloted by William Cranch, who was formerly in charge of the Washington property. Morris spoke to them out of the window, sending his compliments to Officer Dunwoody and advising him to have patience. Not long afterward Dunwoody himself arrived with six men, two of whom remained in the copse, "in ambush." Well armed with sledge hammers and pick-axes, they were determined to break in the house. The situation demanded all of Morris's persuasive powers and adroitness. From his second-story "observation tower" he dissuaded them by diplomacy and threats from forcing the doors or windows of "Castle Defiance." All night on December 15 certain men (C. Tunis and others) lurked around the hills and in the valleys, building a fire among the rocks on the river bank. This time the dogs gave the alarm. That day Morris considered "pregnant with fate." He began to fear the arrival of Baker, the sheriff.

There was never a moment of peace. Men tried to bribe their way into the house in order to arrest him. Behind every tree he imagined a spy. Constable Hunt (appropriately named) he described as being "as cunning and active as Lucifer." A Frenchman threatened to shoot him at the window if he did not pay a note which had been protested several days before. Morris suspected even his coachman of having been tampered with, but he did not let this servant come near him. A messenger, Thomas (not his son), was not above suspicion as he evidently did not deliver a note sent by him to John Nicholson. "If ever I could have had a previous idea of such things happening to me," he wrote despairingly to his fellow bankrupt, "I would sooner have wheeled oysters all my days than incurred the risk."

His mind was so perturbed that he found it difficult to attend to business. "It is hardly worth while," he felt, "to submit to the drudgery of business"; nor was there much incentive in his affairs themselves. Although he still retained some stock in the North American Land Company, the Pennsylvania Property Company, the legally involved Washington lots and was at this time in possession of the block on Chestnut Street, he was unable to borrow money or pay taxes. Real estate was not accepted as security. Two hundred thousand acres in North Carolina, bought for $27,000, were sold for a year's taxes. "I believe I shall go mad," he said. "Every day brings forward scenes and troubles almost insupportable."

At last he feared that he would lose his new Chestnut Street home on which he had lavished so much money uselessly. In September he wrote his partner: "My Chestnut Street house and lot, these grounds ["The Hills"], and some ground-rents are advertised by Mr. Baker for sale on the 15th instant, and what to do I am at a loss, . . . If this thing takes place, it is of little consequence whether I am taken or not. . . . Can you assist me to raise five hundred dollars to send off Mr. Richard [a servant or clerk], otherwise his two years' labor will be lost? I have been scheming and trying, but without success. No man, it seems, can command—rather say, spare—so large a sum. . . . What shall we do? Powerful exertions must be made, for at all events we must relieve all who have served us and who will continue to serve us." This shows Morris's concern for his servants even in the midst of his own financial worries. He requested a postponement of sales on his property, for, as he said, "A sale at this time will not answer any good purpose. No property, however valuable, commands money." At last he had learned that fact, but the knowledge came too late. The sale was postponed several times—to November and later to December. In the meantime a society was being formed to buy the Chestnut Street house.

In Washington the half-finished houses were being plundered or occupied by squatters. Morris tried to negotiate loans for twelve to eighteen months, to save his Washington property, which was mortgaged to the Bank of Columbia and assigned to the Trustees of the Aggregate Fund to hold until payments were made. "Alas poor Washington City! Alas poor proprietors!" he lamented in a letter to Nicholson. "I believe if you or I were the owners of the Heavenly Paradise, no security we could offer in this world would be accepted." His interest and belief in the capital remained as enthusiastic as ever. To another correspondent, Gustavus Scott, he wrote feelingly: "I wish to God I had the same command of money as formerly. I would make the City of Washington flourish by my own exertions, but the devil of it is that men who use money lose the command of it, and it gets into the hands of Holdfast, who never parts with it." In part payment of debt for his services in connection with the Washington property, Lovering, whom Morris had trusted implicitly, took all the materials for six houses on Pennsylvania Avenue and for other houses as well. The Commissioners and others involved seemed to prefer sacrificing lots by forced sales to holding them for an adequate purchase price. The Trustees of the Aggregate Fund wished further security from Morris and Nicholson but would not accept real estate as collateral, the only kind they possessed. During the time of his self-imposed imprisonment at "The Hills," Robert Morris escaped long enough to meet some of the Trustees at a tavern near Germantown, but found them timorous, fearing to incur censure if they extended the time of payment upon an uncertainty.

Again in December the Philadelphia property was advertised for sale. Even "The Hills," "Castle Defiance" itself, mortgaged to the Pennsylvania Insurance Company, was finally sold by the sheriff to Reed and Forde, from whom Morris leased the house and garden. The marble palace, which had consumed so much of his fortune and which was still unfinished, was sold to satisfy the creditors. On the night of December 9, during the fateful week of espionage and dire events, the entire square on Chestnut Street, divided into building lots, was sold at auction. Thomas Billington bought the building materials and later, in 1799, took down the costly and magnificent

ruin, "Morris's Folly." The marble decorations were scattered among
the different buildings in the city. The fine high relief tablets, representing Tragedy and Comedy, were placed in semicircles over the
windows in the wings of the Chestnut Street Theatre, then under
construction. A row of houses on Race Street were ornamented with
garlands of sculptured flowers. Another home was decorated with a
carving representing two cherubs with pen in hand on each side of a
palette. These fragments of Jardella's work were all that remained of
Robert Morris's dream palace.

By the end of January the furniture at "The Hills," even the shrubs,
the exotic plants, the lemon and orange trees in the hothouse had all
been attached. His own personal plate and furniture he assigned to
Thomas Fitzsimons, his next-door neighbor in Philadelphia, to whom
he was deeply in debt, and to whom he had written, "I do not want
any Trustee or other person between you and me." He sold and
delivered to Mr. Sansom all movables in the Chestnut Street house,
and those at "The Hills" to Mr. Forde before the sheriff had attached
all his possessions there.

Even more than these tragic losses of his own, Robert Morris regretted that others were involved in his ruin. Gerald Cottringer, who
had attended to his business in these days of financial disaster, was
arrested on November 13. Charles Young, another friend of his, was
lodged in jail, where Morris feared that he and Nicholson might soon
join him. The prisoner of "Castle Defiance" talked to Young's son
sympathetically from his chamber window. To the father he philosophized: "Jail or sacrificing property by forced sales does not enable
debtors to pay their creditors, whereas lenient measures and time may
enable them to acquit everything most honorably." This situation of
his friends and adherents continued to cause Morris infinite distress.
The agents of the North American Land Company were in want.
Friends had lost money in this and other ventures. "Is it possible that
I can be in a situation to cause any man's ruin?" the former Financier
asked, grieved and perplexed at such a circumstance. To Nicholson,
his partner in affliction, he stated frankly: "Unhappily our misfortunes, or as many will call it, misconduct brings consequences upon
others which we alone ought to face, and I wish to God they were

confined solely to us." "These ill-fated notes have singed our best friends," he lamented in another letter, and continued: "My name inspired confidence, and to protect the honour and credit of that name, I am called on and abused beyond all bearing to do what is out of my power to do."

With regard to certain creditors of Nicholson's, notably Sheriff Boone of Washington and Mr. Higbee, Robert Morris felt most sympathetic and remorseful, much more so, apparently, than did his partner. "I will go to jail sooner than let Higbee pay the debt," he informed Nicholson with righteous indignation.

Every letter from Morris to his partner began to sound the *leitmotif* of "gaol" or "Prune Street," the prison on Walnut and Prune (Locust) streets where debtors were imprisoned. He spoke of receiving a letter, in which he "read Prune Street in every line." His sanguine nature seemed crushed beneath the perplexities, the threats, the ruin that overwhelmed him. He who had borne so much for his nation and himself for more than forty years, building up a prosperous business, a large fortune and a highly esteemed reputation, now saw everything devoured by "the vultures," "the rascally muskrats," and "the sly old foxes." He was threatened with a domestic attachment on the household goods his family were using. Humiliated past all bearing, in utter desperation he said, "I am pestered to death with letters that set me almost mad. All the world seems to be engaged in hunting up my property, attacking, plundering, pestering, and persecuting; in short, I believe the best way to get rid of trouble is to go at once to [Prune] Street." In writing to General Harry Lee he lamented: "The world say that I am to be ruined and determine to make good their words by totally withdrawing that confidence which is essential to the preservation of my property from the cruel sacrifices which threaten it in every quarter."

Yet despite all these anxieties and perplexities, he preserved his balance and his patience. To his partner he wrote: "We are both under the power of the same paw and I fear it will fall equally heavy on both, and there is no one to help either of us; if our afflictions are as heavy and follow as quick as those of Job, we must follow his example and bear them with patience and resignation. This I can do perfectly as to myself, but when I think of my family my soul is wrung to the quick."

In the Prune Street prison was a former friend and partner of Morris, concerning whose fate he felt not the slightest anxiety; that was James Greenleaf, held in jail with only one suit against him and "near to getting out." Up to the very day of his imprisonment he had continued to play the role of Mephistopheles. He had attached one thousand shares in the North American Land Company, in the hands of Willink & Company and all other stock in Holland belonging to Morris and Nicholson. Like their evil genius he had pursued them, cautioning the world against buying their property. Although Greenleaf was in Morris's debt by bond and on account, the latter had brought no suit against him, but finally the miscreant, chief cause of Morris's financial ruin, was brought to justice. Morris hoped that "Master Jimmy" would come out if he went in, as he did not wish to be under the same roof with such a scoundrel "lest it should fall to crush the guilty, and the innocent be involved in the same fate."

The last of January Robert Morris felt the net tightening around him. Nevertheless he ventured one day to leave his castle for the city. Previously he had gone on several occasions to the tavern, the Butcher's Arms, to meet friends or business associates. Once at least he had walked there and back, more than ten miles, and once had ridden in John Nicholson's carriage. But he was always glad to return to the haven of "The Hills." This time he seemed especially happy to get back safely as he felt himself pursued and surrounded by spies and other enemies. The last time he escaped from his fortress was on February 4. "I got safe here," he told Nicholson the next day, "and found it the only place of calmness and quiet my foot was in yesterday. It has made me more averse to the city than ever, and I detest Prune Street more than ever. Therefore, keep me from it, my dear friend."

Robert Morris's nemesis proved to be George Eddy, who was his "special bail" man, a small creditor but stubborn and unyielding, incited to obstinacy by Charles Eddy, his brother, who insisted that he prosecute Morris. On January 31, 1798, his birthday according to the old calendar, Morris received an especially threatening letter from

Eddy, in regard to which the poor harassed debtor wrote: "Perhaps it is right that I should be fretted and vexed on this the anniversary of the day on which I was born, as it would have been far better never to have seen the light than at this time of life to experience what day by day I go through." In the meantime he warned Molly that George Eddy's friends "pursued measures to force a surrender." He informed her of the danger so that she might face the situation bravely. He need not have feared her faltering. His sons tried to extricate him, but it was too late. To Thomas his father gave excellent advice: not to over-strain but "to keep within bounds." "You will grow rich fast enough," he assured his son, "and enjoy yourself much more."

All through January and February Morris steeled himself to meet the inevitable. On February 5 he sent word to Nicholson: "I shall pre-pare for Prune Street, but I hope you will be able to keep clear as you have no false friend for bail, which is unhappily the case of R.M." The following day he considered his fate fixed; "hard and cruel Fate it is," he lamented. Although he admitted that the punishment of his imprudence in the use of his name was perhaps what he deserved, he felt its effects upon his family "most tormentingly." "On their ac-count," he said, "I would do anything to avert what I see must happen next week, except an act that would still affect them more deeply." Evidently Morris, despairing, contemplated suicide but cast the thought from him, realizing how deeply that would hurt his wife and family.

On the evening of February 14, St. Valentine's Day, George Eddy arrived, planning to send for his brother to take the prisoner into custody. Even at that tragic moment Morris continued his corre-spondence with Nicholson. "George Eddy is in the house," he stated. "My fate is fixed." Realizing that further resistance was vain, he sent for Sheriff Baker to surrender himself to him rather than to Charles Eddy, Morris's implacable foe. The sheriff permitted Morris to re-main at home under guard until the next day. That night of respite Morris catalogued his few remaining possessions: bedding and cloth-ing, two bales of nankeen, a quarter cask of wine, some bottled wine, a part of a barrel of flour, coffee, a small amount of sugar, a parcel of old books and newspapers, materials for a steam engine (an invention in which he had been interested), a microscope, an old chariot in Richmond, a share in the Library Company, a share of stock in the Bank of North America, and his father's old, worn-out gold watch, from which he did not wish to part if he could avoid it. With meticulous care he recorded these few items—all that remained of his vast fortune, his millions of dollars and millions of acres, his elegant furniture and handsome homes, the result of a lifetime of hard work. Just as he was preparing to leave for prison, forty dollars arrived from John Nicholson, but it came too late and was returned to the donor. Robert Morris's doom was sealed.

CHAPTER XVII

THE HOTEL WITH THE GRATED DOOR

❖　　❖　　❖

THE Philadelphia prison to which Robert Morris was taken on February 15, was called "the Wonder of the World." Neat, handsome, and well-kept, it was "no inconsiderable ornament to the city." It was a large stone building two stories high, on a lot four hundred by two hundred feet. From the entrance in the middle of the building a passageway, eleven and a half feet wide, led to the eight rooms on each floor, where the prisoners were housed. Each room had two windows arched with stone and barred by double gratings. On the east and west were two wings, ninety feet in length, with five rooms on each floor, almost the size of those in front. A stone building on the south side, which had been designed for a workhouse, housed the debtors as it was considered wise to separate these prisoners from the criminals or other law-breakers. A separate yard on the south side of the lot was appropriated to the use of the debtors and furnished, as was the other prison yard, with pumps, baths, sewers, and other necessities. Under this yard on the north side ran a natural watercourse. The prison buildings were kept scrupulously clean. They were whitewashed two or three times a year; the passages and rooms were swept every morning and washed twice a week in summer and once in winter. The beds, filled with red cedar shavings, were clean and (considered) comfortable.

The prisoners were kept clean, well clothed, and well employed. The men and women occupied separate buildings. They washed every morning and received clean linen once a week. In summer they used the out-of-door baths. Clean towels for the prisoners hung in the passageways. The men shaved twice a week and had their hair cut once a month. In the winter they wore woolen jackets, waistcoats, and trousers; and in the summer, garments of coarse linen, manufactured in the prison workshop. The diet was plain, cheap, and wholesome. Molasses was considered "very salutary to the health of the prisoners as well as useful in gratifying them with a small luxury." Consequently one-half pint of molasses was distributed to every four prisoners on Tuesdays, Thursdays, and Saturdays.

The convicts or regular prisoners were given employment. In the gaol yard was a small industrious community: a nail factory, a blacksmith shop, sheds for sawing and polishing marble and for cutting stone; workshops for shoe-making, weaving, and tailoring. Men were busy shipping logwood, grinding plaster-of-Paris, and beating hemp. Mutely, under expert supervision, the prisoners went about their tasks, silence imposed upon them unless speech was imperative. Since it was feared that the example of the indolent, often foul-mouthed debtors might "corrupt the morals" of the convicts, a prison wall had been erected to prevent the debtors in their apartments from overlooking this scene of activity.

Such was the jail to which Robert Morris was led by Sheriff Baker. The ironical situation with regard to debtors' prisons was this: the prisoner, who was there because he had no money to pay his debts, was compelled to pay rent for and furnish a room which the law forced him to occupy. While in jail, he was, of course, denied the privilege of earning money to pay his debts.

When Morris first entered the Prune Street Prison, no room was available. He wrote Nicholson in semi-humorous vein that he was trying daily to get "a room for a high rent in this hotel with the grated door." Although his sons were making every effort to obtain suitable accommodations for him, no private "apartment" was available, so crowded was the prison. At first, therefore, he occupied a room with several other inmates. He who had always enjoyed privacy and had offered lavish hospitality to others, now "slept in another person's bed." His confinement in those early days he described as "most disagreeable and uncomfortable." Throughout these days of discomfort there was little self-pity in his attitude. As he told Thomas, one of his chief confidants: "A man that cannot bear and face misfortune should never run risks, but I have been too adventurous and therefore it is a duty to meet my fate with fortitude." At least he had the courage and grace to suffer in silence.

From the first he had many visitors, friends who sympathized with him. Sheriff Boone, Nicholson's creditor, and Wilson Hunt came to see him. On February 26, the day after he moved into his own room, he received a flood of tormenting applications. Here it was more difficult than at "The Hills" to elude visitors, but he could refuse to admit anyone without learning his name and business. A man possessing some of Morris's and Nicholson's notes called several times. The first few times Morris was "not at home." When the persistent visitor returned during a storm, Robert Morris, although admitting he was at home, refused to see him. Evidently the creditor resented this treatment. "If a man had a soul as big as a louse," Morris told Nicholson, "he would have smothered his resentment."

Among the visitors he welcomed in his whitewashed prison room were Alexander Hamilton, who admired Morris although he was not a close personal friend of his; Gouverneur Morris, sincere and loyal, who dined with his old chief; and George Washington, who seemed genuinely saddened by his friend's misfortunes but apparently made no effort to relieve them.

In 1798, a few months after the beginning of Morris's imprisonment, Washington arrived in Philadelphia to superintend the organization of his last army. War with France threatened as a result of the European and Egyptian wars then being conducted with such phenomenal skill by Napoleon Bonaparte. The youthful United States of America discovered even so early in its history that it could not remain isolated from the rest of the world; that a threat to other countries also implied a threat to this nation, especially to its all-important commercial enterprises. Thus, realizing the imminent danger and wishing to be prepared, the Congress again called Washington from his retirement at Mount Vernon to organize another army. Distressed at his friend's imprisonment, Washington arranged to make his first call at the debtors' prison to see Morris. An air of expectancy enveloped Prune Street when word was buzzed about that General Washington was coming. Morris himself, with so few pleasures and honors in these days, also felt the tension of expectancy. Unwilling to be selfish in his enjoyment of this distinguished guest, he invited Nicholson to join them for dinner. In preparation for the visit, Morris had a fire blazing on the hearth and a borrowed mahogany table set in front of it. The dinners he had previously ordered. As he waited with tautening nerves, Robert Morris must have thought of Washington's farewell dinner little more than a year before and of the many occasions when he had entertained his friend and chief in his own elegant home. What a contrast between this visit and those others! Finally sounded the long-expected knock on the door. As Morris grasped his old friend's hand, tears were in his eyes. Washington warmly returned the pressure of his handclasp although words came haltingly to express his sadness at Morris's unhappy situation. Then they sat down before the fire under the whitewashed vault of the prison room to chat of other days. Later Washington expressed his sympathy to Mrs. Morris in a letter in which he "prayed that Mr. Morris would soon work his way through all his difficulties."

Another acquaintance, Samuel Breck, who went to see him at this time, has recorded his feelings on the occasion in his famous *Recollections:* "I visited that great man in the Prune Street debtors' apartment, and saw him in his ugly whitewashed vault. In Rome or Greece a thousand statues would have honored his mighty services. . . . In America, republican America, not a single voice was raised in Congress or elsewhere in aid of him or his family."

Morris's most attentive visitors were the members of his family. Every day no matter what the weather, his Molly and Maria came to visit him. They generally brought food and dined in his room. Soon they moved to a house near the prison so that they might spend as much time as possible with him. Mary Morris was a thoroughbred, patient and uncomplaining, unswerving in her affections and her loyalty. Through all those dark days she maintained her own dignity and her faith in her husband. Maria's sparkling presence also brightened many weary hours for her father.

By the summer of 1798 the illustrious prisoner had settled into a routine of work, exercise, and meditation. In his cell, a fairly spacious room, he had a writing desk, a bedstead with a mattress and adequate bedding, a settee, chairs and mirrors as well as his account books, letter books, and cases and a carrying press. Here he continued his voluminous correspondence with Nicholson, whose flood of notes daily inundated Morris's room. Much of his natural good humor seemed restored to him. He tried to turn a sunny face to others, no matter how much he suffered alone. In requesting his partner to visit him at "the hotel with the grated doors," he said: "We will show you how we live here that you may be prepared to bear your fate should it be decided that you are to become a boarder at this hotel." Sometimes he was able to lay aside cares and forget that "the front door was locked." Almost daily during his first years in prison he pleaded with Nicholson to visit him. Morris addressed him as "brother sufferer in lawsuits," and twitted him about his legal knowledge. Soon after he had entered Prune Street, Morris mocked: "As you are a *great* lawyer, instruct me how to parry the *little* stroke threatened against the property." Several times he referred sarcastically to "those who are lawyers or who *think* they are." His experience at that period made him caustic in his comments on the legal profession. He wrote his partner: "We shall not get lawyers to defend us or our property, for I believe they are as unwilling to work without pay as any class of man you meet with." Usually he seemed in merrier mood. On Nicholson's birthday, July 5, he sent him a cheery note: "I made a frolic yesterday. I hope the future anniversaries of your birthday will be numerous and passed in full possession of liberty." In May he suggested a party on the banks of the Schuylkill. He would like to go, he said, but could not get out. In January of the following year he invited Nicholson to take a walk and dine with Mr. Banks and him. "We return the compliment of a venison dinner to the gentlemen of Number 3 in this Hotel," he told his partner, "and they will be glad to see you here at 3 o'clock." Occasionally Nicholson called on him, but more often he failed to appear through fear of arrest. He felt that his own situation was too precarious. Sadly Morris sent him this message after having expected a visit from him: "Another Sunday hath passed away and you would not risque a visit at this gloomy mansion."

In writing of Greenleaf, Robert Morris remained bitter: "If I get possession of James Greenleaf's room and he comes back, he will not get it again unless he turns me out of the House and I should thank him to effect that." At another time when he evidently had to communicate with his former partner (Greenleaf) on business, he spoke of his soul's revolting at the thought of writing that miscreant. "The right hand refused to perform its functions," he admitted to Nicholson.

During his imprisonment Morris remained amazingly well. He took good care of his health, exercising every day. One morning in March he walked three miles and every day when the weather permitted, he walked fifty times around the prison yard—"fifty times the length of my tether," as he expressed it. A proof of his essential common sense and balance was his ability to make his prison life so normal. He read, wrote, looked over his accounts, led a fairly social life with his family and fellow prisoners.

This normality was the more amazing in view of the fact that an epidemic of yellow fever ravaged the city and particularly the prison. In 1798 there were almost four thousand deaths in Philadelphia from this plague. Inmates of Prune Street died daily—men Morris knew, with whom he had recently dined, yet he remained apparently unafraid. So did Mary Morris and Maria, who through the summer of 1798 while the fever raged continued their daily visits to the prison until they walked in and out the corridors "between piles of coffins." That summer the prison was a pesthouse; men died like flies. Robert Morris prayed for cold winds to halt the epidemic. For himself he apparently felt no danger, but he feared for his family who so loyally visited him and could not be induced to stay away. At last a court order was issued permitting his removal to the country "when the danger of the situation required it." It is difficult to conceive the official interpretation of "danger." Two rows of coffins of yellow-fever victims extending from the floor to the ceiling in the corridors outside his door might be construed as a mild menace. It was hard to walk anywhere in the building without stepping on a dead man. Yet Morris was never removed from the prison, apparently never thought of asking that favor. His health was good; his mind, vigorous; his spirits, unbroken; his patience, phenomenal. During the worst of the epidemic he remained in his own room away from the other inmates. In September he wrote: "Our prisoners are gone, except the sick, Banks, Rittenhouse, and myself. They all have the fever, but still I am not alarmed although in the house with it. I keep upstairs and avoid all intercourse as much as I can." Although the wife of the man who cleaned his room became ill with the fever and died, Morris seemed immune and unperturbed. In a note to John Nicholson he remarked: "It is wonderful but, notwithstanding the danger is now at my chamber door—for Hofner is in the room I formerly occupied—I feel no kind of apprehension, and my only anxiety is for my wife and daughter and these poor sick people. I hope my life will be spared, for the sake of my family, until I get my affairs settled." Soon after he sent this letter, Mr. Hofner died in the room opposite him and Mr. Allison just below, but his own health was never better than during that period when death was all around him. When cold weather came in October, he dug in the prison garden, leaving his windows open to air the room while he was out. On his return he made a good fire from a bucket or two of slaked lime. Thus by exercise, fresh air, and common precautions he kept well.

In the fall of 1798, Robert and Mary Morris were saddened by the death of their son William, the victim of a bilious remitting fever. He died the morning of October 9 and was buried in the family vault in Christ Churchyard. Only after his death did Morris realize his worth. "His value to the family I never counted until he was lost and now I see its magnitude and that it is irreparable," he confided sadly to Thomas. The father felt, so he said, that he had lost a dutiful son, a friend and companion. Old friends had died, too —Benjamin Franklin, James Wilson, and Benjamin Harrison, the elder.

Robert Morris was more than ever intent on family affairs. Charles was again in distress, at Morrisville without a change of clothes or a cent in his pocket. Always sanguine, his father hoped his son, now

ROBERT MORRIS'S DAUGHTERS, MARIA AND HETTY

Portrait by Gilbert Stuart

twenty-one years of age, might yet do well. Very soon Robert Morris discovered that Charles was not wilfully indolent or mischievous, but merely a misfit, who heard the call of the sea—a longing inherited from his great-grandfather, Andrew Morris, "saylor."

In June, 1799, Mrs. Morris and Maria, now nineteen, visited Hetty, Mrs. James Marshall, in Virginia. The following letter from Robert Morris to Maria reveals his affection and enthusiastic interest in their visit and in all family matters:

"Philada., June 26, 1799

"Your letter of the 17th inst. gave me, my dear Maria, great pleasure so that your hope in that respect is fully answered, and I thank you for the account you give me of your niece and nephews, the boys I know and have formed great expectations of them from a certain originality of character that was discernible even at the youthful period when I saw them, the little girl altho small now, will I suppose at a future day make up by rapid growth as generally is the case when they are under-size at first. I observe that Henry in your opinion retains the same natural character he had when he left us—altho his Person is altered by growth, if we can but so fix his habits as that he may ever retain his innocence, love of truth and purity of mind, it will be a great happiness for him and his connections. . . .

"Altho my journey with you, your Mother and Mrs. Tidball to Fredk town was not quite so tiresome to me as to you as I had not the jolting and squeezing, yet it was attended with an anxiety of mind which is more than equivalent to personal fatigue and especially as it continued not only for the rest of your journey but untill I heard of your safe arrival. Are you not surprised that I have not had a line from Tom since he was married altho it was on the 28th of May, I suppose he defers writing to any of us untill he gets back to his own home at Canandaigua.

"This city continues healthy but I am told is remarkably dull, little of either business or pleasure going forward and the families that usually go into the country for the summer season are on the move, altho there has been no hot weather until now. Mr. LaTrobe is as I am informed going on briskly with his work for watering the City. They are now laying the Pipes through some of the Streets, but I doubt if he can be in time for the hot season so close at hand. Count de Tilly is gone, and Bingham gave him Twenty thousand dollars and five hundred pounds a year for which he gave up all claims to the Countess who it is said despises him for it being now convinced what was the attractive charm that drew his attention to her. Thus you see, my dear, that large fortunes do not always bring happiness, on the contrary misery to the possessor is frequently the result and this unfortunate young lady is one instance of it. I hope when any worthy young man is smitten with you that your virtues will be the alluring charm and that will be a treasure sufficient for any man who has sense to estimate their value for on that foundation he may lay the structure of happiness which Wealth cannot give and he who wants that degree of sense is not worthy of my adorable Maria. I think your sister has been happy in her choice. Mr. Marshall is a man of a sound heart, strong mind, & clear head, I am warmly attached to him for his virtues which are of the purest kind. . . . I have taken great pains to get from hence but the fates still work against me through the medium of Mr. Thos. Ross & his clients, whether I shall bring them too or not, I cannot yet tell but nothing shall be left undone on my part. I have had my hair cut lately, grow fat, & look young again, at least People tell me so, but time is slipping along for all that. I expect by the next mail to hear from your dear Mother on whom may Heaven shower a plentiful share of its choicest blessings and in the distribution not forget my dear children. Adieu my dear Maria, keep up your Spirits, and enjoy everything that the scene around you affords, for the happiness of virtuous and amicable beings such as you, I am most truly,

"Your Affectionate Father
"Robt Morris

"Miss Maria Morris
"P.S. Charles arrived here this morning, he has been out to Robert & then came here, he is thin but healthy and from what he says I begin to think the sea is the thing of all others that best suits him. He

was in a severe Gale of Wind with his Prizeship which was intended for this Port but after being 13 days on the coast and without bread on board they were obliged to go into New York, he suffered hardships but is not discouraged, he says he is advancing fast towards being a good Seaman and wants to be at Sea again. He dines with Robert today, breakfasts with me tomorrow morning and then sets out to join Capt Truxton at New York.

"R. M."

It must have been a satisfaction to Robert Morris to feel that his fair-haired, blue-eyed son, who had caused him so many heartaches, was now happily established in his chosen career. Rumor runs that the young midshipman died several years later in South America.

A little more than two months after this letter was written, yellow fever broke out again in Philadelphia. Thereupon Robert went down to bring his mother and sister home. Just before they left Winchester, they received this cordial invitation to visit former President and Mrs. Washington at Mount Vernon:

"Mount Vernon, September 21, 1799

"Our Dear Madam—We never learnt with certainty until we had the pleasure of seeing Mr. White (since his return from Frederick), that you were at Winchester.

"We hope it is unnecessary to repeat in this place how happy we should be to see you and Miss Morris under our roof for as long a stay as you shall find it convenient before you return to Philadelphia; for be assured we ever have and still do retain the most affectionate regard for you, Mr. Morris, and the family.

"With the highest esteem and regard, and best wishes for the health and happiness of the family you are in, we remain

"Dear Madam

"Your most obedient and very Humble Servants,
"Geo. Washington
"Martha Washington

"To Mrs. Morris
in Winchester"

It was comforting in the midst of so many trials for Mary Morris to think that Washington retained his friendship for her and her husband. Unfortunately she could not accept the invitation at that time and thus lost her last opportunity of seeing their old friend.

Soon after his family's return from Virginia, Robert Morris mentioned with apparent pleasure that Henry Nixon was "paying his addresses to Maria." He was the son of John Nixon, President of the Bank of North America, who had first read the Declaration of Independence in the State House Yard. Robert and his wife and child had moved to Philadelphia, staying for a while with Mrs. Morris in the small house she had rented on Twelfth Street, not far from the prison. Robert was suffering from a lingering complaint. Before long there was in Tom's family a little Sally, named for her mother. These were the chief interests in Robert Morris's life while prison walls enclosed him.

Dreams of other days—days of power and splendor and service for others—rose unbidden. Robert Morris remained too strong a man, however, to live in memories of the past. His face was always turned forward. Yet his spirit chafed against the inactivity forced upon him. His chief concern was his inability to earn money to provide for his family. That thought was always uppermost in his mind. In 1799 he lamented the protesting of a bill for £389. "What is to be done for subsistence?" he cried. "I counted on this as a means to carry me through 1799." From time to time he suggested business plans, among others the purchase of some bills of exchange with a view to selling them again and making some profit. He knew, however, that he ran the risk of being declared bankrupt and losing his investment if the creditors heard of it and issued a process against him. Nor had he wholly abandoned his real estate ventures. To Nicholson he confided: "I have much in agitation about the Genesee, a nice card is to be played and probably also a bold game, but if trump comes to the right hand, the contest will end as it ought." Still resourceful even in prison, Morris conceived designs for recouping some of his losses and at least providing a living for his wife and children.

If only he were free! Although others were "getting discharges from this place," Morris remained, neglected by the nation he had helped establish. Apparently he did not try to use undue influence to secure his release. He made no appeal to Washington or friends of other days—friends he had helped when their fate and that of the entire country depended upon his assistance. As galling as was his situation to a proud spirit, he remained independent, preferring to bear alone the consequences of his own errors of judgment. The mechanics of Philadelphia, more considerate than the Congress, his creditors or even his friends, wished to raise a fund to liberate him, but he refused to consider their generous offer. The creditors were too numerous and the debts too great—approximately three million dollars.

In his later years in jail he had a larger, more comfortable room in which there were three writing desks, a table with drawers, a breakfast table, a mahogany dining table (borrowed), a Windsor settee and eight old Windsor chairs, three trunks of papers and one of clothes, three pine chests, and a mahogany letter-case. There were also, presumably, a bed and some room to move around and entertain visitors. Space was evidently not at a premium.

During those later years his two former partners joined him in "the hotel with the grated doors." Both James Greenleaf and John Nicholson were imprisoned for debt. The latter published *The Supporter* or *Daily Repast* while in prison. In his last days there, he was considered insane. On December 5, 1800, Nicholson died in the debtor's apartments.

While Morris was an inmate of Prune Street, William Wood, the comedian, was imprisoned for seventy days. The actor gives a revealing description of the famous prisoner at this period: "His person was neat, and his dress, though a little old-fashioned, was adjusted with much care. One side of the Prune Street debtors' prison was neatly laid out as a garden and well kept, affording an agreeable promenade for the luckless inhabitants of this Bastile during a large portion of the day. Mr. Morris appeared cheerful, returned my salutation in the politest manner, but in silence, continuing his walk, and dropping from his hand at a given spot a pebble on each round, until a certain number which he had in his hand was exhausted. For some mornings the same silence prevailed, until at length, observing my languid deportment, he inquired whether I was ill and added with some severity, 'Sir, this is an ill place for one so sickly and apparently so young.' . . . From this time he spoke to me almost daily, and always with great kindness. On one occasion he unbent much more than usual and offered some remarks which embraced much good counsel. While I offer this little picture of the morning walking-party on one side of the prison, I must not forget a riding-party on the other, nearest to Fifth Street—which I was occasionally permitted to overlook. Mr. James Greenleaf, who had been the partner of Mr. Morris's enterprises and with them of his misfortunes, had the privilege of forming a small circle and indulging himself with a rapid ride on a fine horse each morning. It was quite amusing to observe with what skill habit had enabled him to make those swift evolutions within so very limited a space." There was more reason than Wood suspected for the two parties remaining on opposite sides of the prison yard. Certainly that arrangement suited Morris, who thus did not have to watch "Master Jimmy's" equestrian show-manship.

Ordinarily Robert Morris's patience and resignation were amazing for so energetic and independent a nature. He had, of course, much time to meditate. Although he was too essentially sane and well-balanced to brood over his wrongs, yet he could not refrain from lamenting: "If I had contented myself with those purchases [lands in the Genesee country] and employed my time and attention to disposing of the lands to the best advantage, I have every reason to believe that at this day I should have been the wealthiest citizen of the United States; that things have gone otherwise I lament, more on account of others than on my own account, for God has blessed me with a disposition of mind that enables me to submit with patient resignation to his dispensations as they regard myself."

His friends had not entirely forgotten him, however, nor had his political opponents. Thomas Jefferson, who opposed so many of Morris's Federalist policies, considered him for Secretary of the Navy in his cabinet, "if," as Jefferson said, "he could get from confinement and the public gave him confidence." But when Jefferson was inaugurated, the Financier of the Revolution "still languished in a debtors' prison," and it is questionable whether an indifferent public could have had its confidence restored at that time. In Congress Morris's friends agitated the passing of the Bankruptcy Act, according to the terms of which "a man could be adjudicated a bankrupt and thereupon be released." But there were enemies of the bill and of Morris himself, those who had lost money in his financial failure. On April 4, 1800, the Bankruptcy Act was finally passed. A year elapsed, however, before Robert Morris regained his freedom. Through some error he did not apply promptly for the benefit of the act. There were certain preliminaries, moreover, that had to be attended to before he might be discharged. The amount of his debts, proved before the Commissioners, totaled $2,948,711.11. At last the proceedings were certified and on October 15, 1801, two-thirds of Morris's creditors agreed to his discharge.

CHAPTER XVIII

HOPE DEFERRED

❖   ❖   ❖

EVEN before his creditors had agreed to his discharge, Robert Morris was released from prison. On August 26, 1801, after serving three years, six months and ten days in the Prune Street Gaol, he regained his freedom. He was sixty-six years old, penniless and humiliated, dependent upon his family for subsistence. To Thomas he sent this message a few months later: "I now find myself a free citizen of the United States without one cent that I can call my own." He was not, however, without plans and a few prospects of employment. It was rumored that President Jefferson intended to offer him the position of Collector for the Port of Philadelphia, but that offer did not materialize. He inquired among the merchants of the city about acquiring "a means of subsistence"—without result.

He was still concerned about the Washington lots and the unroofed, half-ruined houses in Morris Village on Capitol Hill. Respectable New York names, he felt sure, would aid his plan for selling the Washington property, but New York seemed prejudiced against purchasing lots in the capital. That city still resented the removal of Congress. Morris found it hard to inspire confidence in the value of the property offered for sale. This was unfortunate since there was no want of money or enterprise in New York. Robert Morris, still resourceful, wished Aaron Burr, Vice-President of the United States, to look at the lots and write his opinion to his friends as a method of inspiring confidence.

In January, 1802, Morris journeyed by stagecoach to Washington, where he conferred with the President, Thomas Jefferson, and the Vice-President, Aaron Burr. According to his letters home, the latter received him "with his usual animated warmth of heart, which has uniformly indicated a desire to serve me." He again enjoyed the social life of the capital, dining with the President. Later he visited Mount Vernon but did not remain there since Mrs. Washington was not well. At Tom's quarters, where he stayed, he played cards and chatted with old friends—Colonel Howard, General Dayton, and Mr. Wells. Robert Junior was also residing in Washington at this time at Steele's Hotel, and Hetty and her family were living there. Thus Robert Morris was surrounded by his children. Hetty especially was quite overcome at her father's arrival. He reported to Mary Morris that the Marshalls' four fine children were all healthy and strong. How he delighted in the physical well-being of his family! He himself was not so robust as he had been in earlier years. He suffered particularly from an inflammation of the eyes, which had afflicted him many times before, and for which he had recourse to calomel.

Back in Philadelphia in April, he was again "on the lookout for something to do" as he had no desire to remain idle and needed money to provide for himself and his family. A few weeks after his return he sent word to Thomas, "I am meditating on a business, which if I can bring it to bear will afford me sufficient supplies of that necessary article [money] to lay by annually something for the support of your mother after my death." But this plan, too, proved abortive. At sixty-seven dreams are less apt to come true than at twenty-seven. He sometimes gave advice to the various companies with which he had been associated. To the Trustees of the Land Company he suggested that a little more territory be purchased from the Indians in the Genesee country, for a few hundred dollars, as a small portion of the Indian reservation cut into the company's lands.

Although saddened by his prison experience, Robert Morris remained unbroken. A spirit like his could not be entirely quenched by the indifference of his friends, the treachery of those he trusted, or the slights of a nation he had helped create. Often, however, he was low-spirited. In such a mood as this, a year after his release, he accepted an invitation to visit Gouverneur Morris, now United States Senator from New York, at Morrisania. There he enjoyed "good eatables and drinkables" as well as the best of society. Two charming young ladies, Misses Sally and Katy Ogden, Gouverneur's nieces, were there and a French abbé, M. Jouliner. This cheerful family served to restore his health and spirits. It made him especially happy to hear his host praise Thomas so highly. He enjoyed, too, the visits in the neighborhood and horseback rides through the country around Morrisania.

After his guest's departure, Gouverneur Morris told the story of that visit and its magical restorative powers. According to this report, Robert Morris came to Morrisania "lean, low-spirited and as poor as a commission of bankruptcy can make a man whose effects will not pay a shilling in the pound. I sent him home," the letter continued, "fat, sleek, in good spirits and possessed of the means of living comfortably the rest of his days. So much for the air of Morrisania." Of course it was not the air of Morrisania alone that wrought this magic, but the kind heart and the ingenuity of his host. Gouverneur Morris proved his most loyal and faithful friend. His device for providing a comfortable living for his former chief was a clever one. Since there was some flaw in the title of the Holland Company, this astute lawyer took advantage of the situation to secure an annuity of $1,500 to be paid Mrs. Morris as dower rights during her life. This enabled Robert and Mary Morris to live in modest comfort in a small house in Philadelphia on the east side of Twelfth Street between Market and Chestnut. There the former Financier resided with his family for four years and there his benefactor, Gouverneur Morris, visited him and they "dined around" together as in the olden days.

His life was filled with small domestic details, nothing concerning the family too minute to be of interest to him. To Thomas he sent frequent letters. According to his report, Henry went gunning in December and was shot in both legs by a countryman who was aiming at a rabbit running in Henry's direction. The poor boy was confined to bed "with poultices on both legs while every day some shot was extracted." The next account of Henry's activities was of his becoming an apprentice to the dry goods business a few years later. On March 4, 1802, Maria Morris and Henry Nixon were married and on December 23 of that year their son John was born, the first of a family of ten.

Robert Morris was devoted to his daughter-in-law Sally, Thomas's wife, and to her two little girls, anticipating their visits with great impatience. In January, 1802, the grandchildren arrived for a visit. While they were there, the roads were often so muddy that no one could cross Market Street without being mired above the ankles. The one advantage of this bad weather was that it postponed Sally's departure. After she had left, Morris spoke of missing little Sally, his "great favorite," who had walked with him every morning to Dunlap's Corner. He wrote Thomas that he was now "solitary instead of being enlivened by her engaging pranks." When a year later a son was born to Sally and Thomas, Grandfather Morris was afraid their little daughters might become jealous of the baby brother and warned his son against showing favoritism.

The Marshalls soon after this moved to their new home, the French chateau which they had built at Happy Creek in Fauquier County, Virginia. There, years later, on a wall designed expressly for it, was hung the portrait of Hetty and Maria Morris, painted by Gilbert Stuart. There, too, their large family of sixteen children were born and reared.

Robert, in the meantime, had moved to Philadelphia, where he wrote his brother Thomas for advice and assistance. "As I am moved to town and have commenced a new career," so the letter ran, "I must for one year at least try what can be done, and to enable me to do this, I *must* get money in some shape or way by means of that stock [the Indian annuities]; therefore if you cannot borrow money on it you must sell it for what you can get." There seemed an opportunity to sell, as a Scotch parson and his parishioners, one hundred fifty families, were willing to pay ready money for three thousand to four thousand acres of land in the Genesee country if they could obtain grazing farms at a moderate price. By the end of 1803 the citizens of Philadelphia had "gone mad" over settling and making fortunes in East Florida (a beginning of the Florida boom). Robert planned to go if he had to walk, and his father, the spirit of enterprise still alive within him, felt "much inclined to go with him." Remembering the fertile acres in Georgia, Morris considered purchasing land and planting cotton there. If he went, he planned to take Molly to Hetty's for a visit.

A proposition was made to Robert Morris in August, 1803, to assist in establishing a new bank in Philadelphia on the same principles as the Merchants' Bank of New York. He was to be appointed President, with a handsome salary. What a surging of the old hopes and energies this proposition must have caused! This was just the type of work for which he was well suited. But again he was disappointed. As a new bank was established by others at this time, the old banks became alarmed and created difficulties for the new project. It was hard to find directors who were willing to serve. When at last the list of directors was complete, the public had lost interest in the institution. Very few subscribed as the majority of the citizens seemed to think there were already adequate banking facilities for the community. Only one thousand instead of ten thousand shares were sold. Thus another plan for obtaining a livelihood or regaining a fortune failed Morris. He remained a victim of the caution and pessimism of the period. Two years later Robert Morris thought that the best business for him might be purchasing fine articles at public sales and selling them again, a business for which his taste and mercantile experience admirably fitted him, but unfortunately this required some capital.

On his birthday in 1805 Morris spoke of being "happy and contented except for some erroneous conduct" in the course of his life. No man, he felt assured, had better children or more delightful grandchildren. Robert had a new son, Morris's third grandson within as many years. On that birthday Robert Morris, serene grandsire, expressed himself as "with philosophic patience thankfully enjoying the happiness of all." What a blessing that he was able to end his active, glorious, tragic career on that note of calm and contentment! Only a truly great nature, tolerant and wise, could have attained this degree of philosophic tranquillity—could have read the history of the Revolution with his name omitted and not felt resentful; could have wrought "God out of sorrow and good out of infinite pain."

Another year and he was gone. On May 8, 1806, he died in their small dwelling on Twelfth Street, calm and lucid to the last. A few days later he was buried in the family vault in Christ Churchyard.

For many years his will was sought. Only recently, in 1939, it was found yellowed with age and cracked by heat, in a forgotten vault near the furnaces beneath the Philadelphia City Hall. With it were discovered the wills of six other Signers of the Declaration of Independence, Benjamin Franklin's among the rest. In this collection of manuscripts the will of Robert Morris was considered the most valuable as it was written entirely in his own handwriting.

"The Last Will and Testament of Robert Morris of the City of Philadelphia, made the 13th June, 1804 and witnessed the 16th June when he declared and acknowledged the same to and before Captain Henry Kenyon and Mr. Gerald Cottringer.

"To be opened after his Death by his dearly beloved Mrs. Mary Morris.

"I, Robert Morris of the City of Philadelphia, formerly a merchant, etc., do now make and declare this present writing to contain and to be my last will and testament, hereby revoking all wills by me made and declared of precedent dates.

"Imprimis I give my gold watch to my son Robert, it was my father's and left to me at his death and hath been carefully kept and valued by me ever since.

"Item. I give my gold headed cane to my son Thomas, the head was given to me by the late John Hancock, Esq. when President of Congress and the cane was the gift of James Wilson, Esq. whilst a member of Congress.

"Item. I give to my son Henry my copying press and the papers which were sent to me a present from Sir Robert Harries of London.

"Item. I give to my daughter Hetty (now Mrs. Marshall) my silver vase or punch cup which I imported from London many years ago and have since purchased again.

"Item. I give to my daughter Maria (now Mrs. Nixon) my silver boiler which I also imported from London many years ago and which I have lately repurchased.

"Item. I give to my friend Gouverneur Morris, Esq. my Telescope & Espying glass being the same that I bought of a French refugee from Cape Francois then at Trenton and which I since purchased again of Mr. Hall, officer of the Bankrupt Office.

"Item. I give and bequeath all the other property which I now possess or may hereafter acquire either real or personal or all that shall or may belong to me at the time of my death to my dearly beloved wife, Mary Morris, for her use and comfort during her life and to be disposed of as she pleases at or before her decease when no doubt she will make such distribution of the same amongst our children as she may then think most proper.

"Here I have to express my regret at having lost a very large fortune acquired by honest industry, which I had long hoped and expected to enjoy with my family during my life and then to distribute it amongst those of them that should outlive me. Fate has determined otherwise and we must submit to the decree, which I have done with Patience and Fortitude.

"Lastly I do hereby nominate and appoint my said dearly beloved Wife Mary Morris the sole Executrix of this my last Will and Testament made and declared as such on this 13 day of June 1804."

Mary Morris, the "dearly beloved wife" who had shared his years of prosperity and of humiliation, lived twenty-one years after his death. She resided on Chestnut Street, above Tenth, leading a retired life with her children and grandchildren. Frequently she received visits from noted men whom she and her husband had entertained in their years of splendid hospitality and others whom that husband had helped and she met now for the first time.

When Lafayette arrived in Philadelphia in September, 1824, on his tour of the United States, his first private call was on Mrs. Morris. While the city blossomed with flags and martial music resounded in his honor, he stole away from all the pageantry to the quiet house on Chestnut Street to do honor to another great man and his wife, his "dearest partner" through fortune and misfortune. During that visit he presented his hostess with a fan he had brought from Paris, a fan with carved ivory sticks inlaid with silver and decorated with three exquisite painted medallions. On that occasion he also requested her as a particular favor to him to attend the civic ball in his honor to be held on October 5 at the Chestnut Street Theatre. Although she made it a practice not to appear publicly, she smilingly yielded to his request.

What sad memories were hers as she drove up to the theatre and saw the marble relief work from their "dream palace" over the windows in the wings! An album of old pictures must have opened before her inward eye—pictures of Assembly balls, of dinners and other festivities in her own hospitable home, with the "host of America" beside her; levees at the President's mansion, with Robert Morris at Washington's right hand; grim pictures of a husband hounded by creditors and at last enclosed by prison walls. Some of the pictures were fading; eyes were growing dim. It was best to close the album. This was Mary Morris's last public appearance, this ball in LaFayette's honor, which she graced with her usual dignity and charm.

During her last years, an admirer of Robert Morris, George Lloyd Champion of Camden, South Carolina, wrote a friend of the family about property in that state, worth about $15,000, which really belonged to the estate of Robert Morris. He wished and had the means, he said, to procure it for the family (but not for the creditors), because of his unbounded respect for the great Financier of the Revolution. For eleven years this correspondence continued between Champion and Henry Nixon, relative to buying up part of the estate and reselling it to give the money to Mrs. Morris, but this property, like all of Morris's other estates, was tied up in bankruptcy.

In the meantime Mary Morris died on January 16, 1827, in her seventy-eighth year. She was buried in the family vault beside her husband.

Upon the marble slab above the vault may be read the following inscription:

THE FAMILY VAULT
OF
WILLIAM WHITE AND ROBERT MORRIS
THE LATTER WHO WAS FINANCIER OF THE UNITED STATES
DURING THE REVOLUTION

At the foot a bronze tablet bears this legend:

Robert Morris
Signer of the Constitution of the United States of America
Deputy from Pennsylvania
To the Federal Constitutional Convention

Close to the marble sarcophagus cling evergreen shrubs, forming natural immortelles around the tomb. Here begins the Garden of Remembrance with its lawns and trees shadowed by Christ Church. This is the only memorial to Robert Morris and his great-hearted services to his country. Above the grave, chime church bells, while within the sanctuary itself look down the faces of Morris, Washington, and other great men of their day from a stained-glass window—a window which is, like the patriots depicted thereon, "Dedicated to God in each Crisis."

CHAPTER REFERENCES

CHAPTER I

For information concerning the firm of Charles Willing I am indebted to: Thomas Willing Balch, *Letters and Papers*, Phila., 1922; and Burton Alva Kunkle, *Thomas Willing and the First Financial System*, Phila., 1937.

The letter from Henry Callister has been lost, but its contents are known. It is referred to by Dr. Oberholtzer.

There are several versions of the elder Morris's death, but that given here is based upon the "Narrative of Jeremiah Banning," found in Boogher's *Repository* and upon a letter from Maria Morris Nixon, the Financier's daughter, also found in the *Repository*.

The facts concerning Robert Morris's date of birth were derived from a letter to the author from Mr. J. F. Smith, Head Librarian of the Liverpool Public Libraries, whose letter I quote (in part):

"Robert Morris was born on the 20th January, 1734/5 [actually 1735], and was christened at St. George's Church, Castle Street, Liverpool, on the 28th January. The entry in the Register runs:

" 'Robert, son of Elizabeth Murphet and Robert Morris.'

"He is said to have been born in Chorley Court, off Dale Street, but confirmation on this point is lacking.

"The year 1734 has always been given hitherto as the year of his birth, but an examination of the Register makes it quite clear that 1735 is actually the year as the church was not consecrated until the 1st August, 1734, and the first baptism took place on that date. The error, of course, is due to the fact that in the old style the first three months of the year were dated as the year before.

"We have had many previous requests for information on Robert Morris, particularly from America, but it is only recently that we have been able to establish these facts, and the first time they have been communicated."

There is also a discrepancy in the day of birth, Robert Morris himself always claiming January 31 as his birthday. There was a difference of eleven days between the old calendar and the new.

The letters quoted here are from *Letters and Papers of Thomas Willing* by Thomas Willing Balch, Phila., 1922, pp. 48, 52, 74, 60.

Other material is based upon: Charles Henry Hart, *Mary White—Mrs. Robert Morris, An Address* (From the *Shippen Papers*, ed. Thomas Balch, Phia., 1855); Letters from Tarring and Feathering Committee from Thomas Scharf and Thompson Westcott, *History of Philadeplhia*, Vol. I, pp. 286 and 287; Willis J. Abbot, *Story of Our Navy for Young Americans*, New York, 1910; and J. F. Cooper, *History of the Navy of the United States*, Phila., 1839.

CHAPTER IV

Letters to and from Reed, Hooper, Hancock, Harrison, and Washington are from *Revolutionary Letters*, 1776 and 1777.

Letters to Robert Morris from Mary Morris and letters from Morris to his wife are from the Robert Morris Collection in the Huntington Library. They were written between December, 1776, and the last of February, 1777.

Information concerning the interview with the Quaker, Abel James, was obtained from a letter written by a descendant of Mr. James to Dr. Ellis Paxson Oberholtzer, and attached to the front of his biography, *Robert Morris, Patriot and Financier*, in the Pennsylvania Historical Society in Philadelphia. Kind permission to use this material was granted by Nicholas B. Wainwright, Librarian of the Society.

CHAPTER V

Letters from Mary Morris to her mother are from the Robert Morris Collection in the Huntington Library. They were written in March and April, 1777.

The scene at "The Hills" is a composite of several visits by noted men to Morris that summer. While the conversation itself is not authentic, the scene is based upon facts—an accurate description of "The Hills," and scattered remarks by friends in letters.

The scene at Betsy Ross's is based in part upon the painting by Charles H. Weisgerber, "The Birth of Our Nation's Flag," and upon historical records of the event. The actual conversation is not authentic.

Letters from Deane, Tilghman, and others are from *Official Letters*, 1777 and 1778.

CHAPTER VI

Letters in this chapter are from *Official Letters*, 1777 and 1778, and from *Revolutionary Letters* for those years.

Letter from Johnstone, June 16, 1778, is also found in *Secret History of the American Revolution* by Carl Van Doren, p. 98.

The incident in the home of Don Mirailles, found in various sources, is based primarily on the *Life of Robert Morris* by David Gould, Boston, 1834.

CHAPTER VII

Letters from *Official Letter Book*, 1781, *Private Letter Book*, 1782, and *Official Diary*, 1781–1784.

Letter from Washington, June 4, 1781, is from Jared Sparks, *Diplomatic Correspondence*.

The quotation concerning Morris by Carlo Botta, is from *History of the War of the Independence of the United States of America*, transl. George Alexander Otis, New Haven, 1841, Vol. II, p. 368.

Account of the visit of Peters and Morris to Washington, found in many sources, is based largely on conversations by Thomas Morris with his father and reported by his son, from Henry Simpson's *Eminent Philadelphians*, pp. 705–707.

CHAPTER VIII

Letters from *Official Letter Book* and *Official Diary*, 1781.

CHAPTERS IX AND X

Letters from *Official Letter Book* and *Official Diary*, 1781 and 1782.

CHAPTER XI

Letters from *Official Letter Book*, 1781–1783, and *Official Diary*, 1781–1784.

Quotation concerning Morris is from Carlo Botta, *History of the War of the Independence of the United States of America*, Vol. II, p. 368.

Statement of Accounts and Farewell to the Inhabitants of the United States of America, found in the Rare Book Room of the Library of Congress.

CHAPTER XII

Letter to Washington, October 19, 1781, from Henkel's *Catalogue of Confidential Correspondence of Robert Morris*.

Letters to Ridley and De Basseville, from the Henry E. Huntington Library; also letters from Robert Morris to Mary Morris and his son Robert, and from Mary Morris to her husband—all from the Huntington Library.

Letters from Sarah Livingston Jay to Mary Morris and to Katherine Livingston from Boogher's *Repository*, Vol. I; also letter from William Carmichael to Morris from the same source.

Quotations from Chastellux and Broglie found in various early lives of Morris and in Oberholtzer's biography, also, from Harrison's *Annals*, pp. 188–189.

CHAPTER XIII

Material in this chapter was derived largely from William Maclay's *Journal*, pp. 48, 63, 66, 162, 271, 296, 329, 336.

Letters from Morris to his wife, from the Robert Morris Collection, Huntington Library.

Letter from Washington to Lear, from Henkel's *Catalogue*, Vol. I.

Quotations and other material concerning John Paul Jones, from A. C. Buell's *John Paul Jones, Founder of the American Navy*, Vol. II, pp. 15, 16 and 319.

Information about Gilbert Stuart is from *An Illustrated Descriptive List of His Works*, Vol. II.

CHAPTER XIV

Letters from *Private Letter Book*, 1790–1795, 1795–1797.

CHAPTER XV

Letters from *Private Letter Book*, 1795–1797.
Excerpt from Henry Latrobe's *Journal*.

CHAPTER XVI

Letters from *Private Letter Book*, 1797–1798.

CHAPTER XVII

Quotation from Samuel Breck's *Recollections*, p. 204.

Letters from *Private Letter Book*, 1798–1801.

Letter from Robert Morris to his daughter Maria, June 26, 1799, included by the kind permission of Mrs. George L. Harrison, from her *Annals of Charles Custis Harrison and Ellen Waln Harrison*, published privately, p. 208.

Description of Morris in Prune Street Gaol by William Wood from Westcott's *Historic Mansions*, p. 373.

CHAPTER XVIII

Letters to Thomas Morris from his father (July 13, 1802) and from his brother, Robert Morris, Jr. (March 22, 1803), in Huntington Library.

Letters of Gouverneur Morris, 1802.

Description of fan presented by Lafayette to Mary Morris, from *Annals of Ancestry of Charles Custis Harrison and Ellen Waln Harrison*, included by permission of Mrs. George Harrison.

The will of Robert Morris was found in the Will Record Book #1, 1802, Philadelphia City Hall. The actual will was on display in City Hall in May, 1940, not long after its discovery in a forgotten vault beneath that building.

ACKNOWLEDGMENTS

I wish to express my sincere appreciation of the assistance rendered me by many institutions, agencies, and friends, in the preparation of this work.

I am especially indebted to the following libraries:

To the Manuscript Division of the Henry E. Huntington Library, San Marino, California, for so generously placing at my disposal the facilities of that department and the services of their capable and willing staff, and for permission to print extracts of letters from the Robert Morris Collection;

To the Historical Society of Pennsylvania in Philadelphia for the use of their library, particularly the Dreer and Conarrhoe Collections of Letters to and from Robert Morris, and for their kind permission to use certain material acknowledged elsewhere in this biography, and the portrait of Robert Morris I;

To the Pennsylvania State Library in Harrisburg, Archives Division;

To the Library of Congress, especially Dr. Donald Mugridge of the Manuscript Division;

To the Library Company of Philadelphia and the Public Libraries of New York and Philadelphia.

I wish to avail myself of this opportunity to thank the following persons for their whole-hearted cooperation: Mr. J. F. Smith, Chief Librarian of the Liverpool Public Libraries, Liverpool, England, for information concerning Robert Morris's birth and parentage; Dr. Frank H. Garver, Professor of American History at the University of Southern California, for his kind recommendations; Lieutenant Colonel Robert Morris of Harrisburg, a great-great-grandson of the Financier, for his kind permission to use photographs of the two Gilbert Stuart portraits in his possession, more specific acknowledgment of which is made elsewhere in this book; Miss Caroline Cooke, a great-great-granddaughter of Robert Morris, for her very friendly and valuable cooperation; Mrs. George L. Harrison, author of the privately circulated *Annals of the Ancestry of Charles Custis Harrison and Ellen Waln Harrison*, for her gracious permission to print a letter from the Financier to his daughter Maria, and for other interesting information; Miss Bartlett Cowdrey of New York City for her advice concerning the Gilbert Stuart portraits used in this volume; and my good friend, Miss Helen S. Johnson, for her unfailing help and interest;

Also all my friends for their constant, unwearying faith in me and in the consummation of this task;

All authors who have presented data concerning the life of Robert Morris, especially Dr. Ellis Paxson Oberholtzer for his pioneer work in this field, which greatly simplified my research.

I am most deeply indebted to the inspiring life and works of my dear father, without whose earlier efforts on this subject this biography would never have been written.

BIBLIOGRAPHY

MANUSCRIPTS AND SPECIAL COLLECTIONS

Conarrhoe Collection of Robert Morris's Autograph Letters. Pennsylvania Historical Society, Manuscript Division, Phila.

Confidential Correspondence of Robert Morris, The. To be sold Tuesday, January 16, 1917. Stan V. Henkels, Auction Commission Merchant, Phila.

Dreer Collection of Robert Morris's Autograph Letters. Pennsylvania Historical Society.

Morris, Robert, *Account of Property.* Pennsylvania Historical Society.

——, *Address to Citizens of Pennsylvania,* July 7, 1779. Special Collection of the Pennsylvania Historical Society.

——, *Application to Friends for Pecuniary Relief for the Southern War.* Pennsylvania Historical Society.

——, Collection (consisting of 320 manuscripts purchased from the sale at the Anderson Galleries of the Sessler and Madigan Collection; 216 letters from Robert Morris and 21 from Mary White Morris, others to Morris. Period: 1774–1837). Henry E. Huntington Library, Manuscript Division, San Marino, Calif.

——, Correspondence, 1776–1783 (miscellaneous). Library of Congress, Manuscript Division.

——, *Letters to John Hancock.* Pennsylvania Historical Society, Phila., 1848.

——, Letters from and to Robert Morris (miscellaneous, 5 boxes). Library of Congress.

——, *Official Diary,* 3 vols. Library of Congress, Manuscript Division.

——, *Official Letter Book,* 7 vols. (3,024 letters). Library of Congress, Manuscript Division.

——, *Private Letter Book* (2,702 letters). Library of Congress, Manuscript Division.

——, *Statement of the Accounts of the United States of America during the Administration of the Superintendent of Finance,* Phila., 1785. Library of Congress, Rare Book Collection.

New York Historical Society Collections, Letters to Robert Morris, 1775–1782. New York, 1878.

Papers of the Continental Congress, Letters of Robert Morris. Library of Congress, Manuscript Division.

Pennsylvania State Archives, Robert Morris Collection, consisting of deeds, leases and letters. Pennsylvania State Library, Harrisburg.

Will Record Book #1, 1802. Department of Wills, City Hall, Phila.

BOOKS, SKETCHES, AND PERIODICALS

Abbot, Willis J., *American Merchant Ships and Sailors*. New York, 1902.

Balch, Thomas Willing, *Thomas Willing—Letters and Papers*. Phila., 1922.

Ballagh, James Curtis, *White Servitude in the Colony of Virginia*. Johns Hopkins University Studies, Series 13, Baltimore, 1895.

Barton, George, *Little Journeys around Old Philadelphia*. Phila., 1925.

Boogher's Repository (ed. Horace Wemyss Smith), Vol. I. Phila., 1883, in Library Company of Phila.

Botta, Carlo Giuseppi, *History of the War of the Independence of the United States of America* (transl. George Alexander Otis). New Haven, 1841.

Breck, Samuel, *Recollections*. Phila., 1877.

Buell, A. C., *John Paul Jones, Founder of the American Navy*, 2 Vols. New York, 1900.

Delaplaine, Joseph, *Repository of the Lives and Portraits of Distinguished American Characters*. Phila., 1815.

Faris, John T., *The Romance of Old Philadelphia*. Phila., 1918.

Fisher, Redwood, *Revolutionary Reminiscences Connected with the Life of Robert Morris, Esq.* Gilpin Library of Pennsylvania Historical Society, Phila.

Fiske, John, *The Critical Period of American History*. Boston, 1888, 1916.

Gould, David, *Life of Robert Morris*. Boston, 1834.

Guttridge, G. H. (ed.), *American Correspondence of a Bristol Merchant*. University of California, Berkeley, 1934.

Harrison, Mary (Mrs. George L.), *Annals of the Ancestry of Charles Custis and Ellen Waln Harrison*. Printed for private circulation, Phila., 1932.

Hart, Charles Henry, *Mary White—Mrs. Robert Morris—An Address*. Phila., 1878.

———, *Robert Morris, the Financier of the American Revolution—A Sketch*. Phila., 1878.

Heiges, George L., *Robert Morris in Manheim—Historical Sketch*. Manheim, 1933.

Hill, Charles L., *History of American Shipping*. New York, 1883.

Jameson, J. Franklin, *The American Revolution Considered as a Social Movement.*

Joyce, J. St. George, *Story of Philadelphia.* Phila., 1919.

Kennedy, John M., *Robert Morris and the Holland Purchase.* Batavia, 1894.

———, *The Genesee Country.* Batavia, 1895.

Kunkle, Burton Alva, *Thomas Willing and the First American Financial System.* University of Pennsylvania Press, Phila., 1937.

Lacey, Louis, *The History of Liverpool from 1207–1907.* Lyceum Press, Liverpool.

Lee, Richard Henry, *The Life of Arthur Lee.* Boston, 1829.

Lewis, Lawrence, *A History of the Bank of North America.* Phila., 1882.

Life of Robert Morris, the Great Financier, with an Engraving and Description of the Celebrated House, Partly Erected in Chestnut Street. Phila., 1841.

Long, J. C., *Mr. Pitt and America's Birthright.* New York, 1940.

Longacre, James B., *The National Portrait Gallery of Distinguished Americans,* Vol. IV. Phila., 1839.

Lownes, Caleb, *Account of the Alteration and Present State of the Penal Laws of Pennsylvania.* Boston, 1799.

Maclay, William, *Journal.* New York, 1890.

———, *Sketches of Debate in the First Senate of the United States in 1789–1791.* Harrisburg, 1880.

Morris, Gouverneur, *Diary and Letters* (ed. Anne Cary Morris). New York, 1888.

Robert Morris Memorial. Fairmount Park Art Association, Pub. No. 65, Phila., June 18, 1926.

Oberholtzer, Ellis Paxson, *Robert Morris, Patriot and Financier.* New York, 1903.

Repplier, Agnes, *Philadelphia—The Place and the People.* New York, 1925.

Roosevelt, Theodore, *Gouverneur Morris* (American Statesmen Series). Boston, 1898.

Scharf, J. Thomas and Westcott, Thompson, *History of Philadelphia,* Vol. I. Phila., 1884.

Schuckers, J. W., *A Brief Account of the Finances and Paper Money of the Revolutionary War.* Phila., 1874.

Stuart, Gilbert, *An Illustrated Descriptive List of His Works,* Vol. II (comp. Lawrence Park). New York, 1926.

Simpson, Henry, *Eminent Philadelphians.* Phila., 1859.

Snyder, Freas Brown, *Robert Morris—An Address Delivered before the

Lansdowne Chapter, Daughters of the American Revolution. Lansdowne, Pa., 1930.

Sparks, Jared (ed.), *Diplomatic Correspondence of the American Revolution.* Boston, 1853.

———, *The Library of American Biography.* New York, 1854.

Sumner, William Graham, *Finances and the Financier of the Revolution.* New York, 1891.

———, *Robert Morris.* New York, 1892.

Trevelyan, Sir George Otto, *The American Revolution.* New York, 1922.

Turnbull, Robert J., *A Visit to the Philadelphia Prison.* Phila., 1796.

Turner, Orasmus, *Pioneer History of the Holland Purchase.* Buffalo, 1849.

Van Doren, Carl, *Benjamin Franklin.* New York, 1938.

———, *Secret History of the American Revolution.* New York, 1941.

Van Tyne, Claude Halstead, *The American Revolution in the American Nation* (ed. A. B. Hart). New York, 1905.

Waln, Robert, Jr., *Life of Robert Morris* (in Sanderson's *Lives of the Signers of the Declaration of Independence*). Phila., 1823.

Westcott, Thompson, *Historic Mansions and Buildings of Philadelphia with Some Notice of Their Owners.* Phila.

INDEX